Proceedings from the Third International Conference of the
Nordic Association for Canadian Studies, University of Oslo 1990

The Arctic: Canada and the Nordic Countries

Edited by
Per Seyersted

The Nordic Association for Canadian Studies Text Series
Volume 6

The Nordic Association for Canadian Studies Text Series:

Volume 1   *Canadiana.* Edited by Jörn Carlsen and Knud Larsen. Århus 1984

Volume 2   *Canada and the Nordic Countries.* Edited by Jørn Carlsen and Bengt Streijffert. Lund 1988

Volume 3   *Essays in Canadian Literature.* Edited by Jørn Carlsen and Bengt Streijffert. Lund 1989

Volume 4   *Multiculturalism and Canadian Culture and Communication Policies,* by Joy Cohnstaedt. (Lund 1989)

Volume 5   *The Canadian North: Essays in Culture and Literature.* Edited by Jørn Carlsen and Bengt Streijffert. Lund 1989

Volume 6   *The Arctic: Canada and the Nordic Countries.* Edited by Per Seyersted. Lund 1991

Drawings by Heather Spears.

Copyrights the authors, the artist, and the Nordic Association for Canadian Studies/L'Association Nordique d'Etudes Canadiennes.

Published by the Nordic Association for Canadian Studies/L'Association Nordique d'Etudes Canadiennes.

Secretariat: Bygglovsgränden 6, 222 47 Lund, Sweden.

Printed in Sweden by Studentlitteratur, Lund.

Lund 1991

ISBN 91-971343-3-3   ISSN 1101-6957

Contents

3

Preface

It was in 1984 that representatives from Denmark, Finland, Norway and Sweden founded NACS/ANEC, the Nordic Association for Canadian Studies/Association Nordique d'Etudes Canadiennes.

Already that same year we organized, at the University of Aarhus, the first of our triennial international conferences. A number of the papers presented there were published as Volume 1 in the Nordic Association for Canadian Studies Text Series.

Our second such conference, in 1987, was held at the University of Lund. The Proceedings were brought out as Volumes 2, 3, 4, and 5 in our series.

When we got to our Third International Conference, 9-12 August, 1990, the turn had come to Norway and the University of Oslo. Our base was the Soria Moria Conference Center overlooking Oslo and the Oslo Fjord, but on the first day we had the opening ceremony downtown in the University Aula, and then went to Bygdøy for a guided tour of the Viking ships and the "Fram," and for a reception at the residence of the Canadian Ambassador and dinner at the Maritime Museum.

As in Aarhus and Lund, there were about 200 participants, and once again, nearly half of them had come from Canada and the United States, and a good number from England, Germany, Holland, France, and Italy. The rest came from our Nordic countries, and we were particularly happy to be able to welcome this time representatives also from both Iceland and Greenland.

During the three days of the conference we had a very full program, with six keynote lectures, about ninety papers and addresses, readings by ten poets, filmshowings, and concerts by the "Breakwater Group" from Newfoundland and the student group "Cakes and Ale" from the University of Oslo. The conference participants represented an impressive range of disciplines. We were fortunate in having distinguished speakers and lively audiences, and many a session at Soria Moria was continued informally around the coffee stands or outside on the terrace.

What made it possible for us to bring this event off was the devoted work of a group of NACS/ANEC members, and the generous financial support by the Canadian Government, the Norwegian Government (through five different ministries), la Délégation Générale du Québec à Londres, and a number of Norwegian and Nordic cultural foundations and institutions. The addresses of the Canadian Ambassador to Norway and Iceland and of representatives from the Norwegian Government, the University of Oslo, and the International

Council for Canadian Studies, and the participation of three of the Canadian Ambassadors to our Nordic countries, lent extra distinction to the conference.

About sixty papers, some of them in expanded form, were sent to us for inclusion in the Proceedings. Having secured the necessary funding we are now able to publish them, and they will appear as Volumes 6, 7, and 8 in our Text Series.

Here, in Volume 6, we have collected 25 papers dealing with the theme of the conference, "The Arctic: Canada and the Nordic Countries," a natural topic in view of the growing importance of that part of the world and the geographic position of our countries. Seventeen of these papers were given as part of four panel discussions, which also form the four sections of this collection. Seven of the remaining eight--including the keynote lecture by Chief Billy Diamond--were presented at other sessions, but have been added to the one or the other of the four parts where they thematically belong.

Finally, there is the keynote lecture given by Knut Vollebæak, State Secretary, Norwegian Ministry of Foreign Affairs; just as his address opened the Conference, it serves as an Introduction to this volume.

The first of the panel discussions dealt with "Economic Development of the Arctic: Challenges for Canada and the Nordic Countries." It was chaired by Dr. Odd Rogne, Director of the Norwegian Polar Institute. The second discussed "Indigenous Peoples and the State: Rights Achieved in Canada and the Nordic Countries." Presiding here (and also contributing a paper) was Dr. Carsten Smith, former Chairman of the Norwegian Sami Commission. Wanting to have expert and representative panelists to discuss these topics, we turned to the Cree Indians of Quebec, the Norwegian Sami Parliament, the Northern Norway Institute of Trade and Industry, and the Governments of Canada, the Northwest Territories, and Greenland, and we were fortunate in that all of them graciously accepted our invitation for them to send speakers to these sessions.

The third panel discussion dealt with "Current Problems Related to the Northern Fourth World: Canada and the Nordic Countries." It was chaired by Dr. Tom G. Svensson of the University of Oslo, who also had proposed this meeting. The initiative for the fourth session came from Dr. Jack Stagg, Director General, Constitutional Development and Strategic Planning, Indian and Northern Affairs Canada, who wanted to discuss with Dr. Rogne "Comparative Approaches to International Arctic Cooperation: The Experiences of Canada and Norway." Chairman here was Mr. Graham Mitchell, Canadian Ambassador to Norway and Iceland.

We are grateful to Heather Spears, our unofficial "conference artist," for letting us use her sketches of speakers, performers, and listeners. Among these latter, participants will recognize Drs. Helge and Anne Stine Ingstad, who at Soria Moria were made the first Honorary Members of our Nordic Association for Canadian Studies. We also wish to express our sincere thanks to Ms. Majliss Johnson who typed the manuscript on her PC.

We are indebted to the many who gave us invaluable advice in connection with the planning of the sessions directly connected with our theme. Among the experts on the Arctic I turned to, the following must be particularly mentioned: Dr. Tore Gjelsvik, former Director of the Norwegian Polar Research Institute; Director General Dagfinn Stenseth, Norwegian Ministry of Foregin Affairs; Mr. Brian Long, Director, Academic Relations, Foreign Affairs and International Trade Canada, and Drs. Jack Stagg, Graham Mitchell, Odd Rogne, Tom G. Svensson, and Carsten Smith.

Per Seyersted
Oslo

Anne Stine Ingstad

Helge Ingstad

11/08/90

Introduction

The Growing Importance of the Arctic

Knut Vollebæk

On behalf of the Norwegian Government and the Minister of Foreign Affairs, Mr. Kjell Magne Bondevik, I have the honour to welcome The Nordic Association for Canadian Studies to Norway and to our capital, Oslo.

Although far from the Arctic Circle, Oslo has strong ties to the Arctic and the Norwegian Polar tradition. Fridtjof Nansen and Roald Amundsen lived in this city and planned their Arctic travels and expeditions here. Later today you will see their ships *Fram* and *Gjøa* at Bygdøy. These vessels tell more than many words about Nansen's daring drift across the Arctic Ocean and Amundsen's bold venture through the Northwest Passage, capping centuries of search for a Northern Searoute to the Far East. You will also see the Viking ships, the means of transportation for the first visitors from the Old to the New World a thousand years ago. On the shores of Newfoundland, at l'Anse aux Meadows, the Norwegian explorer Helge Ingstad has excavated their settlements, and thereby established the undisputable facts about the common heritage between Canada and the Nordic countries.

It goes without saying that we in the Nordic countries are proud to share this common heritage with Canada. And we share more than historic ties. We have similiarities of geography, common values, and parallel social and political developments. We share a likeminded perception of international challenges and of the role of our countries in international politics. Although divided by the High Seas, Canada and the Nordic countries are all countries of the North. And the North, as the Canadian poet and scholar Henry Beissel has put it, is where all parallels meet.

But our common heritage and traditions should not be taken for something granted. These are qualities that we need to renew and care for. We therefore need occasions like this conference to rediscover each other. My compliments go to the organizers of The Third International Conference of the Nordic Association for Canadian Studies for their dedication and efforts in maintaining this dialogue across the Atlantic.

We have here the opportunity to draw on the experience of ranking members of our academic and professional communities. Your insight is highly appreciated and needed, not least in a field of study that is the subject for this conference. The growing importance of the Arctic demands that more efforts are put into research on a number of issues, ranging from international security, legal questions, resource management, environmental protection or the safeguarding of the rights and values of indigenous people. These are matters that occupy the day-to-day agenda in Canadian politics, and which I can assure our Canadian friends are not unfamiliar to the Nordic Governments either. They represent common challenges which we need to address in a concerted fashion.

A few decades ago the Arctic was still an area of marginal interest even to the governments and general public of the littoral states surrounding the polar basin. This has changed radically. The developments in the Arctic have caught the attention of governments, economists, community planners, corporate executives and scientists. Our concern for the state of the Arctic environment is growing as well. The need and desirability of cooperation on issues relating to the developments of the Northern areas are being recognized. Increased diplomatic acitivity and search for new ways of establishing international cooperation in the scientific as well as in the environmental fields reflect this. The complexity of Arctic challenges underlines the need for common efforts, sharing of insights and experiences, imagination and new thinking. Also in our day and age the Arctic calls for a pioneering spirit, technological creativity and new approaches to the political, legal and security problems which confront us.

The Arctic is an area which holds out both prospects of fruitful and peaceful cooperation as well as a potential for conflict. Maintenance of stability and security in the Arctic is the basic challenge in an age when the Arctic is acquiring increasing strategic importance. Dynamic forces are at work both in the field of military strategy and resource exploitation. There is mounting pressure on the unique and vulnerable environment of the Arctic. There are increasing demands for Arctic science and research, in the fields of both natural and political sciences. Rational managament of resources, protection of the environment, and maintenance of stability are in turn linked up with questions of jurisdiction and sovereignty. One matter of priority will be to work out solutions to the questions of jurisdiction and sovereignty, since solving these matters no doubt would facilitate circumpolar cooperation and stability.

Norway's strategic position in the North is determined by our geographic location, our sovereignty over the Svalbard archipelago as well as Norway's jurisdiction over large sea and shelf areas. We are facing long term challenges of developing our natural resources while handling questions of environment, international law and security. Needless to say, we consider it of the greatest importance that developments here should take place peacefully, conflicts be avoided and stability be maintained. At a time when we have embarked upon the historic efforts of designing a new and hopefully more secure policy framework in Europe, the Arctic should not become a new arena for confrontation and conflict. We therefore hope that the changes we are witnessing in Europe will not leave the military aspects of the North untouched. While Norwegian security will benefit from a CFE treaty in a general way, it will not change the fact that we are neighbouring the largest military establishment of the World. A tangible evidence that the time of confrontation is gone, and that the North will not be the arena of conflict, would be if the Soviet Union started to reduce its naval forces in the North, as we have repeatedly urged them to do. In the meantime we will continue to work with our Allies in meeting our security needs, both in terms of defence and in the field of disarmament. We have also worked with our Soviet neighbours in increasing the security in the North by establishing a framework for avoiding unintended incidents between our naval forces by negotiating a treaty for this purpose that now is ready to be signed.

Questions concerning environmental protection, scientific research and economic relations in the North have become important elements in the dialogue between the Arctic countries - where the Nordic countries and Canada play an important role. Scientists from the Nordic countries, Canada, USA and the Soviet Union have been actively engaged in the work of developing a better organized and more coordinated approach to scientific research in the Arctic through the establishment of an International Arctic Science Committee. A founding meeting for the IASC is scheduled to take place in Resolute Bay in the Canadian Arctic later this month. IASC represents the first multilateral cooperation agreement in the Arctic since The Agreement on the Conservation of Polar Bears of 1973 between Norway, Denmark, Canada, USA and the Soviet Union. It will constitute a useful basis for coordination of scientific data and information in the years to come. Norway has offered to host the secretariat of the IASC.

The Arctic has for a long time been considered the last wilderness, untouched by the pollution which is a threat to our environment elsewhere on this planet. However, research on the Arctic environment has shown that those days are gone. Longdistance transport of pollution is now a matter of grave concern. The challenge to preserve the Arctic environment is vital. Pollution knows no boundaries. Sufficient measures can therefore not be taken by each of our countries alone. Confronted with these problems even superpowers become small. Hence, more than in any other field, we here need to work together, both among each other as well as together with other countries in Europe and America in our efforts to reduce this threat to the Arctic environment.

On this background the initiative taken by Finland to focus on the environmental challenges in the Arctic was both timely and welcome and rightly deserved the support it received by all our governments. The meetings in Rovaniemi and in Yellowknife with the participation of the eight Arctic and Nordic countries have clearly demonstrated their commitment to safeguard the Arctic environment.

We also welcome the participation of representatives of the indigenous peoples of the North in the "Rovaniemi process." It is highly appropriate that those who live in the North, and who are most directly affected by the threat of environmental pollution of this area, participate in this important process.

The Norwegian Government is dedicated to contribute so that the Rovaniemi process will yield substantial results. We are presently preparing a proposal for a monitoring system for the Arctic environment. This system can become a basis for a continuing review of the Arctic environment in general and also make it possible to assess its changes over time. We will thereby be in a better position to know where our efforts are most needed and to monitor the effect of those measures implemented. Norway is hosting a workshop in Oslo this fall to work out a proposal for such a monitoring system to be decided at the forthcoming ministerial meeting of the Arctic and Nordic countries next year.

Norway has already established such a system on behalf of the United Nations Environmental Program (UNEP). This has provided us with invaluable experience which may be used when developing a similar system for the Arctic. The Arctic monitoring system would naturally be linked up to the existing UNEP system.

Cross border pollution is a matter of grave concern in Northern Norway. The pollution from the Kola peninsula has emphasized the need for practical cooperation to halt further degradation of the delicate environment in this particular area. Norway and the Soviet Union have established bilateral cooperation to deal with environmental issues at large. In June, the Norwegian Government launched an initiative to establish a dialogue between Norway, Sweden, Finland and the Soviet Union on the issue of industrial pollution. We are pleased to note that the first reactions to this initiative have been positive, and that concrete measures are presently being considered to reduce the emissions.

The threat of radioactive pollution in the Arctic is another source of serious concern. The Chernobyl accident and accidents involving nuclear submarines off the coast of Norway have reminded us that the possibility of nuclear pollution indeed is a problem we need to take seriously. It should therefore come as no surprise that Norway – as well as the other Nordic countries – has reacted strongly against current Soviet plans to transfer all their nuclear tests from Kazakhstan to the Arctic island of Novaya Zemlya as from 1993.

We have repeatedly brought our concern on this issue to the attention of the Soviet authorities and strongly requested that their plans not be implemented. We do not want a nuclear test site on our door-step. We think it is wrong to use the fragile environment of the North as an area for testing these weapons. A step to move these tests to Novaja Zemlya would be a step in the wrong direction. At the present day and age we should be more concerned with ending all nuclear testing than with planning for the continuation of such tests. Norway favours an urgent agreement on a comprehensive nuclear test ban treaty which would prohibit all nuclear test-explosions by all States in all environments at all time. Our strong reactions to the Soviet plans are thus consistent with a policy which has been pursued by Norway for a number of years in all relevant international fora.

The question of securing a rational resource management is vital to the peoples of the North who depend on living resources on land and in the sea for their livelihood. To Norway the ecobalance of living marine resources thus is essential for a continued settlement in the coastal regions of the North. Through national measures, bilateral cooperation with other countries, as well as through international organizations at regional and global levels it is important to contribute actively to the protection and rational management of living resources in the sea. The critical question is to find the right balance between conservation of living resources on the one hand and resource utilization on the other. Developments in recent years have clearly demonstrated the importance of seeing management of living resources in the broad ecological context, covering the interrelationship between different species and the entire environment which must be protected from pollution and degradation.

To the Norwegian government it is a matter of high priority to increase international understanding for the contents and objectives of its policies on rational utilization, management and conservation of living marine resources in accordance with the principles of sustainable development set out in the report of the World Commission on Environment and Development.

The Svalbard archipelago is Norway's arctic area. This group of islands is among the easiest accessible Arctic areas in the world, not only because of climate and geography, but also by virtue of the principles of equal treatment and access accorded to nationals of the parties to the Svalbard treaty of 1920. The archipelago of Svalbard represents therefore a unique possibility for Arctic research on a wide variety of subjects. Through the years scientists from a number of countries have done extensive work on the islands which each year are visited by a large number of scientific expeditions. The Norwegian Polar Research Institute has concentrated the main part of its research activity on the archipelago together with extensive activities by Norwegian universities and other research institutes.

One important reason why Norway was granted sovereignty over Svalbard following World War I was the prevailing desire to keep the archipelago outside great power rivalry. The Svalbard Treaty prohibits the establishment of naval bases and the use of the archipelago for warlike purposes. In accordance with the provisions of the Svalbard Treaty Norway's overriding objectives are directed towards the maintenance of peace and stability in the area, and the orderly development of economic activities while preserving the area's unique natural environment.

Opening the Arctic to economic development and cooperation is to a large extent also a question of infrastructure, not least in relation to transport. The interest for commercial navigation in Arctic waters is growing. More than one hundred years after Sweden's Adolf Nordenskiöld passed through the full length of the Northeast Passage, and 90 years after Norway's Roald Amundsen first passed through the Northwest Passage, the prospects for a more extensive use of the Northern searoute to the Far East may become the next challenge facing the circumpolar nations. Development of sea lines of communication along the northern shores of Canada and the Soviet Union opens new and fascinating prospects for the communities along these routes. However, we need to consider carefully what prospects the development of commercial traffic in Northern waters might hold for the future of these areas.

Towards the end of the 20th century we have witnessed a growing concern for the environment of our planet. The World Commission on Environment and Development, chaired by Norway's former Prime Minister, Mrs Gro Harlem Brundtland, outlined in its report the difficult choices we are facing.

The response to the Brundtland report is encouraging. We know that the countries represented here today are among those which have been most active in pursuing international actions in the follow-up of the Brundtland report, not least when it comes to the Arctic environment. We also have common interests in finding answers to the challenges of Arctic resource utilization. We should cooperate in meeting the challenges facing indigenous peoples in the Arctic particularly concerning the problems of pollution of the Arctic and the contamination of the food chains in these areas.

Although not a full list of questions and areas for contacts and cooperation, these matters suggest what we could do to give tangible substance to a continuing dialogue which will reflect the increasing importance of arctic questions and challenges to our countries.

The great Arctic explorer Vilhjalmur Stefansson in 1922 stated:

> We shall not come to the northward limit of communal progress. There is no northern boundary beyond which productive enterprise cannot go until North meets North on the opposite shores of the Arctic Ocean as East has met West in the Pacific.

Although Stefansson's words may have a slightly different ring to-day than when they were spoken, his vision still appeals to our imagination. Certainly we have not reached the northern limit of communal progress. The age of the Arctic is only about to begin.

In Stefansson's words we may well discern an appeal to us, to move forward across the Arctic Ocean toward a pattern of wider cooperation and stability. We surely shall be faced with challenges. I feel confident that this conference will represent a valuable contribution towards greater insight into the nature of these challenges as well as the demands which will have to be met in overcoming these challenges. In this spirit I am honoured to speak to you here and I wish you good luck in your deliberations.

Part One

Economic Development of the Arctic: Challenges for Canada and the Nordic Countries

Economic Development in the Canadian North

Jack Stagg

Canada's two northern territories have experienced rapid economic growth in the past twenty years. The economy of the North in real terms increased by almost 200 percent between 1971 and 1988. During the same period income per capita rose from $5,000 to $22,000. Most of this growth has been driven by increasing government expenditures, and by oil and gas and mineral exploration and development activities. Renewable resource development and tourism have been far less significant in terms of northern GDP, but are increasingly important in the Yukon and some of the smaller, more remote communities in the Northwest Territories.

Despite this economic growth, northerners, northern governments and the federal government continue to be challenged in their northern economic development efforts. This stems from the fact that despite government programs and policies, the North's economy remains narrowly based, and by implication underdeveloped and vulnerable. While remoteness and the natural environment are partially to blame, poor infrastructure and a lack of investment in adapting southern production technologies for northern use are also responsible.

In the following discussion I would like to review with you some of the reasons why this situation has developed and how both the public and private sector have attempted to deal with it. In doing so, suggestions of improved approaches to northern economic development will be identified.

In the past twenty years both Yukon and the Northwest Territories have come to rely quite heavily on government and the non-renewable resource sector as sources of investment dollars, income and employment. Development of these sectors fulfilled both national and regional economic development objectives. However, this dependence has led to a variety of economic problems.

For geographic reasons most of the activity associated with these sectors has taken place in Yukon and the Western Arctic. This has left the Central and Eastern Arctic economically underdeveloped, with income being derived largely from government employment, government transfer payments and in some cases, renewable resource harvesting acitivities. Settlements in this region are small and widely scattered. Unemployment in most communities is close to 50 percent. The population is largely Inuit, 55 percent of whom are under the age of 20. Educational attainment is low and most residents are unwilling to move to western communities where the bulk of northern jobs are created. Unless migration patterns or birth or death rates change, the Inuit population of the N.W.T. will more than double over the next 25 years.

Secondly, most of the investment in non-renewable resources is controlled by southern interests. Consequently, most development profis flow out of the territories. Benefits accruing to northerners from the economic development of this sector, though significant in some regions, have largely been in the form of seasonal employment.

Finally, public and private sector investment in the North has, for the most part, not been oriented towards adapting southern production technologies for northern use, or establishing the infrastructure required to support economic diversification. Government expenditures have been largely directed at raising the quality of public services throughout the North. Investment by the private sector has been primarily in the infrastructure required to produce and export non-renewable resources. This had led to the growth of a northern service sector which is strongly regionalized and often adversely affected by changes in government expenditure and world market conditions.

This economic orientation now poses a problem. In Canada today, federal fiscal realitites and soft world markets indicate that growth in both of these sectors is likely to be much slower in the coming years. When viewed against the demography and geography of the northern native population, the employment prospects for the territories are not bright.

While other industrial sectors, such as renewable resources and tourism may be able to pick up some of the slack, these sectors remain largely underdeveloped relative to their potential. Those portions which have been developed are tied to southern markets.

Alternative sources of employment and income now need to be found in order to accommodate the rapidly expanding native population. Both the federal and territorial governments have been reviewing their economic development programs and policies in the past couple of years in an effort to find improved ways to broaden and strengthen the North's economic base--the emphasis being on *improved*.

I say this because since the mid-1980s the federal and territorial governments have jointly managed several economic development programs in the areas of renewable resources, mineral development, arts and craft development, small business development and tourism development. All have been aimed at economic diversification.

While this type of programming has led to the creation of several businesses including an elk ranch, several commercial fisheries, an egg and poultry producing facility, an abattoir and numerous tourist facilities, most of the successes have been among the non-native population in the Yukon and the Western Arctic. Additionally, the actual number of northernes that have derived income and employment from these types of ventures has been quite small compared to the number of northerners unemployed or looking for work.

Participation by native people and organizations in this joint programming has been limited. An inappropriate level of program sensitivity towards such issues as language differences, low educational levels and cultural preferences may be partially responsible for this trend. As well, most native communities face certain geographic realities: their remoteness to each other and to southern Canada, small markets, limited transportation and production infrastructure and climate. These reduce the economic viability of most types of initiatives that would be quite successful elsewhere.

This is not to say there have not been successful native ventures. There have been. However, government efforts now need to be more focussed in order to involve a larger number of native people in economic development programs.

One such effort is the recently announced Canadian Aboriginal Economic Development Strategy (CAEDS). The sole purpose of this strategy is to support native business and employment opportunities. Native people and organizations across Canada will be participating in the design and delivery of the various programs covered by CAEDS. The program will be sensitive to regional variations.

A second effort has been in the area of comprehensive claims settlements. In April of this year final comprehensive land claims agreements were reached between Canada and the Indian people of Yukon and the Dene and Metis of the western Northwest Territories. As well, an agreement-in-principle was reached with the Inuit people of the Central and Eastern Arctic. These agreements provided for a settlement amount of $1.8 billion and the confirmation of land ownership of an area slightly larger than the area of Norway. The settlement agreements provided northern native organizations with a substantial land base to manage and develop as they see fit, something not afforded in the past by the economic development programs designed largely by non-natives.

One of the more important economic development initiatives in the agreement-in-principle with the Inuit of the Eastern Arctic is the commitment of the territorial government to develop a wildlife harvesting assistance program. Most native northerners, and in particular the Inuit of the Central and Eastern Arctic, rely on renewable resource harvesting for food and some of their cash income. Those that do not participate in traditional activities often lack the cash necessary to do so. By developing a program that will offer support for these types of activities, a source of employment and income will be available to natives in small, remote communities currently lacking an economic base. All of this will have to be done in an economically and environmentally sustainable manner so that the resource base is available for use by future generations.

Encouraging import substitution is another way of diversifying the northern economy. Canada has had some success, particularly in the areas of food production. However, small markets, limited infrastructure, climate and remoteness severely limit the types of consumer products which can be produced in the Arctic. In the past, the cost of overcoming these limitations has often exceeded the benefits that would result from local production. This problem is not unique to Canada. Other arctic nations face similar economic development challenges. With science and technology being a growth area for future development both nationally and internationally, information exchanges need to increase. Finding appropriate production technologies that are economically viable through the collaborative efforts of circumpolar nations would benefit all circumpolar residents. It is hoped that this type of international cooperation will be facilitated by the upcoming establishment of the Canadian Polar Commission.

Both the federal and territorial governments have come to realize that past economic development have not resulted in enough economic diversification. In an attempt to address this issue each government has developed new economic development strategies within the past couple of years. All emphasize the need for expanding the economy in the areas of renewable resources and tourism in order to develop a sound and stable northern economy.

From a federal perspective, it is hoped that the settlement of land claims and the transfer of remaining provincial-type responsibilities to the territorial governments, will provide northerners with the tools necessary to control the direction of northern economic development. Both these processes were progressing well until the recent rejection of the final claim settlement by the Dene/Metis which, unless resolved, will be a major setback for all parties concerned. The federal government, however, will continue to support northerners' economic development efforts through initiatives such as joint economic development programming, CAEDS and the sharing of revenues from oil and gas development.

Both the Yukon and Northwest Territories governments will be placing increased emphasis on the acquisition by northerners of the requisite skills and training required to participate more fully in the northern economy. Increased environmental scrutiny will also by a priority in order to ensure that the resource base is available for use by future generations. The federal government will be a partner in this effort through the various regional land-use planning commissions and the upcoming Arctic Environment Strategy.

All of these efforts should result in a broader and stronger economic base in the North, where stable, sustainable renewable resource industries supplement and complement the non-renewable resource sector.

Economic Development of Northern Norway

Roald C. Halvorsen

My subject is economic development, or rather the sound economic development, of Northern Norway. To start with, I need to look a little bit back into Norwegian history.

From the beginning of the industrialization of our country, Northern Norway has contributed mainly as a supplier of raw materials, especially those with which the area is richly endowed: fish and minerals. It is significant that most of these materials, after being taken out in the North, have been transported to the South to be processed and sold there. Jack Stagg mentioned the problem of the difference between regions as regards skill and competence. In Norway, traditionally, the competence, the skill, the capital, the decision making, the market intelligence, and the market contacts have all been in the South, while Northern Norway has contributed only with raw materials. Consequently, the whole industrial infrastructure in Northern Norway has been based on the exploitation of these raw materials. The other industry built up there has been completely dependent on that primary activity. This, I believe, is a common feature, and indeed in many respects the definition, of what you could call un-industrialized or Third World countries.

With fluctuating prices and variations in supply of, and access to, the raw materials, it is evident that the infrastructure built up in the North has been hindered in developing in a sound manner. This has led to a military build-up in this area which in turn created possibilities for the local industry in supplying the defense system. The local industry built up has indeed been totally dependent on the military defense system.

The present situation is not very different from what I have sketched here, except that in terms of raw materials our fisheries are now facing a more or less "black sea," with severe consequences for the population living along the coast. We hope this is temporary. Also, the military activity is on a decline, and I am sure we are all very happy for that. But for Northern Norway this is having consequences for the communities which have built up to serve the military in the area.

As a result of these facts, I would say that the whole North Norwegian community is now at the crossroads with respect to the future. We need to do something, and it is my firm belief that the choice is ours and that the opportunities are there. By that I also mean creating what could be called "real jobs," that is, jobs that have not been politically motivated. The challenges and the very considerable possibilities are similar to what we find in other countries stretching towards the Arctic: Sweden, Finland, the USSR, and Canada.

Northern Norway is rich in mineral resources, and it is very rich--even if there is a low procreation at present--in marine resources. It is also rich in fossil fuel deposits. And it is very interesting to see, in Northern Norway as in Canada, the prospect the fish breeding industry is giving us for the future. And not the least, the Arctic presents a maginficent scenery, a magnificent nature which offers possibilities for developing a profitable and economically sound travel and tourist industry, an industry which is still underdeveloped in Norway. Northern Norway is still unpolluted to a degree which with every year becomes more and more rare in the world. We believe we also have the necessary human resources, the people needed for development of our part of the country; some of these people, it is true, are at present in the South--that is where most of the challenging jobs are.

In my view there are two major factors which govern whether or not successful economic development will take place in Northern Norway, and I imagine this applies also to all other Northern or Arctic areas. Both factors have reference to government policies. The first is the political willingness to develop these areas, to ensure a proper setting or the boundary conditions which encourage people to move up North into the Arctic area, and which encourage enterprises to take up the Arctic challenge and work out the possibilities. In this connection it is important to expand Research and Development acitivities ("R&D") related to the North and the Arctic. We need to know more about these areas. We should focus on building up knowledge about inherent business opportunities there, and about how to--under an economic development scheme--preserve the delicate balance of the Arctic nature.

The second main factor is governmental contribution in order to make available necessary venture capital, that is, long term capital, for investment in Arctic projects. Today one of the most significant problems for industry in Northern Norway is that venture capital is lacking.

As regards establishing the necessary boundary conditions which stimulate enterprises and people to settle down, we should look also at such measures as beneficial taxation and wage policies. Some of the counties in the North have implemented this and have gained by it with respect to both people and companies moving there. Equally important is the social infrastructure and the communication and transport systems. Another main feature is the political willingness to take action to preserve the Arctic from the increasing global pollution. A clean and fresh Arctic, free from pollution, will no doubt represent a tremendous sales advantage with respect to tourism, as well as in connection with the breeding and selling of agricultural products, fish products, and so on. I'm sure that if we can have a label on the product that tells us that it is "Produced in the Arctic," this would soon be seen worldwide as a quality mark. We can see it already today.

We in the North should try to identify and develop the really unique business opportunites inherent in, and special to, our areas, and not start something that anybody else in the world can do, and can do better than us. We also really need to look into how to eliminate the disadvantages represented by the long distances to main markets, for example by focusing on developing an industry which produces low volume, light weight products. We are already in the data business, the information technology business, and so on. There are a lot of possibilities.

I am also very concerned about how we can jointly develop close cooperation between the Arctic countries. Facing largely the same problems and challenges, we should establish a common policy towards the exploitation of the Arctic areas with their marine and mineral resources, and we should work out joint development and sharing of experience and knowledge in such fields as exploitation of the fossil fuels, fish breeding, marine biology, pollution, materials technology and building techniques suited to the cold climate, and tourism and travel industry. Finally, we should look into the social infrastructure, all the things people need to thrive, so that they can be creative together and develop the God-given opportunities that the region provides.

Economic Strategy for the Nineties: A Northwest Territories Approach

Peter Allen

Like Norway and many other Scandinavian nations, Canada is a constitutional democracy. Unlike in many of these nations, considerable power rests there with regional or provincial governments. In many ways the Government of the Northwest Territories is a provincial government. We are primary responsible for the NWT's economic and social development and we have the power to raise taxes and introduce new legislation.

Like Scandinavian nations we are an Arctic region. We are also the largest political jurisdiction in Canada, encompassing some 3.2 million square kilometers. This is ten times the size of Norway. We are also sparsely populated. We only have 50,000 people in the whole NWT.

In terms of our economy, we have a Gross Domestic Product or GDP that approaches $2 billion. This is quite a bit smaller than Norway's, at almost $90 billion, but it is quite respectable for our population. In fact, our per capita GDP exceeds that of most Scandinavian nations.

Like in many large and diverse nations, decisions made in Canada in the national interest might hinder, or even impede, development in other areas. Right now, for example, Canada is following a restrictive monetary policy to combat inflationary pressures in central Canada. This means slower development and higher prices for our region. However, the Federal Government plays a major role in economic development in the north and our regional economic policies must complement national objectives.

Economic Overview

Since historic times the economy of the NWT has depended on mining and renewable resource activities. In fact many of our present communities grew around Hudson Bay Company Trading posts; and in many ways the economies of these settlements still revolve around the fur trade and the company store.

With the move of the Government to the NWT in the late sixties, there was a concerted effort to change this. Significant resources were committed to diversifying local economies. Craft shops, sawmills, cooperatives and other types of businesses were directly developed by the government in many communities, providing up to 1200 jobs at their peak. In the eighties, like many other governments, the GNWT closed or privatized these shops because they were not earning profits.

Many people at that time felt the future lay in resource development. Looking at the statistics, it was hard to argue against this. It appeared, at least on paper, that oil and gas, and mining could easily absorb all our unemployed. It was felt that people would move, either on a rotational basis to take these jobs, or they would locate permanently. This did not occur and many of these small communities have the same level of unemployment now as they did then. What went wrong?

Despite the closing of these shops, the rate of growth of the NWT Gross Domestic Product has maintained or exceeded that of the Canadian average, mainly because of oil and gas activities and government expenditures. Other NWT indices such as average and per capita incomes are also in line with the national average. Even though the rate of unemployment is higher than average, it by itself is not a cause for great alarm. As one looks deeper into the figures, particularly on a community by community, or on an ethnic basis, other patterns start to emerge which raise significant concerns.

It becomes clear the basis of the economy is very narrow, and that all people are not benefitting to the same extent. Unemployment in urban industrial centres is negligible, (under 5%), while in the remote communities it can be as high as 50% or more. Not only are there differences between communities but they are even more dramatic between ethnic groups. These differences are compounded by the fact that 56% of working age aboriginal people are in the labour force as compared to 88% for the nonaboriginal population.

Average income statistics demonstrate similar trends with 75% of the income being earned by 60 percent of the population.

Consequently, if economic growth or job creation is not a problem (there is actually a skilled labour shortage in the NWT), what is the problem?

Why the difference in the levels of employment and income between ethnic groups? High costs of living, inadequate transportation infrastructure, a lack of financial services are only symptoms of a much more deep rooted problem. . .a lack of education and training particularly among native people. Nearly three quarters of the aboriginal working age population is functionally illiterate in English.

Why a Strategy Is Important

All governments are facing serious constraints in obtaining new resources. No longer can we afford a shotgun approach to program delivery. Resources must be allocated to the areas where needs are greatest. An economic policy in the NWT based upon the premise that the private sector is the engine of growth is unworkable.

Territorial and Federal programs providing financial assistance to businesses provide for growth. Yet because of a lack of skilled workers it is often necessary to import labour--64% of the NWT labour force was not born in the NWT.

The problem in the NWT is not growth but a poorly integrated economy where a significant portion of the population sit on the sidelines without the skills to participate. Can government afford to wait until the necessary skills are developed? Obviously not; short term solutions must be found to provide jobs for the unemployed now.

With this in mind the government looked at a number of policy options.

Policy Options

Economic policy making to meet the needs of regions with underdeveloped or depressed economies is no science. The array of economic and social circumstances found in the polar regions tend to be surprisingly similar. Numerous approaches to overcome the basic structural problems in these regions have been tried, discarded and tried again. Some have worked better than others, some have not worked at all. Typically policies have fallen into three categories: Resettlement to industrial growth centres, fiscal and taxation incentives to encourage external investment, or industrial developmental subsidies.

Resettlement

The object of a resettlement policy is to relocate people living in remote communities closer to centres of employment and public services. This policy has been implemented in both Greenland and in Newfoundland, Canada. This is an extreme policy and has had disastrous effects where the people relocated lack the skills to fully integrate into an urban industrial environment. Yet this has occurred in southern Canada in the absence of any government intervention as many native people have moved from Indian reservations to the cities forming a new class of urban poor.

Investment Incentives

Instead of bringing people to jobs, fiscal or taxation incentives are offered to attract companies to areas of high unemployment. Distances from markets and high operating costs rule out this as a serious option in the north.

Targeting Strategic Sectors

Direct public intervention in the economy by investing in strategic industries or sectors is a long term approach to creating jobs and income opportunities in high unemployment areas. From a public policy perspective this option is the most complex as it requires commitment of both governments. Furthermore a public/private sector consensus on a developmental plan is required. It also requires a comprehensive analysis of markets, labour supply, technology, capital and distribution channels prior to making investments.

A Policy for the Nineties:
Building on Strengths: A Community Based Approach

In designing an economic policy for the NWT it was important to keep in mind who our target clients are and where they live: working age native people living in communities dependent on traditional acitivities.

After an extensive examination of work and income patterns, four sectors were chosen because they contributed significantly to community and family incomes, exhibited potential for growth and did not require an extensive training effort. The sectors chosen were arts and crafts and other cultural industries, commercial development of renewable resources, and the tourism and travel industry and small businesses.

Arts and Crafts

As a 22 million dollar industry in the NWT, arts and crafts makes up less than 1.5 % of the GDP. Yet it is important because it provides income to those who need it most. In the Baffin Region, one of the poorer regions in the NWT, over 1/4 of working age people derive income from the production of Inuit sculptures. Recent studies have revealed that the artisan base is aging and the skills are not being passed on. To overcome this problem and to revitalize the

industry the GNWT is investing significant money to:
-- broaden the product base by establishing two product development centres;
-- expand training opportunities in the schools and through community based workshops;
-- improve marketing and distribution, and
-- expand production through government sponsored production centres.

Tourism and Travel Sector

In 1988 the value of tourism and travel expenditures was estimated at 57 million dollars. Yet the government believes that the potential in this sector is just beginning to be realized. To tap the potential in this sector the government is embarking on a three pronged program to:
-- improve quality of NWT Tourism products;
-- increase the variety and quality of NWT vacation products, and also
-- continue present efforts in promoting community based tourism.

Small Business

Small business is the NWT's largest employer accounting for 52% of all employment. Yet significant opportunities for growth still exist. By taking the following steps, it is hoped that the potential in this sector will be realized:
-- improving access to capital and eliminating some of the barriers to the establishment of small business in small communities;
-- industry development: providing industry based assistance to overcome some of the common overhead costs associated with industry development - product development, marketing research and development, technology transfer, and to improve integration between industries;
-- Buy North: encourage NWT consumers and business to buy northern services.

Renewable Resources

The renewable resource economy, frequently referred to as the domestic economy, has often been cited as the back bone of the small community economies. It provides food, clothing and shelter, in 1988 valued at more than 54 million dollars. Yet it has not provided a significant source of cash - less than 7.5 million dollars. Great possibilities exist to develop the commercial potential of resources considered surplus to NWT needs, at no cost to domestic consumption.

To develop the commercial potential of these resources the government is taking steps to:

-- improve industry competitiveness, by enhancing technology, training and distribution systems;
-- expand opportunities for value added processing, and
-- expand domestic and renewable resources export markets.

In closing the government believes that we must begin to develop policies which bridge the domestic and the wage based economies, providing a choice for those who wish to complement traditional activities or to work in the wage economy.

Economic development is not only a matter of money, it is also a matter of time. It must be remembered that many in the north are only one or two generations removed from a nomadic lifestyle. We cannot go back, we must provide for economic development which will provide jobs now, utilizing appropriate technology and available resources.

We believe that people living in the NWT, like people throughout the circumpolar world, have the resources and the will to compete on a global scale without compromising the traditions and values that have been important in their survival for thousands of years.

Economic Development As Seen from a Sami Viewpoint

Sven-Roald Nystø

Introduction

In this paper I will deal with the future challenges facing industrial and social development in the areas populated by Samis in northern Norway. Most of the data I will be drawing on is limited in geographical terms to the most northerly part of the country, namely to Nord-Troms and Finnmark. This is not only due to the fact that the majority of the Sami population lives in this area, but also because this is where most of the future challenges are to be found.

The Norwegian Parliament, the Storting, has recently discussed the living conditions in, and prospects for, this area (cf. Committee Report No. 238, 1989-90, and Storting Report No. 32, 1989-90). One of the reasons for this has been the dramatic rate of emigration from the area over recent years - a situation primarily caused by the fact that unemployment levels in the most northerly and north-easterly parts of the country are significantly higher than they are further south. Otherwise, the general living conditions appear to be just as good as in other regional areas of the country. A central point in the political debate concerning the future of northern Norway is the excessive concentration on the *problems* this part of the country has. This has caused people to overlook the *opportunities* it has to offer for positive development. The region has a number of significant advantages to offer - not least its proximity to fish resources, its long tradition in reindeer husbandry, its closeness to foreign markets north of the Arctic Circle, its distinctive natural beauty, culture and location as a basis for tourism, the recorded and potential resources of natural oil in the Barents Sea, and a wide range of mineral resources on the mainland. Added to this is the added quality of life which comes from living in smaller communities where people still feel a sense of responsibility for their fellow man and their environment.

Military and strategic considerations and the need for Norway to stake its claim to natural resources vis-a-vis foreign powers have long influenced the measures which have been adopted for northern Norway. These aspects are now being played down by the Storting which believes that the development of northern Norway is a worthwhile goal in itself, and that the resources this region has to offer make it an important part of the country.

Primary Industries, Modernization and Urbanization

Throughout history, northern Norway has been characterized first and foremost by resources from the sea. The historical picture of the fishing industry has changed over the years, with booms and slumps alternating in an almost rhythmical pattern. Agriculture was also developed intensively from an early date and created its own industry - frequently in the form of a self-sufficient farm economy, but more often through a combined economy of fishing and various forms of agricultural activity.

It was against the backdrop of this fishing and agricultural landscape that the Sami people developed their own economy and culture on the mountain plateaus and fjord sides. This economy was centred around fjord fishing, small holdings, reindeer husbandry and harvesting of the natural resources offered by the land - and often a combination of these. Life was not easy for the Sami community which often found little understanding from the rest of the community around them. From an overall ecological viewpoint, the Sami population displays an astounding ability to adapt. It bases its economy on the mobile exploitation of various different niches of nature - a fact which allows it to resist periods of crisis in the national economy as a whole.

Sovereignty over the northern regions was long disputed. Military and strategic considerations and the need for Norway to stake its claim to the region's natural resources vis-a-vis foreign powers resulted in very heavy colonization by Norway before the turn of the century and brought about the introduction of the mining industry in order to limit influence from the east. However, other considerations also played their part. Right up until the Second World War, northern Norway was seen as the Scandinavian equivalent of America's Midwest. This region offered the poor the possibility of financial rewards and a certain degree of freedom from oppression. The fact that making a living here was linked very considerably to exploiting the land's natural resources made it easy to establish a home in this area.

The development of the community after the Second World War showed very strong signs of modernization and urbanization. There was a significant movement of labour from agriculture and fishing to wage labour. Wheras 40% of employees worked in primary industries in 1950, this figure was down to 11% in 1980, compared to 8% for Norway as a whole. The local Sami community became more closely linked to the national economy and other aspects of national life. The Samis were able to exercise very little influence on

36

the course of this development. Indeed, the Sami way of life, language and culture were seen more as obstacles in this process. Many of the external features of Sami culture were linked to old trades and occupations which disappeared as a result of the adaptions to the economic and social changes. For generations, Sami culture had been regarded as an unimportant and unwanted element of Norwegian society and therefore found itself the victim of a harsh assimilation policy. This made it difficult for the Samis to attach any positive associations to the concept of a Sami identity in their dealings with the country's other inhabitants. This made it tempting for the Samis to shed their cultural heritage, a process particularly evident in the local communities along the coast of northern Norway.

New Political Rights, But Weakening of the Resource Basis for Industrial Activity

The 1970s and 1980s saw a revitalization of the Sami identity in the north. In Norway, this has resulted in the Samis' legal status being anchored in the Norwegian constitution, the passing of a Sami Act and the establishment of a Sami Parliament - the Sámediggi - elected by the Sami people. This has given Samis new political avenues for advancing their claims as a separate ethnic group - a separate people. It has also given Samis greater opportunities to resolve their internal political conflicts. The positive political development in the relationship between the Sami population and the Norwegian authorities has coincided with a worsening in the resource basis for primary industries in the north. Fish resources in the sea are overtaxed, the grazing situation for reindeer has worsened, and there is little opportunity to employ more people in other industries. This has resulted in a high level of emigration southwards. The cumulative effect of this process can be seen as a migrational development from the outlying areas of the country to the centre. The original advantages which northern Norway offered have been turned to disadvantages by industrial policies which have involved high levels of regulation and granting of licences.

As we enter the 1990s, living standards in most sectors of Nord-Troms and Finnmark are on a par with other regional districts in Norway. The critical factor is employment and earning opportunities which are far from satisfactory. The employment market is suffering from a structural imbalance and it is difficult to recruit people for various jobs requiring a high level of training. At the same time, unenployment levels are also high in the fields of agriculture, fishing, industry and construction work. To a large degree women and men work in different parts of the labour market. Many of the women work in the public sector, where jobs are at risk at a time characterized by cuts in local and other public budgets. The motivation to obtain training is lower in this area than elsewhere in the country, particularly amongst boys. Industry lacks capital and banks have made it more difficult to obtain loans for investments due to the large losses suffered in the past. Efforts in research and the field of organizational development lie well below the national average.

It is this situation that most Samis in Norway find themselves in. They live in local communities of varying sizes which have their own special characteristics and in which the differences and variations in culture, population and industry often overshadow the common, uniting features. The Samis' everyday life is very closely linked to the opportunities such communities provide in terms of employment, public and private services, cultural activities and other aspects of social life. Much of this is regulated through national legislation and other state measures which apply to the country's population as a whole irrespective of their ethnic ties. The practical measures which have been implemented for the Sami population as a separate ethnic group are currently rather limited seen from a regional viewpoint. The Sámediggi, as the Samis' representative body, is intended to serve as a platform from which the Samis, within the framework of the possibilities and confines described, can achieve their future aspirations in this area.

Sami Prospects and Opportunities

The Sámediggi's primary aim for the Sami population is to ensure the continuity of the Sami culture against the backdrop of the Samis' status as a nation and as indigenous people. This cannot be achieved without a strong and vital Sami community, a stable population and a diverse business and social life. The Samis' right to self-determination and their influence in society are prerequisites for this. The development of Sami society in the future will require a high level of competence on the part of the Sami people and an adequate understanding of the Sami population in the rest of society. Such a development will ensure that Sami and non-Sami alike will be able to assume their full roles in our multi-cultural society of the future.

The primary goal and condition for future social development in Sami areas is to *guarantee* the resource basis for primary industries such as fishing, agriculture and reindeer husbandry. These basic industries are important not purely as a source of income for part of the population, but also as a vital element in the material basis required to maintain the Sami culture. What is more, the areas and activities associated with these industries and other traditional pursuits linked to the land provide a cultural reference base for Samis in other occupations.

As regards future prospects in the fishing and reindeer husbandry sectors, increased opportunities exist to create new jobs through increased processing of meat and fish. This requires greater attention to product quality and marketing. Over a number of years, a concerted effort has been made to create jobs through building up a Sami arts and crafts industry. Such measures not only strengthen the cultural base for the Sami people, but also provide jobs for women. Even if these measures have resulted in a separate sales and marketing company being established for Sami arts and crafts articles, they have not yet yielded the success hoped for. In addition to organizational and marketing difficulties, there also seems to have been problems on the production side as regards skills and product development. Another factor which has had a particularly strong influence is the continuing debate on the correctness of modernizing traditional Sami products and production techniques for commercial goals. While this question remains unsettled, it will slow down the creation of jobs within the Sami arts and crafts industry.

Tourism finds itself in the same situation. The Samis have so far played only a limited role in this sector. The reason for this is a fear that the Sami culture could be abused by others in attracting tourism. This has been particularly true of developments in Finland. It is therefore vital that Samis are included in the tourism planning process and take an active part in shaping the range of local cultural and other acitivities available. Such developments have been started in Norway.

Sami activities in the field of art and culture will continue to remain heavily dependent on public financial assistance in the future. Jobs created in this sector will be by-products of primary cultural objectives. The potential this sector possesses also depends on the quality of the products it can supply to the market.

There would appear to be a good potential for mining of mineral resources in the Sami districts. This would give rise to a conflict of interests between traditional primary industries and new production industries of an industrial character which would create many new jobs, yet would also leave their mark on the natural environment. This is a continuing debate which in the near future will become a crucial issue for the Sami population. Self-determination will be a central theme in this debate.

An area which appears to offer significant potential for the Samis in the future is research and information technology. Efforts to develop Sami research into an area of prime scientific importance at both national and international level demand systematic, long-term input. So far, however, little political intiative has been demonstrated as regards Sami research work, organizational planning or funding. EDP has been introduced into most Sami institutions, but the potential which exists will take many years to realize.

The greatest challenge for the Sami population would seem to lie in acquiring future-oriented skills. Industry, the public sector and other sectors of the community will demonstrate a growing demand for skilled workers in the future. This makes it essential for the young members of the Sami community to receive training in all areas of activity. This situation will accentuate the tension between traditional Sami ways and more modern life forms. Old strategies for preserving and developing Sami culture will come face to face with new ones. This in turn will place new demands on the Samis' leaders and the implementation of Sami policy. This is a debate which we cannot ignore. Closed strategies are not the answer for our future. An open mind and a willingness to compromise in regard to other communities and cultures will be enriching and inspiring in the long term. The future of the Sami people lies in political *cooperation* between our own and other indigenous peoples, but also with the Norwegian authorities and Norwegian people. By building cooperation on the basis of mutual respect we shall succeed in our goals!

Economic Development of the Canadian North

William S. Grodinsky

We have had a lot of interesting comments made today with respect to economic development of the North. What I will try to do is to simply resumé some of the major challenges, some of the real questions, as titles of areas that really have to be addressed.

The first one is a question of basic commercial and business infrastructures that are required for the North. This is not mere rhetoric. This is very, very important in terms of allowing business, commercial oportunities, economic growth to take place in the North. We heard this morning Mr. Wray talking about some of the difficulties in getting economic development established in the Northwest Territories. I have seen similar examples in Northern Quebec where the inability to get trained accountants, lawyers, secretaries, computer people available locally is an extreme handicap to those who want to promote economic development. It is an important question and really should be addressed. It is translated into traditional costs for anybody trying to promote economic development in the North. It applies also to other professional services such as engineers and architects and mechanics and anyone else who has to provide these types of professional services. It alwyas costs more for Northern residents, Northern businesses, and Northern governments to proceed with projects because they usually have to get people from the South.

Another important question is the question of education. Education is an issue in the North. There is a problem with respect to the level of education, to what people actually know when they come out with certain degrees.

There is also the question--and that is a very important one--of the understanding of certain concepts and certain words. Sometimes people in two different cultures are using the exact same word and it means two different things. There can be agreement on that particular word, but in reality the people are speaking two different languages. So it is a handicap that has to be addressed and has to be looked at as we proceed with economic development.

Another very important area--and that is one where I have had the occasion to work a little while--is the question of vocational and technical education, the question of working towards making vocational and technical education up in the North more available. And this is important because usually, or invariably, the way the courses are presented, the qualifications to enter the course are usually based upon Southern norms. Questions such as class size, the length of training, the people who are actually giving education, those are all based upon the perceptions of people in the South, and invariably they do not reply to what people need in the North. It is important to look at that from the Northern point of view, from the Northern perspective, and to change that system so that it really does answer to the people's needs in the North.

A more fundamental problem is the ability to make traditional attitudes towards the work ethic, to somehow make the importance of traditional activities fit in with commercial activities and economic development. We have the famous story of our goose hunt in Northern Quebec where there is a period of time when basically everything shuts down for a number of weeks. If you go up and want to start a business and presume that things will be running 50 weeks a year, you have got a surprise coming. These are the type of things that people have to realize before there can be successful economic development, and you can adjust and make sure that these things are taken into consideration.

Another real challenge is to push for much more relevant government and institutional support. One particular point that I think has come across in the last little while, at least in Canada, is that there is a scarcity of what is called industrial benefits set-aside programs. In other words, asking an industry or a commercial enterprise to come in--and I am talking about foreign companies who come into the country--and telling them that they have to have some percentage of that work carried out in Canadian regions. Invariably, of course, people will go down South--it is much easier to locate there. It does not take much imagination to say that to promote the development of the North, we should perhaps ask people, force people to look more closely at developing those industries and commerces in the North.

The preferential contract question I think was dealt with very helpfully by Gordon Wray this morning. It is an important issue. He made the very interesting point that there are two types of preferences: there is a preference with regard to the actual price that is bid with respect to a contract, and there is a second preference when a consideration is given to the actual cost of doing business in the North, which at times can be more important than the original preference. It takes into consideration something that is a reality, and the businessmen and the government people in the North know what the people in the South don't know.

There are a number of other issues with respect to allocation of contracts, allocation of work by government. Government is a major employer, a major

42

hirer of companies, employer of people, and it is very important to make sure that government policy with respect to employment and contracts also follows a social objective. It is important to make sure that contracts are known in the North, so that people can organize themselves to take advantage of them. It is also important that the people who give out these contracts be people who live and work in the North. You can be sure that if the contract office is located in Ottawa, in Southern Canada, it is highly likely that the contracts, whatever they are and notwithstanding whatever preferences are given, will go to companies located in the South. If in fact the contracts are given out of Yellowknife or Whitehorse, people will be looking at it from a different perspective. Those who give out a contract will then of course also be lobbied by people who live in that area, and then there will be much more pressure to give it to a Northern company.

One other issue is to make sure that people take advantage of the situations in the North. There is the question of distance, the question of geography. It helps if air, road, and marine transportation in the North are operated by Northern enterprises. Northern carriers have the expertise; they can serve a distinct market, and they can be preferred by government.

There is also the overall question of looking at a Northern market. Some 30 years ago, our Prime Minister Mr. Diefenbaker was talking about a "northern vision," urging Canadians to look to the North as a new frontier. The frontier is there, and perhaps this vision was a difficult one because it came from Ottawa. If the vision came from the North, then perhaps that vision could in fact be implemented.

One difficult area that has to be dealt with is the question of bias, racism, and discrimination that often affects commercial operations in the North. These are difficult issues to talk about, but having been involved with a couple of them I think that they represent a reality. It is very clear that in Northern Canada, for example, it is much preferable at this point for government to be giving contracts opportunities to people within the establishment rather than to native groups. We have had a number of situations where you have to fight that initial bias and sometimes have to come out public with it, and it is important to know that it always exists.

There was a clear mention made by Jack Stagg with respect to the question of new technology. This is very important. We do have examples of new technology having been used with great innovation in the North. Some of us here have talked about innovative ways of producing energy, and with a little bit of imagination and effort those things could come through.

One final point I think it important to add is the question of private funds available for the North. There have been funds established in Canada, private investment funds, used for selected opportunities in the environmental industry, for example. It may be an idea--and again it takes the right kind of investor and the right kind of people involved--to look at setting up funds specifically for development and investment in the North, and that is an idea I think will have its day at one point in time.

Achieving Sustainable Development in Canada's North

Stephen Hazell and Zella Osberg

1 Introduction

As an approach for reconciling economic development and environmental conservation goals in Canada's North, the concept of sustainable development has figured in initiatives of northern governments and been reflected in emerging comprehensive native claims settlements. The use of the term "sustainable development" over the past few years has created greater interest in the study of environment-economy linkages in the Yukon and Northwest Territories (NWT).

The term "sustainable development" first received wide currency in the 1980 World Conservation Strategy and was popularized by *Our Common Future*, the 1987 report of the World Commission on Environment and Development (the Brundtland Commission).[1] Yet the popularity of the phrase has not led to any clear consensus among scholars, let alone policy-makers, as to what the expression means or demands.

The phrase "sustainable growth" has crept into use by political leaders and business writers as a synonym for sustainable development, notwithstanding the very different sense that the former expression conveys. Speaking at a conference on Canada-United States bilateral relations in the Arctic in Whitehorse, a British Petroleum executive based in Alaska recently applied the phrase (in the context of the Alaskan oil industry) to mean ensuring the sustained production of oil and gas from the Alaskan North Slope.[2] And some scholars have proposed that the creation of trust funds from the profits of northern mineral, oil and gas developments represents a sustainable approach to the development of non-renewable resources--without regard to the environmental implications of such development.[3] Clearly, there is great danger that the term may lose all content through overuse or misuse.

Our Common Future is perhaps a key touchstone for the iteration of the concept: sustainable development is defined in the Brundtland report as "development that meets the needs of the present without compromising the ability of future generations to meet their own needs."[4] *Our Common Future* emphasizes that sustainable development means alleviating poverty--meeting human needs--in an equitable manner. Sustainable development also means meeting those human needs in ways that do not compromise the global ecology--the life-support systems of the earth upon which all creatures depend.

Discussion of sustainable development is frequently restricted to describing goals for the management of renewable resources, perhaps due to the difficulty of applying the concept to the development of non-renewable resources. Restricting the discussion in this manner, however, avoids the broader challenge that sustainable development poses, that is, to re-think cultural values and related economic imperatives in terms of ecological and social sustainability.

Sustainable development is a process, a process that for ecological reasons demands cultural as well as political and economic change. It is not likely to be achieved through "business as usual with a treatment plant."[5] Canada's North lies at the margins of North America, culturally as well as politically and economically. Here the mainstream consumer culture of the west confronts traditional subsistence cultures, and the result is the social dislocation of many native people.

Yet this very cultural, not to mention political and institutional flux in the Yukon and Northwest Territories provides opportunities to reconcile economic development and environmental conservation goals in novel ways that have not occurred to communities and policy-makers elsewhere. For this reason, the paper focuses on developments involving the territorial governments and northern native organizations, rather than reviewing efforts made at federal or international levels.

This paper briefly describes the environmental, economic, and political challenges facing the Yukon and Northwest Territories, highlighting several approaches by the territorial governments to develop economic strategies that incorporate or refine the sustainable development concept. The paper also identifies two concrete examples of initiatives that have potential to lay foundations for durable economic development, ensure environmental conservation and meet economic, social and cultural needs. Note that the paper does not attempt to describe all of the numerous initiatives made by federal, territorial and aboriginal organizations to advance the concept of sustainability, merely a few that are particularly interesting in the context of the current discussion.

2 Challenges in Canada's North

(i)   Northerners and the Northern Environment

Approximately 83,000 individuals live in the Yukon and Northwest Territories--dispersed over an area larger than India--in about 83 communities.[6] Most of these communities remain isolated by the vast distances between them, notwithstanding improved transportation and communication links with other parts of Canada, as well as the United States.

The cultural heritage of the two territories is diverse. In the Yukon 14 per cent, and in the NWT some 58 per cent are of native/aboriginal origin. The balance of the population have come from a wide variety of European, American and Oriental cultures.[7] By and large, most of these northerners want to stay in the North and provide a future for their children and their children's children.

The northern population is growing quickly. In the NWT, for instance, the overall population growth rate is above the national average with the native population growing at three times the national rate.[8] Social stresses within northern communities are also growing, as manifested by high rates of suicide, family violence and substance abuse. Contributing factors such as unemployment are significant. Overall unemployment rates are well above the national average: the so-called underdeveloped communities suffer very high rates. To meet this challenge, the economy of the NWT, for instance, must create 1,140 jobs per year for the next ten years for unemployment rates in the underdeveloped communities to be equalized at 7 per cent and labour force participation rates to be increased from 58 per cent to 84 per cent.[9]

These growing northern communities are placing increasing demands on the lands that support them. Pressures to create jobs through the development of non-renewable resources (oil, gas, mining) and renewable resources (commercial wildlife ranching and harvesting, tourism), as well as pressures to improve transportation services (roads, ports, airports), and such municipal necessities as adequate housing and waste treatment facilities are challenging the way in which northern peoples view their relationship with the land.

Like the people, the lands north of 60 degrees north latitude (60°N) vary dramatically from region to region, settlement to settlement. The diversity in climate, ecology and geo-physical features means that the feasibility and desirability of types of resource development in different parts of the North vary widely as well.

The lands and ecosystems of Canada's North are now subject to new environmental threats. Organic chemicals, heavy metals and acid gases transported long distances from Eurasia and southern North America are contaminating northern ecosystems and wildlife.[10] Among other scientific findings, high levels of polychlorinated biphenyls (PCBs) discovered in the blood of Inuit women and children and the breast milk of Inuit women of Broughton Island have raised concern about the quality of wildlife as a source of food. While the benefits of consuming locally hunted seals, fish, whales and other species appear to outweigh the disadvantages of not consuming them, the trends are disquieting, given the reliance of many northerners on these foods for survival.[11]

Northern ecosystems are especially vulnerable to being affected disproportionally by several global environmental threats. Increasing global atmospheric concentrations of carbon dioxide produced largely by fossil fuel consumption may lead to dramatic climatic and ecological changes in Canada's Arctic. Even conservative models suggest that the warming of the arctic regions at 60°N to 75°N would likely be 2.5 to 4 times as great in the North as between 5°N and 1 3°N.[12] The depletion of the ozone layer caused by chemicals such as chlorofluorocarbons (CFCs) is also most severe in the polar regions.[13]

Northern industrial activities, such as mining, oil and gas exploration, development and transportation in and around the Canadian territories also have significant potential to undermine, if not destroy, northern ecosystems. Already in certain cases, the damage sustained to date appears to be, for practical purposes, irreversible. An evaluation of the Alaskan Prudhoe Bay oil development, for example, found that restoring the industrialized areas was neither economically nor technologically feasible.[14]

Proposals for new developments, such as off-shore hydro-carbon exploration, must come to terms with the significant environmental and logistical limitations posed by the arctic environment. An oil spill in the Canadian Arctic on the scale of the *Exxon Valdez* disaster could be catastrophic. The harsh climatic conditions make clean-up extremely difficult, and arctic ecosystems recover slowly, if ever, from the effects of contamination. Recent studies have concluded that neither the federal government nor industry has the capacity to clean up major oil spills in arctic waters.[15]

The need for sustainable approaches to economic development is acute in the Canadian North with its growing population, increasing demands on natural resources and mounting concern over the quality and integrity of northern ecosystems.

(ii)   The Changing Political Context: Who Makes the Development Decisions?

Over the past two decades, decision-making for economic development of Canada's North has gradually decentralized: power is moving from Ottawa and other southern Canadian centres north to the territorial governments and the public institutions created under comprehensive native claims agreements. As claims are settled and devolution proceeds, there is an excellent opportunity to ensure that new and strengthened northern-based institutions are directed to achieving sustainable development.

Historically, decisions to develop northern resources have largely been made outside the North to serve the interests of, and provide benefits to, people outside the North. The North has been viewed as a last frontier for exploitation and development, not as the homeland of northern peoples with their own development priorities. As a result, most of the economic benefits of industrial development (cash, technical and manufacturing jobs, skills development) have flowed south of 60°N, while the costs of development activities--adverse environmental impacts and social and cultural disruption--have remained in the North. This systemic mismatch in the allocation of benefits and costs, as well as being unjust, clearly has not encouraged the development of sustainable economies in the North.

The federal government continues to act as the "landlord of the north" primarily through its ownership of federal Crown lands. (In the NWT alone, this applies to 97% of the territory.) In this capacity, the federal government has final authority on a wide range of matters including the issuance of land use permits and leases for activities such as construction of airstrips, mining exploration and production and oil and gas production wells.[16] Federal presence in the north is also reinforced through the administration of its other constitutional responsibilities, such as native affairs, coast guard and shipping, fisheries, defence, international agreements, energy export.[17]

The two territorial governments, however, have increased their administrative and legislative responsibilities with federal consent. The federal government is committed to "enhanced northern political development" and is negotiating the devolution of province-like powers to the territories as well as the settlement of comprehensive native claims.[18] But the devolution process has been slow and the cost to the territorial governments is high, given the federal government's commitment to reducing its deficit through spending restraint.[19]

These evolving territorial governments must also meet institutional challenges unlike any faced by Canadian provinces for they must share any new devolved powers over resource development with the public institutions established under comprehensive native claims agreements. These agreements will have a profound effect on territorial government planning since they have created, or are creating, new institutions of public government to manage native rights recognized for settlements areas.

These agreements are at varying stages of maturity. The comprehensive claim of the Inuivialuit of the western Arctic was finalized and ratified by Parliament in 1984.[20] In 1990, the Dene/Metis of NWT and the Yukon Indians signed final agreements with the federal government, now subject to ratification by Parliament and the native people themselves. Also in 1990, the Inuit of Nunavut (the eastern Arctic) signed an agreement-in-principle with the federal government.[21]

The new management regimes set out in the agreements are of varying complexity but all circumscribe the authority of federal or territorial governments concerning natural resource development. Joint management boards with members appointed in equal numbers by governments and native groups have primary authority to manage wildlife, land and water, as well as to assess the environmental impacts of proposed development projects.[22] The claims agreements will also provide the native organizations of the Dene/Metis and eastern Inuit with new capital--in excess of $1 billion--which will be used in part to fund economic development in the settlement regions.[23]

Of particular interest respecting the decision-making authority over resource use is the Inuit agreement-in-principle because it has clear implications for the decision-making processes of the federal and territorial governments. In practical terms, it provides the Inuit with the potential to govern the pace and quality of resource development within the settlement lands and ensure that development strategies respond to the specific environmental, social and cultural requirements of Inuit communities. And while the various claims agreements do not explicitly refer to sustainable development as an objective, their decided emphasis on the conservation of renewable resources, protection of the environment and assessment of non-renewable resource projects is consonant with sustainable development.

The finalization and implementation of the Dene/Metis and Inuit claims is likely to lead to further decentralization of decision-making authority within the Northwest Territories. Certainly, the Inuit continue to be committed to creating an eastern territory called Nunavut. A proposal to divide the Northwest Territories to take account of its geo-physical and cultural differences has been on the table for some time. The settlement of these claims provides a new opportunity to review the future of the NWT government, possibly leading to division of the Territory into Nunavut and a western territory.

Devolution and the negotiation of comprehensive claims provides northerners with a unique opportunity to create options for sustainability through institutions designed to be responsive to the environmental and cultural needs of specific communities and regions.[24] Northern-based institutions should be better able to ensure that economic and social benefits of proposed developments stay in the North and that any associated environmental and social costs and risks are avoided or mitigated.

3 Achieving Sustainable Development

(i) Territorial Policy Initiatives

In recent years, the territorial governments of the Yukon and Northwest Territories have invested considerable energy in exploring how to develop northern economies in ways that do not compromise the ability of future generations of northerners to meet their needs. Both governments have sponsored extensive consultations throughout their territories to better understand the concerns and aspirations of their citizens as well as commissioning many studies in an effort to chart a sound course for the future.

The term "sustainable development" is used to varying extents in the reports that have emerged from these efforts. Frequently the use of the term is confined to management of renewable resources rather than to any discussion of the overall goals of economic development strategies and its implications for cultural priorities (non-native, as well as native). However, a closer look at these reports reveals an awareness of the issues central to the development of sustainable economies and societies.

The Yukon Government began its quest for a fresh approach to development in 1986 after a particularly tough recession when "we were still painfully aware that a bad day at the London metal markets or an Asian smelter could ruin our lives."[26] Recognizing that economic activity "should serve human goals, not just vague abstractions labelled 'the bottom line,' "[27] four goals for an economic strategy were identified through an extensive territory-wide consultation process entitled "Yukon 2000." Offered as the basis for the 1989 Yukon Economic Strategy, these four goals were: the option to stay in the Yukon; control of the future; an acceptable quality of life; and equality of opportunity for all Yukoners.[28]

The *Yukon Conservation Strategy: For Our Common Future,* released in

1990, presents the Government's recommendations and commitments for achieving sustainable development, building on the work of the Task Force on Northern Conservation, the Select Committee on Renewable Resources and the Yukon Economic Strategy. Among the critical contributions that this report brings to economic strategic planning is not only the recognition that environmental protection and conservation is the keystone to sound resource use but also that cultural heritage and knowledge, non-monetary values, informed decision-making and commitment to the global community are important components.[29]

In the NWT, similar efforts have been undertaken. In 1987, the Legislative Assembly of the Northwest Territories gave the Special Committee on the Northern Economy (SCONE) the task of developing workable recommendations to improve the territorial economy. After extensive consultation, the Committee submitted a report in 1989 entitled *The SCONE Report: Building Our Economic Future.*

At the outset, the *SCONE Report* clarifies its orientation to creating an economic development strategy. It asserts that economic development is "very different from economic growth. It is the kind of economic activity that provides real benefits to local resident--jobs, training, increased opportunities for local business. Where economic growth is ephemeral--here today, gone tomorrow--economic development is longer term. It usually leads to a change in the structure of the economy itself."[30]

In this context, the *SCONE Report* tops its list of key policy and program development recommendations with the recommendation that the Government of the Northwest Territories (GNWT) implement a policy on sustainable development. The Committee made this recommendation because protection of the environment was identified as the single most important issue by communities throughout the Territories.[32]

In 1989, the GNWT also released a discussion paper on sustainable development. A major initiative based on its study of sustainable development will be announced during the 1990 fall session of the Legislative Assembly.[33]

The GNW has responded to the *SCONE Report* and its own studies with a new series of economic strategy papers: *Economy in Transition: An Agenda for Action* and its short-term component, *Building on Strengths: A Community-Based Approach.* In the latter, the theme of sustainability is central to the strategy offered for the development of renewable resources.[34] It is also recognized as an important principle in the strategy for tourism development.[35]

It is noteworthy that a sustainable development policy is being developed separately from the economic strategy papers. Since sustainable development is intended as a way of integrating environmental conservation concerns into economic decision-making, the splitting of "sustainable development" planning from "economic development" planning suggests that the former could well be marginalized, with the latter supporting business as usual.

Nevertheless, both territorial governments have made significant efforts to incorporate principles of "sustainable development" in their designs for the future. How this will translate into program or institutional initiatives remains to be seen. Certainly, it is premature to assess whether the concept has truly influenced official thinking in the territorial governments.

(ii)   Promising Approaches to Sustainability

While the concept of sustainable development can to some extent be refined and described through government policy and strategy documents, the dimensions of the concept can best be explored through application to specific challenges. The following two examples have been chosen because they show promise as models for sustainable northern development. (They may also inspire fresh thinking for similar challenges in other regions.)

Each example appears to acknowledge or take account of three principles for sustainable development that are critical in Canada's North, and, probably, elsewhere. These are to:
-- recognize the importance of environmental conservation and incorporate measures to sustain and protect ecosystems;
-- demonstrate potential to produce economic benefits (jobs, cash, skills training) for the community concerned, and
-- respond to community priorities as articulated by the communities themselves.

Isabella Bay (Igalirtuuq) Conservation Proposal

The community of Clyde River on Baffin Island in the Eastern Arctic has developed a proposal for a conservation plan to protect the endangered Bowhead whale and its critical habitat in the Isabella Bay (Igalirtuuq) area, in cooperation with the World Wildlife Fund Canada (WWF). The specific objectives of the proposal are to establish a whale sanctuary under federal legislation and a Biosphere Reserve under the UNESCO Man and Biosphere Program, and to use territorial legislation to document and protect important archaeological sites in the surrounding area.[36]

It is of critical significance that the proposal is sponsored by the community.

This has been done in full recognition of the economic trade-offs that the community must make to ensure that the conservation plan represents a meaningful effort to conserve one of the environmental assets of the region.

Located 120 km south of the community of Clyde River, the Isabella Bay area provides feeding and breeding grounds for Bowhead whales, and is likely the only site in the world where these whales can be observed on consecutive days. Bowhead numbers dropped from 11,000 to near extinction due to commercial whaling, although such whaling ceased almost a century ago. Despite designation as an endangered species, there are no signs that Bowhead populations are recovering.

The Bowhead whale is a critical component of the marine environment on which the people of Clyde River depend. Archaeological artifacts indicate that these whales have played a significant part in the heritage of the Inuit of Baffin Island for some time. They also continue to represent an important part of the cultural heritage that residents wish to pass on to their children.

Since 1983, the community has been involved with the biological research on the Bowhead undertaken by various government and non-governmental agencies. This work has increased understanding of the whales and their prospects for survival. In particular, this research has revealed an urgent need for conservation action if the Bowhead whale population is to have any chance of recovery.

In 1988, the Hamlet Council and Hunters and Trappers Association of Clyde River formed a committee to develop a conservation plan for Isabella Bay. The plan was endorsed by the community at a public meeting in October 1988 and the details for implementing the plan are now set out in a proposal to the federal and territorial governments.[37]

The proposal addresses not only the issues concerning the survival of the Bowhead, but also the implications for community development. For instance, it is clear that tourists are interested in seeing the Bowhead at close range. Providing such opportunities therefore has economic potential--a fact reflected in the GNWT's long range plans for developing on-site viewing facilities and an American proposal for an air-strip at Isabella Bay to service charter flights.

While recognizing that tourism can create economic benefits as well as raise public awareness and support for conservation efforts, residents of Clyde River have decided to support a very cautious approach to the exploitation of tourism opportunities. The conservation plan notes that these whales are extremely sensitive to disturbances, and so, proposes that tourist activities be introduced in stages with continuous monitoring to identify any negative impacts on the whales. It also gives preference to land-based observation, sets guidelines for boats carrying whalewatchers and contemplates limitations on the number of tourists permitted in the area each year.

The plan looks closely at the influence of local traffic, particularly boat traffic associated with traditional hunting. Preference is given to non-motorized boats and kayaks, but even these must not be used to harass the whales. All boats must avoid the key feeding and breeding areas of the Bowhead whales during the period of use (mid-August to mid-October each year).

The proposed guidelines for use of the conservation area also include prohibitions on low-level flying by helicopters and airplanes, hunting of narwhal and walrus during specified periods, non-renewable resource development and other polluting activities.

The community has also identified how it wants to be involved in the implementation of the conservation plan. The plan proposes that the community of Clyde River supply guides and outfitters, be involved in any tourism management committee and provide shelter for on-going scientific and tourist activities. As importantly, the residents want to be kept informed of and involved in further research efforts and participate in the land use permit review process where Bowhead interests are concerned. Among other advantages, these proposals would assist the development of local resource management skills.

Recognizing the importance of the plan for themselves, for the Bowhead and as a model for other northern conservation challenges and communities, the community of Clyde River is offering to commit people and skills. The plan reflects a commitment to make a significant investment in the future--to restore populations of Bowhead whales--which may only yield substantial economic benefits after many years. Recognizing that the proposed plan does not represent a complete or final solution to the Bowhead crisis, it concludes with an apt quotation from an unnamed poet: "Traveller, there is no path. Paths are made by walking."

Not only does the Isabella Bay proposal support community involvement in achieving sustainable development, it also recognizes the role that cultural heritage plays in nurturing a sustainable society. If one broadens the definition of economic development to include the avoidance of the economic costs of social ills,[38] (much as policy-makers are coming to accept the concept that economic value must factor in the costs of environmental degradation) then it becomes clear that this conservation plan has the potential to add a great more to the regional economy than a donut shop could ever hope to do.

The economic value of participation in traditional wildlife harvesting in Canada's North is widely recognized. But not only does the harvest of wildlife life put food on the table (in communities where even those with relatively good incomes have trouble feeding themselves), provide furs to clothe and fuels to warm, the very exercise in harvest-related activities reinforces the values of traditional lifestyles that maintain physical and mental well-being.[39]

For some time, various organizations, notably the Tungavik Federation of Nunavut (TFN, the Inuit claims organization), the Canadian Arctic Resources Committee and more recently SCONE have advocated the development of a wildlife harvest support program (WHSP) as a means of supporting the domestic or subsistence economy in the NorthwestTerritories.[40] (Such programs to support harvesters are already in place for the Cree and Inuit of northern Quebec.)

These proposals are not conceived as guaranteed income programs that serve to redistribute economic benefits to those most needy, but to insure benefits are received for the performance of hard work in a difficult environment.[41] There are also ecological benefits to encouraging harvesters to stay on the land. They have a strong interest in ensuring that wildlife and ecosystems are not threatened, thus representing a political counterweight to industrial developers who primarily value the non-renewable resources of the North.

TFN has proposed a wildlife harvest support program to provide cash to Inuit who wish to return to the land as harvesters. In this proposal, the family is the beneficiary unit. Eligible families are those on the community list with an income below a specified level. Receipt of benefits would hinge on evidence of effort rather than success in harvesting.[42]

The first assumption underlying this and other similar proposals is that subsistence harvesting in the North is now expensive and that the lack of cash to purchase snowmobiles, rifles and gear is breaking down the hunting economy. A second assumption is that government funds currently spent on social assistance in underdeveloped communities could be more usefully redirected to supporting harvesting, which generates wealth for the harvester, and his or her family and community. Third, a WHSP would maintain and further develop harvesters' hunting, trapping and fishing skills and knowledge of local wildlife and wildlife habitat thereby maintaining a vital link with the land.[43]

A wildlife harvest support program could build in community-specific features. These might include providing apprenticeships for untrained youth, supporting supplementary involvement in the wage economy, and ensuring subsistence support to those within the community who may need it.[44]

In its review of income support programs, the GNWT is currently evaluating the feasibility of a wildlife harvest support program with a working group. This group includes representatives from the Dene Nation, the Metis Association, the Tungavik Federation of Nunavut and the Inuvialuit Regional Corporation. After an analysis of regional harvester surveys, proposals will be made to the GNWT Cabinet in the fall of 1990.

A WHSP would promote the economic independence of harvesters and enhance the renewable resource economy, an economy less prone to the boom and bust cycles. The caribou, moose, seals, and fish that are harvested provide cheap, nutritious country foods that replace very expensive foods imported from the south. So improvements in diet, lifestyle, nutrition and health associated with a WHSP could also result in reduced health care costs, although this is difficult to quantify.[45] There probably would also be spin-off economic benefits from the increased purchasing power of residents, as well as from sales of animal by-products (dog food, oriental medicines, alternate fuels).[46] Not only would a WHSP create useful work in communities with high unemployment and few employment or economic opportunities; social problems linked to unemployment and welfare dependence would also likely decrease.[47]

A WHSP appears to have potential to meet many of the social, cultural and economic requirements of the smaller, more traditionally-oriented communities while furthering conservation objectives. It offers a way of meeting pressing social and cultural needs through small but carefully targetted infusions of cash in support of traditional subsistence economies. In doing so, other costs to the state (social assistance, health care costs) may also be reduced. And because it is conceived as a program that would be tailored to meet specific local requirements, it may prove valuable as a model of sustainable community development.

This program, however, would not meet the needs of all northerners. Even among the native youth, many evince little interest in maintaining traditional lifestyles.[48] Nor is it the solution for all time: the impact of global environmental threats such as climate change, ozone depletion and toxic chemical pollution on northern ecosystems and wildlife cannot be predicted with any accuracy, so country foods produced from northern wildlife may not always be abundant and healthful. And while populations of species subject to harvesting are thought to be more than adequate to meet the additional harvesting pressure resulting from a WHSP at present, future demands from the growing human populations in NWT communities could eventually exceed sustainable yields.[49]

But the Isabella Bay and wildlife harvest support program proposals represent the adaption of environmentally responsive, traditional interests and activities to the exigencies of modern commerce and therefore are of great value in charting sustainable futures. The people of Clyde River are seeking to protect an important traditional cultural and economic asset (the Bowhead whales) while cautiously developing a modern economic asset (tourism). Clyde River appears willing to forego the easy, but perhaps short-lived economic benefits of major tourism efforts now in favour of a long-term approach. The wildlife harvest support program offers northern people the opportunity to engage in the traditional hunting, fishing and trapping economy while addressing the very modern need for cash to make that economy work in the 1990s and the very real human costs of social deterioration typical of welfare ghettos.

4 Conclusion

The global environment crisis so eloquently described in *Our Common Future* is giving rise to a cultural and political crisis: profound changes will be required in the organization of most if not all human societies to avoid the breakdown of ecosystems around the world. Yet most governments of the industrialized west are not demonstrating the leadership required to adapt to the worrisome ecological realities.

Canada's Yukon and Northwest Territories are undergoing dramatic political, economic and social changes without parallel in North America. Devolution of authority from federal to territorial governments, settlement of comprehensive native claims, growing populations, combined with threats to the northern environment and increasing demands for northern natural resources create a dynamic climate for environmental and economic decision-making. In this context, the newly empowered territorial governments are demonstrating a commitment to reconciling economic development and environmental conservation goals in the North.

The social dislocation of native people in northern Canada is largely due to tensions between traditional subsistence culture, with its ethic of conservation and sustainability, and western consumer culture. The Isabella Bay and wildlife harvest support program initiatives can be viewed as ways to resolve these tensions within frameworks that appear to meet criteria for ecologically and socially sustainable development.

Creating cultures with an ethic of sustainability, and institutions that support such cultures are key objectives for the 1990s, the turn-around decade for the global environment. There is evidence that a regeneration of the conservation ethic of native subsistence societies--the symbiotic links with nature and the land that informs their cultures--is underway in Canada's northern territories. These northern approaches to sustainable development, specifically the processes for supporting ecologically sustainable economies and societies, should be of interest and use to others more completely immersed in the mainstream of western consumer culture.[50]

Notes

1   World Commission on Environment and Development, *Our Common Future*, Oxford U.K., 1987.

2   Roger Herrera, British Petroleum, speaking at the 1990 Pearson-Dickey conference, Whitehorse, Yukon, May 11, 1990.

3   Pretes, Michael and Michael Robinson, "Permanent Trust Funds and Sustainable Non-Renewable Resource Management in the Canadian North," *Resources*, 25 (Winter 1989), 7-8.

4   WCED, *Our Common Future*, p. 43.

5   Dr. Bill Rees, personal communication.

6   Based on 1989 figures: 29,845 (Yukon), 53,326 (Northwest Territories), see: Yukon Fact Sheet, Yukon Executive Council Office (Bureau of Statistics); Population Estimates, By Community and Region, Northwest Territories (Bureau of Statistics, Government of the Northwest Territories).

7   Special Committee on the Northern Economy, *The SCONE Report: Building Our Economic Future*, Legislative Assembly of the Northwest Territories (October 1989), p. 11; Yukon Fact Sheet.

8   Special Committee, p. 12.

9   Special Committee, p. 25.

10   *Contaminants in Northern Ecosystems and Northern Diets* (Summary of an Evaluation Meeting held in Ottawa, February 29 to March 2, 1989), Indian and Northern Affairs, Ottawa.

11   *Contaminants (Summary)*, see note 10. Concerning PCBs, see, for example: Kuhnlein, H.V. and D. Kinloch, "PCBs and Nutrients in Baffin Island Inuit Foods and Diets," "Assessment of PCBs in Arctic Foods and Diets," *Circumpolar Health 87 (Proceedings)*; ed. Linderholm at al., *Arctic Medical Research*, Vol. 47: Suppl. 1 (1988) 155-158, 159-162.

12   Roots, E.F., personal communication.

13   Roots, E.F., personal communication.

14   Speer, Lisa and Sue Libenson, *Oil in the Arctic: The Environmental Record of Oil Development on Alaska's North Slope: Executive Summary* (Natural Resources Defence Council Inc., 1988), p.i.

15   Canadian Arctic Resources Committee, *A Submission by the Canadian Arctic Resources Committee to the Public Review Panel on Tanker Safety and Marine Spills Response Capability*, Whitehorse, Yukon, November 27, 1989; *News North*, Monday, July 9, 1990, p. A 12.

16   Canada, *Territorial Lands Act*, R.S.C. 1985, c. T-7.

17   Canada, *Constitution Act*, 1867, R.S.C. 1985, App., *National Energy Board*, R.S.C., 1985, c. N-7.

18   Department of Indian and Northern Affairs, Canada, *Northern Political and Economic Policy Framework*, (Ottawa: Supply and Services, 1988), p. 5. A more recent public statement upholding this commitment: Notes for a speech by the Honourable Pierre H. Cadieux, P.C., M.P., Minister of Indian Affairs and Northern Development, to conference on "Strengthening Canada-USSR Relations: Cooperation in the Arctic," October, 25, 1989, p. 9.

19   The cost is expected to be high primarily because territorial governments will not be able to draw on the range of federal resources that current federal northern programs can. For further discussion, see: Special Committee, pp. 40-42, and, Yukon Executive Council Office, "Green Paper on Constitutionat Development," p. 10. In addition, the territorial governments are faced with meeting rising demands and expectations arising from current responsibilities that must be met with reduced federal funding. Federal funding, which accounts for a significant portion of the territorial governments' revenue, has been reduced through revision of the Formula Financing Arrangements for both territories. See, for example, concerns expressed in: The Honourable Michael A. Ballantyne (Minister of Finance), *1990-91 Budget Address,* (Yellowknife: Government of the Northwest Territories, February, 1990), pp. 9-11.

20   *Western Arctic (Inuvialuit) Claims Settlement Act,* S.C. 1984, c.24.

21   *DenelMetis Comprehensive Land Claims Agreement in Principle* (September 1988), *Yukon Indian Land Claim Framework Agreement* (October 1988), *Agreement-in-Principle between the Inuit of the Nunavut Settlement Area and Her Majesty in Right of Canada* (March 1990).

22   See, for example, Inuit Agreement-in-Principle, articles 5, 10-13,15.

23   Government of the Northwest Territories, *Economy in Transition: An Agenda for Action,* p. 11.

24   Concerning Inuit settlement, see: Fenge, Terry, "Toward Environmentally Sustainable Economic Development: The Potential Contribution of the Inuit Land Claim

Settlement" (unpublished manuscript).

25   Some of the key reports include: Yukon Government, *Yukon Economic Strategy, Yukon 2000: Building the Future*; Special Committee, *SCONE Report;* Government of the Northwest Territories, *Economy in Transition;* Government of the Northwest Territories, *Building on Strengths: A Community-Based Approach.*

26   Yukon, *Yukon 2000,* p.iii.

27   Yukon, *Yukon 2000, p.* 3.

28   Yukon, *Yukon 2000,* p. 3.

29   Yukon Government, *Yukon Conservation Strategy: For Our Common Future,* pp.8-9.

30   Special Committee, p. 2.

31   Special Committee, p. 54.

32   Special Committee, p. 57.

33   This initiative will include the announcement of the membership of a "Round Table" on the environment and economy, the usefulness of which will, of course, depend on its composition and mandate.

34   Government of the Northwest Territories, *Renewable Resources: Building on a Tradition (Building on Strengths)*, pp.1,14.

35   Government of the Northwest Territories, *Tourism: The Northern Lure (Building on Strengths), p. 13.*

36   Community of Clyde River (Northwest Territories), *Igalirtuuq: A Conservation Proposal for Bowhead Whales at Isabella Bay, Baffin Island, NWT*, (January, 1990), p. 1. Note: the source for the discussion that follows in this paper is this proposal.

37   Note: this proposal is the same as that noted in note 36.

38   For some discussion on such socio-economic costs and the concept of "social sustainability" see: Osberg, L."Sustainable Social Development" (Dalhousie Working Paper, dated May 28,1990).

39   Freeman, M.M.R., "Environment Society and Health," *Circumpolar Health 87 (Proceedings)*; ed. Linderholm et al, *Arctic Medical Research,* vol .47: Suppl.l (1988), 53-59; and Ames, R.et al, *Keeping on the Land: A Study of the Feasibility of a Comprehensive Wildlife Harvest Support Programme in the Northwest Territories,* Canadian Arctic Resources Committee (Ottawa: 1989).

40   Special Committee, p.57.

41   Ames, p. 67.

42   Ames. p. 84.

43   Fenge, p. 36.

44   Ames, pp. 89, 99.

45   Ames, p. 101.

46   Ames, pp. 96, 97.

47   Ames, p. xxi.

48 Economic Development and Tourism, *1988 NWT Economic Review and Outlook (Government of the Northwest Territories), p. 4.*

49 Ames, p. 43; Usher, *P., A Strategyfor Supporting the Domestic Economy of the Northwest Territories (prepared for the Special Committee on the Northern Economy, Yellowknife: 1989),* pp. 19-23.

50 For further discussion along these lines, see: Griffiths, F., Oran R. Young, "Sustainable Development and the Arctic," *Working Group on Arctic International Relations: Impressions of Co-Chairs* (1989).

Canadian Arctic Gas Development and Environmental Tradeoffs

Gregory P. Marchildon

Introduction: Gas on the Arctic Horizon

After a decade of inactivity due to sagging demand, low prices, popular objections to northern pipeline construction, and nationalistic pressures against exporting energy to the United States, it appears that Canadian arctic gas production--and the construction of pipelines to reach lucrative southern markets--is imminent. Gas producers are gambling that the time is right to begin drilling into the huge natural gas reserves that lie underneath the permafrost and the Arctic Ocean.

The principal stimulus is an increase in demand for natural gas in the United States. After years of surplus supply, the United States now faces a permanent shortfall between domestic gas production and consumption. Supplying 98 percent of imports to the United States, Canadian gas exports to that market have nearly doubled during the past four years. In 1988 alone, gas exports to the United States grew by a record-breaking 30 percent; they now constitute 37 percent of Canada's total annual production.[1]

This level of activity, augmented by the promise of an even brighter future, was the reason that three of Canada's largest gas companies recently sought permission to export 9.2 trillion cubic feet (tcf) of gas from the Canadian arctic to the United States. Their application for permission to export constituted the largest the National Energy Board (NEB), the Canadian government agency responsible for monitoring energy exports, had received since it was created in 1959. In October 1989, the NEB approved the companies' plan which amounts to the export of 90 percent of the present proven natural gas reserves in the Mackenzie Delta region and 10 percent of total Canadian proven reserves. The estimated cost of the project is $10.9 billion of which more than half, $6.1 billion, will be spent on pipeline development alone.

As Shell Canada President Jack MacLeod has stated publicly, however, the NEB's export approval is only the first small step towards the construction of the megaproject. The NEB's decision does not include approving the construction of an arctic pipeline, and hearings on this issue alone could take two years. Many other hurdles, including environmental hearings, aboriginal objections to the project as well as the difficulty of raising finance for the project, must also be cleared for the project to become a reality.[2]

Nevertheless, what was once a dream to some and an ecological nightmare to others will likely become a reality. The objections heard during the days of the Berger inquiry, which first considered the construction of an arctic gas pipeline in the 1970s, are appreciably muted today.[3] Justice Thomas Berger was appointed head of a federal Royal Commission in 1974 to consider the impact of various pipeline proposals through the Mackenzie Valley region of the Western Arctic. After numerous community hearings throughout the North, the Commission concluded in 1977 that a pipeline from the Mackenzie Delta to Alberta (which would hook up to the existing southern pipeline network) could, with the appropriate restrictions and environmental safeguards, benefit the people that live in the arctic, but urged that construction be delayed for ten years to permit the settlement of aboriginal land claims.

The largest indigenous group inhabiting the gas producing region, the Inuit of the Western Arctic (the Inuvialuit), settled their land claim with the Canadian government in 1984. According to this agreement, the Inuvialuit received title to 35,000 square miles of land in the Western Arctic. Of this amount, 5,000 square miles involves ownership of the subsurface including natural gas and oil. An Environmental Impact Screening Committee was created pursuant to the agreement to review all economic development projects in the Inuvialuit Settlement Region (see Appendix). One-half of the permanent members of the Committee must be nominated by the Inuvialuit while the other members are nominated by the Canadian government as well as the territorial governments of the Yukon and Northwest Territories.[4]

The Inuvialuit, originally the group most opposed to pipeline construction during the Berger inquiry, now support the Mackenzie Valley gas development. They do so because their land claim settlement ensures them an economic return and gives them some control over the pace and direction of development. The Inuvialuit are also determined to protect their more traditional livelihood and can use the Environmental Impact Screening Committee to protect the ecosystem of the animals upon which this livelihood depends. Shortly after the agreement was signed, the Inuvialuit Development Corporation purchased shares into two Western Canadian oil and gas drilling companies to begin learning about the industry. They are considering establishing a refinery that would serve their own regional needs in place of purchasing expensive oil and gas products from the south. These moves are intended to ensure that the Inuvialuit will have the economic opportunities which will permit them to remain in their arctic homeland. The Inuvialuit also want some of their number to continue making a living through the traditional pursuits of hunting and fishing even at the same time that many will work directly or indirectly within the hydrocarbon industry. As the chairman of the Inuvialuit Development Corporation stated in 1985:

> We're in a stage right now of developing ourselves, but the centerpoint is still protecting the land and wildlife. If all business fails, we can go out on the land and get our food. You could go bankrupt and still enjoy yourselves out on the land.[5]

The two other indigenous groups inhabiting the Western Arctic have not reached a final land claim agreement with the federal government but are likely to do so in the near future. The 13,000 Dene and Metis make up approximately 45 percent of the total population of the Mackenzie Valley. In 1988, the government of Canada entered into a land claim agreement-in-principle with the Dene and Metis and since that time both sides have been negotiating the details. On April 9, 1990, negotiators initialled the final agreement to settle the Dene-Metis comprehensive land claim and now only ratification and signature are necessary to implement the final agreement. The terms agreed upon are a transfer of 70,000 square miles of the Mackenzie Valley to the Dene and Metis of which 3,900 will include subsurface ownership as well as a transfer of $500 million. The Dene and Metis will also share in resource royalties, the most important of which will be natural gas. They will receive 50 percent of the first $2 million of resource royalties and 10 percent of the remainder. Mirroring the environmental provisions in the Inuvialuit Final Agreement, an Environmental Impact Review Board with wide powers to evaluate economic development projects in the Mackenzie Valley will be established with half of its members nominated by the Dene and Metis.[6]

Because they have little ownership or control without the land claim agreement, the Dene and Metis are trying to stall the Mackenzie Delta gas development until the final agreement has been signed. However, both groups will likely support the Mackenzie Delta project once their claims are resolved for the same reason as the Inuvialuit. Extremely high unemployment and grinding poverty are pressuring both groups into accepting largescale gas development if they can be assured that they will benefit directly from the development. Only ownership of part of the land upon which the natural gas is extracted and transported can provide this type of long-term guarantee. In addition, the Dene and Metis will have some control over the nature and the pace of gas development through their participation on the Environmental

Impact Board. Southern environmental groups and the nationalist Council of Canadians, although still opposed to the development, must tread carefully because of the Inuvialuits' new position and their potential conflict with the Dene and Metis after their land claims with the federal government are resolved.[7]

Canadian Gas Exports in Global Terms: The Significance of the American Market Using Conventional Energy Forecasts

What is under discussion in the case of the Mackenzie Delta project is a non-renewable resource of growing global significance. Currently, natural gas is the third major source of energy in the world, only slightly behind oil and coal, and its importance will increase markedly in the years ahead. According to projections made by the International Energy Association (IEA) for 1995 and 2005, real oil prices will begin to rise as oil production capacity outside the Middle East goes down (assuming that OPEC can control production enough to permit increases in the real price of oil). Thus the world demand for natural gas will grow faster than the demand for all other major energy sources: oil, coal, nuclear, and hydro. The implications for nations such as Canada, Norway, and the USSR--all of which produce (and are capable of producing) much more natural gas than they consume--are obvious. According to conventional estimates, the production of natural gas will expand at record levels during the 1990s.[8]

Although international trade in natural gas is a relatively recent phenomenon, it may eventually rank second to oil in terms of its value in international energy transactions. Canada is the third-largest producer of natural gas in the world and is ranked ninth in terms of proven reserves. In contrast, most of the major OECD nations are net importers. The Western European nations are supplied by Norway, the Netherlands, Algeria, and finally the USSR, the world's leading producer of natural gas. Because it costs ten times more to transport than oil, natural gas is generally delivered through pipelines within geographically proximate regions. The current pipeline system links European customers with suppliers in Norway, the Netherlands, and the USSR, and it is likely that North Sea and arctic gas will continue to dominate the market for many years to come. Given this pipeline infrastructure, the high transport cost of gas, and the potential availability of Middle Eastern gas, it is unlikely that Canadian gas will be exported to Europe in the near or distant future. Further, although Japan's demand for natural gas is growing rapidly, delivery costs and the recent discovery of natural gas in Australia make it an improbable market for Canadian gas. Thus the future viability of Canadian arctic gas exports depends primarily on demand and supply conditions in the United States.[9]

Canadian producers have been exporting natural gas in sizeable quantities to the United States since the OPEC crisis, and to a lesser degree, so have Algerian and Mexican producers. However, the U.S. gas market has fluctuated markedly during the past decade. Demand for natural gas fell steadily from 1979 until 1986 due to sluggish economic growth, conservation efforts, and a rapid fall in oil prices.[10] The decline of natural gas consumption in America, coupled with deregulation during the Reagan administration, made the market increasingly unattractive to foreign gas suppliers. The Algerian and Mexican governments decided against lowering export prices and vacated the market; in contrast, the Canadian government began in 1984 to loosen its previously tight controls on gas exports and essentially became the only foreign gas supplier of any consequence to the United States. Rapidly expanding since 1986, growth in gas exports to the United States now represents the fastest growing component of Canadian gas production.[11] The IEA projects that there will be a gradual rise in U.S. natural gas consumption in coming years. Due to the very low level of proven gas reserves, however, production of natural gas in the United States will continue to decline.[12] The situation has obvious potential for the Canadian gas industry.

Since it went into effect in January 1989, the Free Trade Agreement (FTA) between the United States and Canada has bolstered the trade in fossil fuels by forbidding minimum export prices or taxes, and by prohibiting either country from restricting exports except in an emergency.[13] In March, 1990, the NEB announced that Canadian gas exports would no longer have to meet the test that they are of "net benefit" to Canada before being permitted. This decision, loudly decried by the Council of Canadians and central Canadian gas consumers, removed the last "nationalist" restriction on energy and made NEB practice consistent with the principles enshrined in the FTA.[14]

Now that American gas consumers are guaranteed the same "national" treatment as Canadian consumers, American reliance on Canadian natural gas will become even greater. Not surprisingly, American energy officials are now talking about replacing some of the United States' imports of crude oil with Canadian natural gas. Constance Buckley of the U.S. Department of Energy's fossil fuels program has noted that "[t]here is a consensus that proved and potential reserves in North America are sufficient to allow [American consumption] to increase and can be used to displace foreign oil." Although deregulation had gone some distance toward creating a continental market in natural gas, Buckley points to the FTA as instrumental in galvanizing the gas industry into a "true North American marketplace."[15]

According to industry analysts, the price of natural gas must rise from its present price of $2.35 (Cdn) to at least $3 (Cdn) a thousand cubic feet (tcf) in order for the Mackenzie delta megaproject to pay for itself. These prices are based on long-term contractual commitments for Canadian gas by American fimms. Present short-term natural gas prices are much lower; for example, the spot-market price for gas in 1989 was as low as $1.30 (Cdn).[16] The feasibility of Canadian arctic gas exports, therefore, depends centrally on the future price of natural gas which in turn hinges on world energy supply and demand conditions.[17] There is much evidence that these conditions will favor natural gas over other energy sources.

Beyond the Conventional Projections: Factors Favoring Natural Gas

The IEA's projections concerning natural gas consumption differ little from those of other international, national, and private organizations. All, however, are likely too low in their estimates of future natural gas consumption and production relative to other energy sources. In examining each energy source, it becomes evident that natural gas will be the favored alternative in most situations in the United States and Canada.

As the majority of the potential power from hydro has already been exploited in the United States, the IEA projections assumed that Canadian hydroelectric power would be available for export south at levels established during the 1980s. It now appears, however, that American utilities will not be able to import Canadian hydroelectric power in the quantities previously estimated. In the case of Quebec Hydro, Canada's largest exporter of hydroelectric energy, drought and low water levels have forced it to cut back its export commitments for the next ten to fifteen years.[18] Moreover, oil consumption will continue to decrease *relative* to other energy sources; since the OPEC crisis of 1973, United States security interests have dictated a move away from dependence on oil imports.

Utility companies have consequently tended to rely more on the one fossil fuel that is abundant and relatively inexpensive in the United States: coal. At this time, more than 50 percent of the electricity now generated in the United States comes from coal. This trend may be logical from a short-term economic or national security perspective but it has imposed a tremendous environmental cost; coal-powered electricity generation is the main source of the sulfur dioxide (SO_2) and nitrogen oxide (NOx) emissions, popularly known as acid in rain, in the United States.[19] These emissions are now beginning to be regulated such a manner as to make coal a less desirable energy source relative to natural gas. Although the IEA and other energy organizations have not yet "discounted" coal in their projections, we should begin to do so. As Canada's Energy Options Advisory Committee concedes, "conventional forecasting often does not effectively incorporate changing values (such as an increasing interest in the environment) into its analysis."[20] This conservatism is particularly rain, striking when we examine recent shifts in opinion concerning the use of nuclear energy, the need to take action on acid rain and global warming, and major technological breakthroughs in energy generation.

The factors described below are those which are not taken into consideration in conventional forecasting such as that employed by the IEA. All directly or indirectly are concerned with evidence of environmental damage, changing perceptions of ecological threats, and the increasing desire to change our fuel consumption patterns to lessen these existing and potential threats. The argument presented here is that these environmentally-induced changes in consumption will favor natural gas relative to other fossil fuels and nuclear power. The result will be reflected in higher levels of natural gas production and consumption during the next decade or two than those predicted in conventional energy forecasts. This will likely result in higher natural gas prices making the Mackenzie Delta project feasible, thus increasing the pressure for large-scale exploitation of natural gas in the Canadian arctic.

The Nuclear Problem

The IEA projections are based on the assumption that nuclear-generated electricity consumption will actually grow faster in the 1990s than in the 1980s, because the nuclear industry will be able to reduce public concern about the safety of nuclear power.[21] This seems an unrealistic assumption at best, given the negative publicity of the Chernobyl accident and the increasing hostility of ever-larger segments of the population against the industry.[22]

It is significant that the Energy Options Advisory Committee, recently established in Canada to examine energy issues and evaluate the nation's energy options for the future, was able to agree on virtually every issue raised *except* the nuclear option.[23] Although proportionately Canadians rely more on nuclear power than Americans, the continued growth of Canadian environmental groups which are unequivocally opposed to the use of nuclear energy may soon have the same impact as anti-nuclear groups in the United States. Energy analysts must therefore consider the possibility that nuclear energy may eventually be removed from the Canadian portfolio of energy sources. What is more significant in terms of higher-priced Canadian arctic gas, however, is the changing balance of energy use in the United States.

Indeed, in the United States, public pressure has for some time forced policy makers to minimize the use of nuclear energy. There is little likelihood that the United States will be able to continue its nuclear program at the present level much less expand it during the 1990s given the degree of political opposition this would engender.[24] Any further retreat in nuclear energy usage in the United States will produce greater pressure on all the major fossil fuel energy sources: coal, oil and natural gas. Existing and future legislation aimed at lessening acid rain and the dangers posed by global warming will load the dice in favor of increasing the use of natural gas.

The Acid Rain Problem

The 1980s witnessed a popular mobilization against acid rain in both the United States and Canada. In Canada, the destruction of life systems in hundreds of lakes as well as thousands of acres of maple trees, attracted so much public and media attention that, by 1982, 77 percent of the Canadian population viewed acid rain as the nation's most serious environmental problem.[25] Although acid rain was not as pressing an issue in the United States, environmental groups, often joining together under umbrella organizations such as the National Clean Air Coalition, were successful in applying increased political pressure for remedial action.[26] Governments in both nations have been compelled to enact legislation that restricts S02 and NOx emissions.

Between 1980 and 1984, the Canadian federal government spent $41 million (Cdn) on acid rain research. Total expenditures since that time have averaged about $30 million annually, more than half of which comes from the federal government. More significantly, Canada has recently introduced legislation that will halve S02 emissions by 1994. Since roughly 50 percent of Canada's S02 pollution originates in the United States, the Canadian government has tried to pressure the Reagan and Bush administrations into taking remedial action. So far, however, the Canadian government's remonstrances have had little effect. During the Reagan administration, the link between U.S. emissions and Canadian acid rain was flatly denied. More recently, President Bush refused to enter negotiations on an acid rain accord between the two nations until American clean air legislation is in place.[27]

During the past few years, domestic pressure in the United States has produced legal measures such as mandatory scrappers for smokestacks. Only recently, however, has it resulted in a legislative scheme that would substantially reduce SO2 and NOx emissions in North America. After two months of debate, the United States Senate approved a Clean Air Bill on April 3, 1990, that is expected to halve acid rain emissions within 10 years. Although some difficulties remain, the Clean Air Bill will likely pass Congress. The new legislation will then open the way to a Canada-U.S. acid rain treaty that, in Prime Minister Mulroney's words, "will be an international instrument that will allow [Canada] to put the application of the document before international tribunals."[28]

The immediate consequence of the Canadian and American acid rain legislation will be to put severe pressure on the coal-fired utility industry in both nations--especially in the United States, where more than 50 percent of the nation's electricity is generated by coal. On a much smaller scale, Ontario, New Brunswick, and Nova Scotia, the Canadian provinces most dependent on coal-fired electricity, will also be forced to consider alternatives. Whatever fuel source is chosen, however, any change in the makeup of Canadian energy consumption will have little impact on Canadian energy production relative to the tremendous shift that will result from new clean air legislation in the United States. The immediate impact of the legislation will be an increase in the relative price of coal-generated electricity. To a lesser but still significant degree, oil will also be penalized under this new legislation relative to natural gas.

The Global Warming Problem

Global warming has supplanted acid rain, the issue of the 1980s, as the chief environmental concern of the 1990s. The buildup of carbon dioxide (CO_2) in the atmosphere, largely the result of human activity during the industrial age, is causing the world to warm at a pace that will significantly alter ecological patterns on the planet. According to Professor Irving Minster of the Center for Global Change at the University of Maryland, "the concentration of CO_2 in the atmosphere has increased at an average annual rate of about 0.4 percent" during the past 30 years. Very recent scientific observations now suggest that the rate "may have jumped dramatically in the past two or three years, approaching 0.7-0.8 percent during 1988."[29] Although not solely responsible for the "greenhouse" effect--emissions of other trace gases into the atmosphere such as methane, ozone, and NOx also influence the atmosphere--CO_2 emissions are central to the problem.

Global warming will cause small glaciers in the polar regions to melt, raising sea levels between 0.5 and 1.5 meters. This will cause flooding of extensive land regions near sea level. In addition, patterns of rainfall and snowfall will change as entire ecosystems adjust to higher temperatures. Such changes are expected to occur by the next century if CO_2 and other trace gas emissions remain unregulated.

During the past few years, environmental groups throughout the world have been actively educating the general public about the dangers posed by global warming--and have been pressuring national governments to take legislative action. Although no specific legislation has yet been introduced in the United States, the issue of global warming is being addressed in the various comprehensive environmental protection bills now before Congress. The proposed National Energy Policy Act, for example, would require a 20 percent reduction in CO_2 emissions by the year 2000, and would set the United States on a course to reduce CO_2 emissions by up to 50 percent through international negotiation and treaty. By the same token, the prospective Global Pollution Control Act would attempt to decrease CO_2 emissions by 35 percent by 2010.[30] The Canadian government has recently shown sign of concern as well. Canada's environment minister announced in April, 1990, that the federal government "will set a national target and timetable by this fall" for reducing CO_2 emissions as part of its strategy to combat global warming.[31]

The issue is not whether both nations will have CO_2 emission legislation in place within the next few years but how it will be framed. The U.S. and Canadian governments will be required to either lower CO_2 emissions by a tax policy that imposes the costs of these externalities on utility companies and others discharging CO_2 into the atmosphere, or they will place a cap on the amount of CO_2 that companies will be permitted to release. Coal combustion releases twice as much CO_2 into the atmosphere per unit of energy produced compared with natural gas; fuel oil releases more than 40 percent. As a consequence, either regulatory approach will translate into higher costs for coalpowered energy and fuel oil relative to natural gas. In addition, recent technology is making natural gas more efficient and flexible as an energy source than coal or oil.

Gas Turbine Technology: The New Energy-Convertor

According to Robert Williams and Eric Larson, research engineers at the Center for Energy and Environmental Studies at Princeton University, we are in the midst of a revolution in electricity-generating technology that "may soon radically transform the power industry, in both industrial and developing countries."[32] New gas-powered turbine power systems, in both a portable (modular) or stationary format, have proved to be extremely energy efficient. For example, some recent gas turbines can produce electricity at an efficiency rate 50 percent higher than that achieved by conventional gas turbines. The new gas turbines are also capable of releasing substantially less SO_2, NO_x, and CO_2 into the atmosphere than coal-fired plants per unit of energy produced. Such gas turbines have been developed to the point that they are now being sold commercially.

According to Williams and Larson, the gas turbine will likely assume a significant role in central station and cogeneration power applications in both industrial and developing countries during the next 20 to 40 years:

> The gas turbine will be much more widely used both because the changing circumstances of the electric power industry are especially conducive to the gas turbine and because improvements in gas turbine technology are making gas turbines more competitive. In a wide range of circumstances, new, highly efficient, gas turbine-based power plants will be able to provide electricity at lower cost and with less adverse environmental impacts or safety problems than coal or nuclear steam-electric plants.[33]

Nonetheless, a word of caution is in order concerning the difficulty inherent in predicting the adoption of one technology over another. Rarely do we correctly predict even short-term shifts in technology and history contains numerous examples of short-lived technologies.[34] At this time, a great deal of research and development is also being devoted to cleaner coal-powered energy convertors, as well as to solar and wind-powered energy convertors. Although at present these renewable-energy convertors make up an insignificant percentage of total energy generation in North America, developments in the near future could make them an important element in the global energy portfolio. Until that time, however, it is clear that the abundance of natural gas relative to fuel oil in North America--in conjunction with gas turbines that are flexible and efficient--can serve only to substantially increase the present level of gas production. And at least for the 1990s, it is safe to assume that gas turbine technology will accelerate the shift from coal and oil to natural gas.

An Environmental Tradeoff? Some Policy Proposals

When the above-mentioned environmental effects and technological changes are considered, it seems clear that there will be sufficient demand for natural gas to justify the Mackenzie Delta megaproject on strictly economic grounds.

Moreover, the newfound support of the Inuvialuit combined with the formal establishment of a continental market for energy through the Canada-U.S. FTA at a time when gas reserves are shrinking in the United Sates, makes the development almost inevitable. The irony may be that existing and new legislation to thwart acid rain and global warming, by providing the main stimulus to natural gas demand and, therefore, underwriting the Mackenzie Delta project, could also do irreparable environmental damage to the Canadian arctic.

In contrast to the Berger inquiry of the 1970s, there has been surprisingly little debate on the environmental aspect of the proposed Mackenzie Delta project. Although objections were made by a few members of Canada's Energy Options Advisory Committee concerning the economic and environmental viability of energy megaprojects in general--in a report that was intended to canvass all the major aspects of Canada's energy future--the potential threats to the arctic environment were not addressed. Those undiscussed environmental effects may be severe.

To begin with, the laying of the pipeline itself may cause a certain amount of environmental damage. Precautions will be taken so that the proposed pipeline does not interfere with migratory patterns of certain arctic wildlife, but it is impossible to know in advance the project's precise impact. In making its assessment of the various Mackenzie Valley pipeline proposals of the 1970s, the Berger inquiry placed great weight on disruption to bird and mammal wildlife caused by the construction of the pipeline itself. The proposed routes through the Yukon and Alaska were believed to be particularly damaging in this respect. The Mackenzie Valley route was favored by the Berger Commission but its environmental impact was largely unknown at the time.

Perhaps an even greater danger emanates from the nature of the drilling operations themselves. First, there is no way to eliminate the possibility of gas and water blowouts in drilling operations. Such blowouts are particularly damaging in the arctic environment. Since natural gas exploratory drilling began in the Canadian arctic, there have been at least three major blowouts. In one case, a Panarctic project at Drake Point on Melville Island, engineers worked for two weeks to cap a highpressure gas well that blew out of control. One month later, it blew out again, but this time the company was unable to stem the flow of gas for one year with a consequent loss of 30 million cubic meters of gas. A short time later, another Panarctic well on King Christian Island near the magnetic North Pole caught fire. The 350-foot flame could not be extinguished for three months, and approximately 270 million cubic meters of gas were burned off.[35]

Vehicle activity around the drilling site itself can cause extensive damage to the tundra. Wheels churn up the thin, fragile layer of moss and lichen, exposing the soil underneath to the sun's heat and melting the permafrost. Within a short time, tire tracks turn into muddy channels which can remain for decades.[36] Natural gas development in the U.S.S.R. has already caused precisely this form of damage to the Soviet arctic. In certain regions, the damage to the permafrost caused by vehicle traffic is so extensive that it cannot be reversed. As a consequence, thousands of miles of tundra in the Soviet arctic are permanently damaged.[37] Given that the companies operating in the Canadian arctic must rely on vehicles to transport equipment and men from landing strips and home bases to drilling platforms, we should expect similar damage to permafrost in the Canadian arctic if the Mackenzie Delta project proceeds.

Because most of Canada's arctic gas will actually be drilled in the Arctic Islands, it will have to be transported in some form to the head of the pipeline in the Mackenzie Delta. This will involve transport over or through the Arctic Ocean, one of the most fragile ecosystems in the world.[38] Although a gas spill is not as destructive to polar environments as oil spills, continual transport of gas still poses a deadly threat. One attempt to transport gas through the Arctic Ocean has already failed because of environmental opposition. In 1983, the Greenland Inuit supported by some Canadian Inuit blocked a Canadian project to use an icebreaker supertanker to ship liquified gas from the Arctic islands.[39]

Despite these difficulties, there remain at least two compelling public policy reasons for arctic gas development to proceed from the perspective of the inhabitants of the Mackenzie Valley. The first is the economic benefit to a region plagued by unemployment particularly if the residents of the region play a direct role in the development. As this can only be ensured on a permanent basis through land claim agreements such as the Inuvialuit Final Agreement of of 1984, this implies that the land claim agreements with the Dene and Metis should be finalized before the Mackenzie Delta gas project is permitted to proceed. The land claim agreements also provide the aboriginal peoples of the arctic some control over the nature and pace of the development. This should ensure the protection of their own environment and with it the continuance of more traditional livelihoods. The land claim agreements, through the environmental review boards, are the institutional vehicle through which the Inuvialuit, Dene and Metis will police the activities of the resource companies in the Mackenzie Valley. Given the commitment of the aboriginal groups to preserving the arctic environment for future generations, the boards will be a more effective method of minimizing environmental damage than any agency created by the federal or territorial governments.

The second reason it should proceed is that the replacement of coal and nuclear powered energy generation by natural gas power plants is, at present, the most effective strategy in dealing with the nuclear, acid rain and global warming problems. To the extent that this involves an environmental tradeoff, numerous safeguards should be built into the Mackenzie Delta project to minimize environmental impact to the greatest extent possible. A first step would be an in-depth study of the impact of gas development from the Urengoy gas field to the Yamal Peninsula of western Siberia. The Soviet Union did not ban travel over bare arctic tundra until 1989 and their mistakes as well as experimentation with new tundra vehicles might provide valuable information. The NEB will in fact be conducting an environmental assessment of the Mackenzie project and if the project is felt to adversely affect the environment a more comprehensive review must be undertaken.[40] At this stage, the NEB should only allow the project to go ahead if the strictest environmental safeguards are imposed.

In another sense, it is very misleading to speak in terms of an environmental tradeoff. If the more pessimistic predictions are realized, global warming will adversely affect the arctic regions of the world in the next few years. This melting of the polar regions will then generate major environmental disruptions throughout the world. The Inuvialuit homeland along the western Arctic Ocean as well the Mackenzie Delta itself would be on the front line of such disruptions. Although the northern aboriginal peoples did nothing to cause global warming, they may be the first to suffer the effects of it. They therefore have an inherent interest in seeing that the global warming problem is dealt with effectively and as soon as possible.

References

1   J. DeMont, "Opening the Tap," *Maclean's,* February 26,1990, 32-34.

2   "Natural gas exports get green light," *Montreal Gazette,* October 20, 1989, p. D-6; D. Hatter, "Conditions may stymie Arctic gas export plans," *The Financial Post,* October 18, 1989; G. Kubish, "Tapping the Delta: The NEB approves the largest gas sale in Canada's history," *Western Report,* October 30, 1989; Interviews with Jack MacLeod, *The Financial Times of Canada,* August 28, 1989 and October 23, 1989; R. Zarzeczny, "How our secure gas supplies could go down the pipeline," *The Financial Times of Canada,* August 14,1989 .

3   T.R. Berger, *Northern Frontier, Northern Homeland: Report of the Mackenzie Valley Pipeline Inquiry* (Ottawa: Minister of Supply and Services, 1977); T.R. Berger, "The Mackenzie Valley Pipeline Inquiry,"*Queen's Quarterly,* 83:1 (Spring 1976). Discussion

concerning the possibility of Canadian arctic gas exports to the United States began in earnest with the OPEC crisis in 1973. Intensive exploration of the most promising arctic regions--the Mackenzie Delta and the Arctic Islands--only began in 1968, the same time that an enormous amount of oil and gas was discovered at Prudhoe Bay on Alaska's North Slope: See the report for the Canadian-American Committee prepared by Judith Maxwell, *Energy from the Arctic: Facts and Issues,* (Montreal and Washington: C.D. Howe Institute and the National Planning Association, 1973).

4   Government of Canada, *The Western Arctic Claim: The Inuvialuit Final Agreement* (Ottawa: Indian and Northern Affairs Canada, 1984). For commentary on the legal implications of the agreement, see J.M. Keeping, *The Inuvialuit Final Agreement* (Calgary: The Canadian Institute of Resources Law, 1989) .

5   Randy Pokiak, chairman of the Inuvialuit Development Corporation, quoted in C.S. Wren, "Corporate Fever Hits the Eskimos," *New York Times,* May 26, 1985.

6   "Agreement Reached On Dene-Metis Land Claim," Indian and Northern Affairs Canada Communique, Yellowknife, N.W.T, April 9, 1990; "Summary of the Provisions of the Dene/Metis Comprehensive Land Claim Agreement-in-Principle," Indian and Northern Affairs Canada, Dene/Metis Information Sheet No. 1, April 1989; Background to Dene/Metis Land Claim, land claims file, Canadian Embassy, Washington, D.C.

7   The Council of Canadians, while opposing all of the NEB's energy export approvals of the last few years, were particularly opposed to the Mackenzie Delta export application: G. Koch, "Resurrecting the NEP," *Western Report,* February 5, 1990, p. 15.

8   International Energy Agency, *Energy Policies and Programmes of IEA Countries, 1988 Review* (Paris, OECD Publications, 1989), 30-31.

9   On the significance of a single Canada-U.S. energy market to Canadian producers, see L.A. Coad and D.H. Maerz, *Continental Natural Gas Market: Canadian Export Capacity in the 90s* (Calgary: Canadian Research Institute, 1989) and G.C. Watkins, ed., *Petro Markets: Probing the Economics of Continental Energy* (Vancouver: The Fraser Institute, 1989).

10   Gas prices did not fall as much as oil prices during this period, however. While consumption of gas fell 7 percent between 1985 and 1986, gas prices fell 30 percent. The loss of consumption can be "attributed largely to fuel switching by electric utilities and large industrial users": See A.K. Waldman, "Natural Gas Imports: Federal Policy and Competition for U.S. Markets," *Natural Resources Journal,* 27:4 (Fall 1987) 789.

11   New Policy Guidelines and Delegation Orders from the Secretary of Energy to the Economic Regulatory Administration and the Federal Energy Regulatory Commission Relating to the Regulation of Imported Natural Gas, 49 Fed. Reg. 6684-6689: See A.K. Waldman, *op.cit., p.* 791; Also see H.C. Jenkins-Smith, "An Industry in Turmoil: The Remaking of the Natural Gas Industry," *Natural Resources Journal,* 27:4 (Fall 1987), and L. Kummins, Congressional Research Service Issue Brief, "Natural Gas Regulation:

Overview and Issues," October 26, 1989.

12   As of 1987, the United States has a Reserves/Production (R/P) ratio of 11.5. This compares with an R/P ratio for Canada of 36.8 and an R/P ratio of in excess of 100 for Norway. The R/P ratio is derived by taking the natural gas reserves remaining at the end of 1987 and dividing them by that year's production. The result is the length of time that those remaining reserves would last if production were to continue at that year's level: *Oil and Gas Journal,* 28 December 1987.

13   See Chapter Nine of the FTA between Canada and the United States, in particular, article 904. The impact of the FTA on energy trade between the two nations is summarized by E.A. Carmichael, "Energy and the Canada-U.S. Free Trade Agreement," *Trade Monitor,* no. 4 (May 1988); and on pp. 48-54 of Energy, Mines and Resources Canada, *Energy and Canadians into the 21st Century* (Ottawa: Minister of Supply and Services, 1988).

14   L. Diebel, "Board scraps special test on gas export," *The Toronto Star,* March 16, 1990; F. Dabbs, "Maintain analysis on gas export deals," *The Financial Post,* March 20, 1990; G. Gherson, "The rumble over rolled-in gas tolls," *The Financial Times of Canada,* March 26, 1990; T. Philip, "Letting the gas flow," *Western Report,* April 2, 1990.

15   C. Buckley quoted in "Canadian Natural gas seems key to U.S. Plan," *Toronto Star,* April 7, 1990.

16   These estimates were made by Chris Johnston, gas-marketing manager for Esso Resources Canada Ltd. U.S. energy economist Arlon Tussing, for one, believes that the natural gas price has far to go before it reaches (Cdn) $3: See "And Miles to go for the Arctic pipeline," *The Financial Times of Canada,* October 23, 1989.

17   The IEA was established by a group of high energy consumption nations under the auspices of the OECD. IEA participating countries include most Western European nations, Australia, Canada, Japan, Turkey, and the United States.

18   A. Abel and L.B. Parker, "The Greening of U.S. and Canadian Electricity Trade," *Canada-U.S. Outlook,* 1:3/4 (April 1990), 68.

19   In the United States in 1980 for example, 67 percent of all SOx emissions and 32 percent of NOx emissions were generated by electric utilities, the majority of which used coal. This situation has remained relative constant since that time: T. Albin and S. Paulson, "Environmental and Economic Interests in Canada and the United States," in J. Schmandt et al., eds., *Acid Rain and Friendly Neighbors: The Policy Dispute between Canada and the United States* (Durham, NC: Duke University Press, 1988), p. 109. It should be noted that acid rain is more accurately described as acid depositions because S02 and NOx more often return to the earth's surface as dry particles than through precipitation: C.C. Park, *Acid Rain: Rhetoric and Reality* (London: Methuen, 1987); J.M. Lemco and L. Subrin, "The Energy-Environment Tradeoff: The Binational Issue of the 1990s," *Canada-U.S. Outlook,* 1:3/4 (April 1990).

20   See the report of the Energy Options Advisory Committee: Energy, Mines and Resources

Canada, *Energy and Canadians into the 21st Century* (Ottawa: Minister of Supply and Services, 1988).

21   International Energy Agency, *Energy Policies and Programmes of IEA Countries, 1988 Review* (Paris: OECD Publications, 1989), p. 14.

22   The Nuclear Energy Agency Secretariat of the OECD responded to the "fallout" of the Chernobyl disaster by preparing the report, *Chernobyl and the Safety of Nuclear Reactors in OECD Countries* (Paris: OECD Publications, 1987) ; however, negative public sentiment had been of concern to the Nuclear Energy Agency before Chernobyl: See *Nuclear Power and Public Opinion* (Paris: OECD Publications, 1984). On the Chernobyl disaster itself, see D.R. Maples, *Chernobyl and Nuclear Power in the USSR* (New York: St. Martin's Press, 1986).

23   Energy Options Advisory Committee, *Energy and Canadians into the 21st Century, op. cit., p.* 61.

24   See J.G. Morone and E.J. Woodhouse, *The Demise of Nuclear Energy? Lessons for Democratic Control of Technology* (New Haven, Yale University Press, 1989).

25   J.L. Egel, "Canada's Acid Rain Policy: Federal and Provincial Roles," in J. Schmandt et al., eds., *Acid Rain and Friendly Neighbors, op.cit.*

26   J.L. Regens and R.W. Rycroft, *The Acid Rain Controversy* (Pittsburgh, PA: University of Pittsburgh Press, 1988); T. Albin and S. Paulson, "Environmental and Economic Interests in Canada and the United States," in J. Schmandt et al., eds., *Acid Rain and Friendly Neighbors, op.cit.*, pp. 116-18.

27   J.M. Lemco and L. Subrin, *op. cit., p.* 14.

28   Quoted in "Acid Rain Accord Talks On: Mulroney-Bush Meeting," Canadian Press Wire Service (Toronto), April 11, 1990. Derek Burney, Canada's ambassador to the United States, stated that "although there are still hurdles ahead in Congress, I'm confident we will see clean air legislation passed this year and an acid rain accord with Canada." Quoted in "U.S. Senate's acid rain legislation a win for North America: Canadian Ambassador," Canadian Press Wire Service (Washington), April 3,1990.

29   I.M. Mintzer, "Our Changing Climate: Challenges and Opportunities in Warming World," *Canada-U.S. Outlook,* 1:3/4 (April 1990), 77-78.

30   *Ibid., p.* 74.

31   "Must set target, timetable on carbon dioxide emissions: Minister," Canadian Press Wire Service (Ottawa), April 24,1990.

32   R.H. Williams and E.D. Larson, "Expanding Roles for Gas Turbines in Power Generation," in T.B. Johansson, B. Bodlund and R.H. Williams, *Electricity: Efficient End-Use and New Generation Technologies, and Their Planning Implications* (Lund: Lund University Press, 1989), p. 503. Also see E.D. Larson and R.H. Williams, "Steam-Injected Gas Turbines," Paper No. 86-GT-47, Transactions of the American Society of Mechanical Engineers, January, 1986. I thank Irving Mintzer for making me

aware of the "modular turbine" and I am indebted to Eric Larson for discussing its significance in terms of the demand for natural gas.

33   R.H. Williams and E.D. Larson, *op. cit.,* p. 503.

34   For numerous historical examples, see D.S. Landes, *The Unbound Prometheus: Technological Change and Industrial Development in Western Europe from 1750 to the Present* (Cambridge: Cambridge University Press, 1969).

35   These examples come from S. Hall, *The Fourth World: The Heritage of the Arctic and its Destruction* (New York: Alfred A. Knopf, 1987), pp. 187-88.

36   *Ibid.,* p. 196.

37   A popular accounting of the damage that natural gas development has wreaked in the Soviet arctic, particular in the main producing area in the northwest of Siberia, can be found in M. Edwards, "Siberia: In from the Cold," *National Geographic,* 177:3 (March 1990), 10.

38   In 1976, the Canadian government department of Energy, Mines and Resources gave a 90 percent probability of reserves of 580 million tons of oil and 1.1 million cubic meters of gas in the Mackenzie Delta/Beaufort Sea basin; and 220 million tons of oil and 680,000 million cubic meters of gas in the Sverdrup basin in the Arctic islands: D. Sugden, *Arctic and Antarctic: A Modern Geographical Synthesis* (Totowa, NJ: Barnes and Noble Books, 1982).

39   "Tomorrow Slowly Encroaches on Harsh, Scenic Arctic," *Los Angeles Times,* October 11, 1987.

40   Canadian Press Wire Service (Ottawa), February 19, 1990; and T. Philip, "Retracting its tentacles," *Western Report,* May 14, 1990.

ADJUSTED BOUNDARY —————
ORIGINAL BOUNDARY — — — —

INUVIALUIT SETTLEMENT REGION

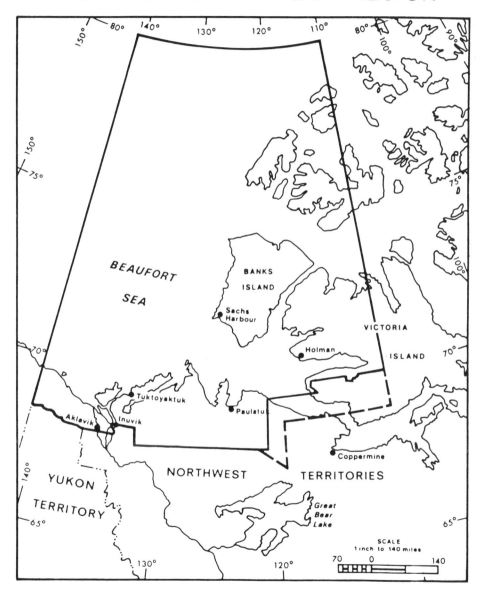

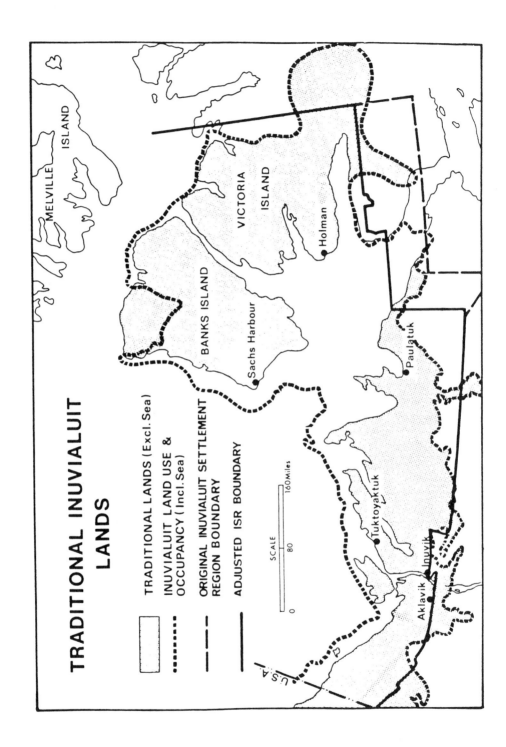

TRADITIONAL INUVIALUIT LANDS

TRADITIONAL LANDS (Excl. Sea)

INUVIALUIT LAND USE & OCCUPANCY (Incl. Sea)

ORIGINAL INUVIALUIT SETTLEMENT REGION BOUNDARY

ADJUSTED ISR BOUNDARY

SCALE

0   80   160 Miles

MELVILLE ISLAND

VICTORIA ISLAND

BANKS ISLAND

Holman

Sachs Harbour

Paulatuk

Tuktoyaktuk

Inuvik

Aklavik

U.S.A.

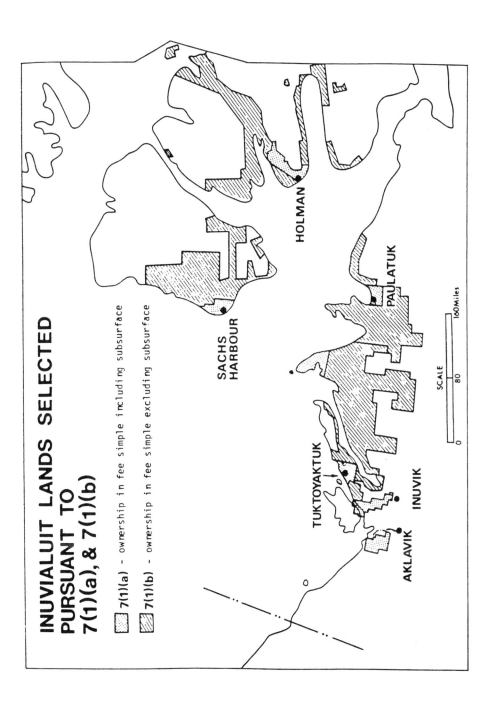

INUVIALUIT LANDS SELECTED PURSUANT TO 7(1)(a), & 7(1)(b)

▨ 7(1)(a) - ownership in fee simple including subsurface

▨ 7(1)(b) - ownership in fee simple excluding subsurface

HOLMAN

PAULATUK

SACHS HARBOUR

TUKTOYAKTUK

INUVIK

AKLAVIK

SCALE

0   80   160 Miles

83

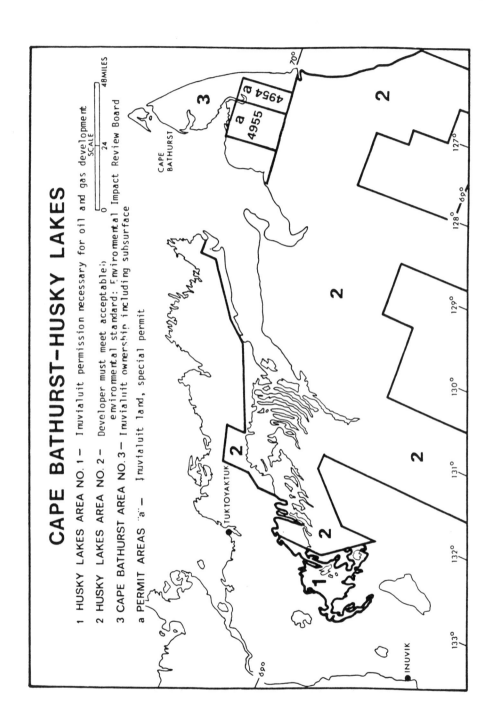

CAPE BATHURST–HUSKY LAKES

1 HUSKY LAKES AREA NO. 1 – Inuvialuit permission necessary for oil and gas development

2 HUSKY LAKES AREA NO. 2 – Developer must meet acceptable environmental standard: Environmental Impact Review Board

3 CAPE BATHURST AREA NO. 3 – Inuvialuit ownership including subsurface

a PERMIT AREAS "a" – Inuvialuit land, special permit

SCALE

0   24   48 MILES

Part Two

Indigenous Peoples and the State: Rights Achieved in Canada and the Nordic Countries

The Development of the North: Confrontation and Conflict

Billy Diamond

When I was approached to give this keynote address, I was asked to speak about the events which led to the signing of the James Bay and Northern Quebec Agreement on November 11, 1975.

In these days of public battle between the Federal and Provincial governments of Canada and the First Nations of Canada, people are more and more interested in how the most important battle in the seventies was climaxed by the signature of an Agreement.

How did we, the Cree People manage to settle? How was the Government able to get us to the negotiating table? What is the nature of the Agreement we signed with Government? How is it being implemented?

We, the Crees of Quebec, are 10,000 People who live in nine communities throughout Northern Quebec. Our traditional territory is approximately 240,000 square kilometers between the 50th and 55th north parallels.

We have a forested area in the south of our territory and it has basic resources which dominate development; hydroelectricity, forestry and mining and in the Cree case, hunting, fishing and trapping.

Our land is less mountainous than that of Norway, and it is dominated by what Canadians have come to refer to by using the Cree word "muskeg" - low wetland and peatbogs. They used to refer to us as the Swampy Cree, I believe your ancestors are known as the Bog People!

We often look to Norway and Sweden for new technology which is designed for this type of environment such as wide-tracked forest equipment designed to use electricity more efficiently. This is the new technology from Norway that we hope we may one day adopt for our purposes.

Hydroelectricity is very important to Norway as it is to Quebec, and the Cree homeland provides approximately 40% of Quebec's capacity of 25,000 megawatts. Unlike Norway, however, where the hydroelectric flooding is mainly confined by mountain walls, in the Cree territory hydroelectric projects flood vast areas and devastate our environment.

The La Grande Project has a total reservoir area of about 14,000 square kilometers of which about 10,500 square kilometers is flooded land. If James

87

Bay Phase Il is completed this total will rise to 25,835 square kilometers of reservoir of which 15,519 square kilometers will be flooded land. This water will be kept in by 668 dikes and channelled by 46 dams. This is the equivalent of putting the whole area of Oslo-Karlstad-Göteborg underwater. It is like submerging the whole of Northern Ireland.

You get my point!

As much as these projects might provide for energy needs in some areas, it certainly creates social and environmental problems in the Cree territory and elsewhere.

In 1970, Robert Bourassa proposed to build the James Bay Project. The Project consisted of three parts: The Great Whale River Project, the La Grande Project and the Nottaway, Broadback and Rupert Hydroelectric Project. He announced his plans, without even consulting with the Cree and Inuit People of Northern Quebec whose lands and ways of life would forever be impacted by these projects.

At that time there were a number of us who had been sent out to residential schools by our parents to learn how to effectively use the white man "wemistigushiw's" system. As the first generation out of high school, we had learned skills which would help our People defend our Rights.

Moreover, we were aware of the constitutional trust relationship, that the Federal Government had towards Indians in Canada, even though we did not trust them.

At that time, Cree society was united by a common language and by a common way of life. It was protected by its isolation, to some degree, from outside interests. This protection was pierced by the paved road, 400 miles long and completed in 400 days, which extended from Mattagami to the La Grande River.

For the first time since the intrusion by "wemistigushiw" contract trappers after the First World War, our homelands were invaded. The first intrusion wiped out the wildlife so that by 1930 my People could no longer go onto the land. There was nothing left on the land to live on.

At that time my People organized and, with the cooperation of Quebec, Canada and the Hudson Bay Company, started a beaver conservation program.

This second invasion into our lands threatened to permanently change the geography. The James Bay Project threatened to destroy eleven major rivers and upset the ecology on an area the size of France. The James Bay Project threatened to permanently diminish the traditional Cree way of life.

How would we counteract this threat?

This time it was up to us, the first generation of Crees out of high school.

We knew that our People had always occupied the Cree territory. We had never signed any treaty and as far as we were concerned we still owned the land.

This is what my People wanted to protect, the land and our way of life. It is for this reason that we called our response to Quebec "Our Land Our Demand." We had always inhabited this land. We were the only inhabitants of the land. Our way of life depended upon the rivers continuing to flow and upon the forests and the animals continuing to thrive.

In order to protect our way of life, we went to Court to attempt to stop the Project. Environmental groups from Canada and from the United States helped us to inform the citizens of Quebec, Canada and the United States about what was happening in Northern Quebec.

In the Courts we found that Canadian law had few legal precedents in the area of Aboriginal Rights. What precedents there were, gave priority to the Royal Proclamation of 1763 whereby the Imperial Crown reserved for itself the responsibility of dealing with Native title, before settlement could proceed.

We also found that Quebec, under the terms of the 1898 and 1912 *Québec Boundaries Extension Acts,* had an outstanding obligation to settle Native "claims" to the territory. Quebec had never fulfilled this condition to the cession of Eastern Ruperts Land from Canada to Quebec. In other words, Quebec's claim to all of Northern Quebec was in jeopardy because it had refused to deal with us.

In fact, Quebec's claim to all of Northern Quebec remains in jeopardy if the Agreement is not respected.

These were the legal underpinnings of our case. First occupancy and unique and continuous occupation of the land played a small part in the proceedings. Quebec attempted to prove that because my People used implements and goods bought in stores, we were no longer Indigenous People.

Before the Courts, however, our story was told articulately and honestly by our People. Mostly by the use of translators, our People related the way in which they lived in harmony with the land and the wildlife and the resources around them.

The Project would destroy our way of life and our People.

After about six months of testimony, we won our case. The Court granted us an injunction to stop the La Grande Project on the basis of the damage caused by it, and our Rights to the territory. We celebrated this decision by Judge Malouf.

This was the longest interlocutory proceeding in Canada and is a hallmark of legal precedent and judicial courage. A judge of the larger society recognized that we, the first inhabitants of the territory had Rights which were potentially stronger than the Rights of Hydro-Québec and Quebec Government.

We thought that we just might save "Matahonan," our name (meaning - place to meet after coming downriver in the spring) for what Hydro-Québec called La Grande II, the place where the works had started.

One week after the Malouf decision, the Quebec Court of Appeal overturned the decision. It decided that the Rights of Quebec society were stronger than the Cree Rights. In making its decision it decided that while we may indeed have Rights that were compromised by the Project, the public interest of the southern society was more important. The damages to us could be compensated for in money.

No one can buy a way of life and culture with dollars.

We then had a choice to make.

We were already heavily in debt to our lawyers for the cost of the defence of our lands.

The Court were letting the works on the La Grande Project proceed. Even if we would win in the Supreme Court of Canada (and we thought we could), the main case argued on the basis of the nature of our Rights, we would lose the La Grande and Eastmain Rivers.

The Project would be built and we would only be looking at monetary compensation for a dead culture and way of life.

We were ready to proceed in Court, but we saw the need to try to limit the damages, seek remedial works and to have certain fundamental Rights recognized. We decided to attempt to negotiate a settlement. We really had no other choice.

The James Bay and Northern Québec Agreement took a total of two years to negotiate. At first we gave ourselves one year to attempt to negotiate an agreement in principle. This we did at a time when there was not yet any Federal or Provincial policy with respect to land claims. We broke new ground.

We thought that through the Agreement, we had secured the means for our People to adapt to the damages caused by the La Grande Project and to the changes which would surely result from increased contact with the larger society.

The index to the Agreement reads like a constitution of a new country and in many ways, this is what it was meant to be.

Firstly, we set up the Cree School Board and took control of Cree education. Up to that point Cree education was administered from Ottawa.

There was a deliberate policy to prevent us from using our language and culture. Education to Indians was third rate, characterized by the use of residential schools to take children away from their communities for eight months at a time and directed towards assimilation.

We set up the Cree Board of Health and Social Services and brought the responsibility for administering health services back from Ottawa to the Cree communities.

The level of health services available to Native people in Canada is similar to that in some Third World countries and is a Canadian shame and embarassment. Our People have shorter life spans, more disease, higher childbirth mortality and we are a neglected area of Canadian life.

In the Agreement we secured special measures for the administration of justice and for setting up Cree police forces.

We set up a program which provides a guaranteed income, albeit a low income, for Cree hunters. The program encourages them to stay in the bush for at least 125 days per year.

This insured that even as southern society was intruding into our life, a system would exist to provide support and allow our traditional life to continue. In fact, even today over one third of our People continue the traditional activities of hunting, fishing and trapping.

The Agreement promised Federal Legislation for Cree self-govemment. *The Cree-Naskapi (of Québec) Act* was finally passed by Parliament in 1984, nine years after the signature of the Agreement. It is a recognition of Cree sovereignty in the area of local government, is constitutionally enshrined, is vibrant and supports our community development.

The Agreement set up a speical regime for the environmental review of proposed future projects. We were too late to get an assessment of the La Grande Project although we understood there would be an environmental review of its effects once it had been built.

This was an empty promise. We know virtually nothing about the long-term effects of the Project.

The Agreement provided special measures for the building of the Cree communities and in order to give Cree people an important part in the economic development of the territory. These commitments were only given by Government to get us to sign the Agreement. They have been consistently ignored and breached by Canada and Quebec.

Finally, the Agreement provided for monetary compensation. The Cree portion of this is approximately 130 million dollars, paid out over twenty years. This was to be a Heritage Fund for future generations of Crees.

In consideration of all of the above, we approved the completion of the La

Grande Project (1975).

We did not approve any other project. In fact, while we submitted environmental impacts for review, we withheld submission of our Rights to such a process. Any future project would require Cree approval. That is my understanding and that was the understanding of my People in 1975 and it still is today.

No new projects without our consent.

Since 1975 we have negotiated three times with Hydro-Québec to allow them to make changes to the design of the La Grande Project.

In 1978 the community of Chisasibi relocated to the mainland to allow a change in the location of La Grande I hydroelectric central.

In 1979 the Sakami Agreement was negotiated because Hydro-Québec could not control the flooding in the Sakami reservoir.

In 1986 we signed the La Grande Agreement to allow for maximizing the electric potential of La Grande. In each Agreement we received compensation and remedial measures.

In each Agreement the principle was the same: "to compensate and remediate damages to our way of life and to our Rights." We only accepted changes we could live with and which would not destroy our way of life.

With respect to the overall James Bay and Northern Quebec Agreement, we have had 15 years of constant struggle to try to force the governments to respect their commitments.

If I had known in 1975 what I now know about the way solemn commitments become twisted and interpreted, I would have refused to sign the Agreement! I would have gone to the Supreme Court and we would have found other ways to block the Project - in the Courts and on the ground.

The Governments of Canada and Quebec have consistently broken the James Bay and Northern Quebec Agreement.

I could go into detail on how this was done but I will only mention the most important problems.

The Agreement provided for the guarenteed continuation of the Cree way of life. The protections for the environment were largely aimed at this.

The protection of the environment in Northern Quebec has been a farce. The regime set out in the Agreement does not work, it has not been well implemented. The Provincial Government has put almost no resources for implementing the regime. Its representatives, because they are Government employees, follow the party line.

No independent expertise is brought to bear on the environmental questions posed by development. There are no public hearings, nor is there funding for third parties to study the questions. The process is bankrupt and allows Hydro-Québec to dictate what will happen. Hydro-Québec and the Government of Quebec want to act as the proponents of projects, as the evaluator, as the judge and as the jury.

For Canada's part, the environmental protection process in the James Bay Agreement, does not exist. Canada began to implement its environmental responsibilities in Section 22 in 1982-1984. In 1984 Quebec nationalists working in the Quebec City office of Environment Canada found a way to interpret Section 22 so that Canada could avoid any and all obligations. This is what they did.

To this day, the Federal Department of Justice refuses to allow the Minister of the Environment to implement Section 22.

As a result of the lack of concern for the destruction of the environment and as a result of the fact that there are no Cree game wardens (almost no game wardens at all) on the territory as provided in the Agreement, the traditional Cree way of life is in danger of extinction. The traditional Cree way of life will end if we do not stop the ransacking of the environment in the Cree territory by southern Canada and the United States of America.

Employment opportunities were to have been opened to the Cree People by the Agreement so that we could become full partners in the development of the territory. Except in the provision of institutional services such as education, health and local government, etc., this has not occurred.

Any successful commercial initiatives are carried out despite Government road blocks and not with Government help and assistance.

In the case of Hydro-Québec, my People have traditionally received the "rock washer" jobs on construction projects. The 15 years after signing the Agreement were lost years in terms of developing programs for bringing Cree People into managerial and operation jobs on the hydroelectric centrals.

In forestry, my People have been trying since before the Agreement to set up logging and wood processing plants. Quebec has resisted our efforts. Rather than working to develop ways in which forestry can be managed on a sustained yield basis, and also done in a way which is compatible with environmental protection and the Cree way of life, Quebec has illegally given forestry concessions to multi-national corporations.

Black spruce forests which take over one hundred years to grow are being clear-cut at the rate of 600 square kilometers per year. The equivalent of one Cree family hunting territory is obliterated each year. The Cree forest is being clear-cut to buy time for southern forests to regrow. Quebec has been overcutting its forests for years.

The Cree forests are being clear-cut to allow for the land to be flooded for future proposed hydroelectric Projects.

These Projects have not received Cree approval and are subject to environmental review.

We, the Cree People, God willing, will stop them.

Forestry operations are destroying the water and the land. From satellite imagery the deterioration in water quality is evident. The Rights that we gained in the James Bay and Northern Quebec Agreement, to continue our traditional way of life, are becoming illusory because the environment in Northwestern Quebec is being destroyed.

Moreover, alternative employment opportunities are being closed off to the Cree People. In the Agreement we set up the James Bay Native Development Corporation which was to open the door to joint ventures with the parent company, the James Bay Development Corporation. This never happened. Rather, the James Bay Development Corporation has taken upon itself a racist mandate to drive the Crees out of regional development.

They want to close the Cree fuel sales business called Cree Energy and are attempting to push us out of business at Radisson Airport.

They want to close the Cree Construction Company and Air Creebec. The James Bay Development Corporation goes around to the non-Native communitites south of the Cree territory in attempts to recruit local businessmen into their campaign.

The Rights we gained in the James Bay and Northern Quebec Agreement are being denied in other ways. We have improved our communities but the fact remains that Federal and Provincial program cuts have resulted in the shortfall of 800 houses. Eight hundred Cree families are without houses and this number increases every year.

The Cree People of Oujé-Bougoumou are still considered squatters on their own lands by Quebec and Canada because the Prime Minister of Canada, Mr. Brian Mulroney, did not do what he said he would in 1985 and recognize them as a *Cree-Naskapi Act* Band.

Three Cree communities still do not have the access roads which were to come from the Agreement. Community infrastructure has run out.

The powers of the Cree School Board have never been fully implemented. The list goes on an on.

Today Quebec announces that it will go ahead with the Great Whale River Project and in two years time, with the Nottaway Broadback Rupert Projects.

First we must look at the unfolding impacts of the La Grande Project.

The Project was so far advanced by the time the Agreement was signed that it was impossible to impose environmental conditions upon it. This was exactly Quebec's plan and at this moment we have no idea how far the consequences of this Project have gone.

We do know that our People cannot eat certain species of fish because they are so contaminated with mercury.

We do know that there are fewer and fewer geese each year.

We know that whole fisheries have been wiped out, and the lands for hunting, fishing, and trapping have been severely reduced.

We know that 40,000 non-Cree People per year are using the hydroelectric infrastructure to hunt and fish on the territory, without controls.

We know that there have been effects to James Bay and Hudson's Bay and to the wildlife of the territory.

But Hydro-Quebec has very carefully prevented the public environmentalists, and other scientists from learning the full impact of the La Grande Project. How can they build another project, cut more trees and flood more land without knowing this?

We know about the destruction of the Amazon forests, but what about the destruction of the northern Quebec forests?

Bourassa says that he is going ahead with James Bay II. Bourassa says that he does not need Cree consent to destroy our rivers and flood our land.

He is wrong - Cree consent is required and we want these Projects stopped!

In the Great Whale River Project, Premier Bourassa intends to flood the lands of the Great River Basin, of the Nastapoca Basin, of the Coates River Basin, of the Boutin River Basin and of the Little Whale River Basin to produce some 3,000 megawatts of electricity to be exported 1,600 kilometers to the United States.

Each of these rivers has an important and virgin fish population. Each of these rivers contributes to the ecology of Hudson's Bay of which Beluga whales, elephant seals, polar bears and arctic char form a part. Rare inland fresh water seals depend on this water.

The flooding of Lake Bienville to turn it into the major reservoir of this project will flood important wetlands and ruin caribou calving grounds. This flooding will cause the natural release of mercury into the water and the environment which, for hundreds of years to come, will contaminate the fish populations, such as they will be, of the reservoir.

The yearly drawdown at Lake Bienville in the wintertime, will leave 375 square miles of mud around the lake. The annual fall in the ice cover on Lake Bienville may become a trap for caribou herds which walk out onto the ice.

The next major complex after Great Whale River will be the Nottaway

Broadback Rupert Project. This Project will produce 9,000 megawatts of power once the 10 proposed powerhouses are completed.

As with the Great Whale Project, the operation of these powerhouses will be in accordance with the demand for electricity in the south. This will involve draining the reservoirs in winter and refilling them during the summer.

The Nottaway River and the Rupert River will be diverted toward the Broadback River system in this Project. The present natural channel of the Lower Broadback River will be the main location for the powerhouses.

The water flow in the Lower Broadback River will be, in the winter, ten times to twenty times the present natural flow. The present plan is to construct the Project by building the upstream powerhouses first. As economically required, the remaining powerhouses proceeding downriver will be constructed.

During the interim period of 5 to 10 or more years, this increased flow will scour out the Lower Broadback River channel. The annual fluctuation in the reservoir depth will be from 20 to 60 feet. As the reservoirs are shallow, this will leave vast bands of mud around each reservoir.

The impacts of this project will be devastating. Many Cree families will lose the most productive parts of most of their hunting, fishing and trapping areas. Because the Nottaway Broadback Rupert Project is to be built on low relief forested areas and on sensitive wetland environments, the Project will cause mercury contamination of the fish in those reservoirs at levels as yet unseen in Northern Quebec.

The diversion channel of the Nottaway River to the Broadback system will not be excavated. The sensitive clays will be pumped out and will completely fill a neighbouring lake. This channel will forever be unstable.

These river basins are presently an intricate and complex pattern of wetland environments and small lakes. They are major nesting grounds for ducks, herons, and all of the migratory waterfowl which come to our northern territory every spring.

The spilling of forty cubic kilometers of fresh water into James Bay and Rupert's Bay every winter will negatively affect the trout populations, white fish populations, cisco populations and will have a negative effect on the ecology of the snow goose staging grounds in Rupert's Bay.

For the Cree communities, the local effects in addition to social problems and damages to the hunting and trapping way of life will include: loss of community water supplies, contamination of local water bodies, local erosion and silting problems, and dangers to transportation.

My community, Waskaganish, will be tremendously impacted by this

Project. Our very existence is at stake.

The traditional way of life of my People will be at risk and with it the heart and soul of our existence.

Moreover, the Projects do not produce clean energy from an atmospheric standpoint. The Projects will allow Quebec and the United States to avoid implementing energy conservation so as to cut down consumption as recommended by the Brundtland Commission. In addition, the rotting vegetation from these Projects will dump 100 million tons of carbon into the atmosphere, contributing greatly to the greenhouse effect.

Major power transmission lines will have to be built and will cut through our territory and urban areas in southern Quebec and the United States. The likely harmful effects of these transmission lines are still being studied.

The real crime about the proposed hydroelectric Projects is that they are not needed and there are much better investments available for the people of Quebec.

It is only because of a few interested parties, including Premier Bourassa, that the Projects are proposed at all. Hydro-Québec is not a publicly regulated company, although it is a public company and has all of its debts underwritten by the Quebec taxpayer.

What Hydro-Québec proposes to do is to spend 62 billion dollars on mega projects and related works over the next 10 years. This is approximately twice the level of spending of that proposed by Ontario Hydro. The Nottaway Broadback Rupert and Great Whale Projects will produce about 11,000 to 12,000 megawatts of power once they are completed.

In Brazil, it is argued by developers, that the enormous population increase in the next century will require the power that they hope to get by flooding parts of the Amazon Basin.

In Quebec the population is expected to start declining by the year 2006. In Quebec, however, Hydro-Québec is actually encouraging consumers to use more electricity.

Seventy percent of Quebec houses are electrically heated. Moreover, Quebec with one third of the population of New York State, uses the same amount of electricity.

In order to increase the demand so that their Projects can be rationalized to the public, Hydro-Québec has aggressively marketed its electricity in the United States and has agreements, which have still not been approved by regulatory boards, for at least 2,000 megawatts of firm power for over 20 years.

Moreover, Quebec has been selling electricity at 1.5 cents per kilowatt hour to aluminum smelters. Aluminum smelters have also been conveniently exempted by Quebec and Canada, from environmental review.

In 1984, when Premier Bourassa was re-elected, Hydro-Québec began to sell what it called "surplus electricity" to the United States, at bargain basement prices. This was not surplus electricity, it was the margin of security of stored water in the reservoirs.

The reservoirs are now, six years later, 25% to 40% under capacity. Moreover, rainfall in Northern Quebec is below normal, perhaps due to permanent climate change.

The alternative for Quebec will cost less than building mega projects. If Quebec cancelled the U.S. contracts, (it will lose money on them anyway) and implemented a program of energy conservation, more employment would be created and our Territory will be saved.

As new technologies are developed using the sun, wind and perhaps fusion, it is more and more likely that the cement and gravel pyramids in Northern Quebec will stand as monuments to the abuse by 20th century man of his environment.

A major related question is that the financing of these Projects is coming from the financial world generally in North America, Asia and Europe.

Any bank, bond fund, brokerage house or investment group looking to invest in the future hydroelectric projects of Hydro-Québec should best look seriously at the global situation before it makes commitments.

The environmental effects of these projects are reason enough to be concerned. You would be supporting a mega project which would result in serious environmental damage and you must live with the consequences.

The viability of the projects is a second issue.

Hydro-Québec's strength is at question. Their bonds are guaranteed by the Government of Quebec which is in fact directly involved in the financing of these projects.

This is a paper tiger ready to fall!

Be advised that we have initiated legal proceedings in Quebec to prevent the construction of the projects or, at worst, we will substantially delay them. We are also involved in proceedings in the American Courts.

Before a decision is taken to invest, there had better be a clear review of the overall situation to look at these legal proceedings, the provisions of the James Bay and Northern Quebec Agreement and the ability of the Crees to block the Project.

Investors in Hydro-Québec would also be best advised to look and see who really own Northern Quebec - the Crees, Canada or Quebec.

Don't underestimate us - others have, much to their detriment.

This is what we are facing as Cree People in Northern Quebec. Our future looks black. Will we be able to protect and promote our language, culture and way of life?

Sixty-five percent of the population of the Cree People are under the age of 25 years. These people realize that hydroelectric development does not promote the long term health of our way of life. The dams are built and not one Cree works on their operation.

They know that forestry must be controlled by the Cree People if it is to be made compatible with Cree hunting.

These young people are the same ones who are being drawn away from the land, away from their family hunting territories. They are the ones who will stand up to protect the Cree Rights.

They will not be a lost generation. They see the confrontations at Kanesatake (Oka), Kahnawake, Akwasasne, Lubicon Lake, Restigouche, Rapid Lake, the Inuit of Labrador, the Indians of British Columbia and the Algonquins of Northern Quebec, and they realize that if the Native People of Canada are to protect and promote their way of life, they will have to do it themselves.

The Governments, Quebec and Canada, will not look out after our interests. They never have and they never will. The future generations clearly see Government as the enemy.

The news reports you see in Canada about Native reactions on the ground to Government inaction reflect years of frustration, racism and neglect.

How long can a people be suppressed, discriminated against and have their legitimate rights ignored before they react.

The similarities between what is happening in South Africa and Eastern Europe to that of the Native People in Canada is not exaggerated.

Canada has a form of institutional racism and apartheid which is a shame to the Nation as a whole and to the International World.

The "Intifada" in Canada by the Native People is *not* an isolated event. The Kanesatake situation may be resolved but this is clearly the last generation of Native People who will accept passively the indignity of having their Rights ignored, their culture destroyed and Human Rights lost!

Ottawa and Indigenous Rights

Jack Stagg

I listened this morning to a very moving and compelling statement made by Chief Diamond on his problems with Quebec and the federal governments over his claims settlement and his fears that more development in the James Bay and Northern Regions will further destroy the life of his people, the Cree First Nation. I have worked for the federal government for more than 15 years--not, mind you, in areas dealing directly with Chief Diamond--and it disturbs me a great deal to think that any possibility exists wherein the Chief Billy Diamond will not be treated fairly. It also saddens me to know that we now have a situation at Oka where police, troups, and guns are involved in the dispute between the Mohawks First Nation there and two levels of our government in Canada. We, as Canadians, or at least I, are not accustomed to thinking about myself as mean-spirited, racist, and uncaring as some are portraying us in the international press. It is disturbing, and it is embarrassing.

But outside of all of that I am particularly concerned with the possibility that what is happening at Oka and with the James Bay Crees will tear down some of the very positive things we have tried very hard to work on and to achieve amongst Canada's First Nations in our North. I agree with Chief Diamond that we cannot isolate the problems at Oka and in other parts of Quebec from the rest of Canada. As Chief Diamond has said this morning, how can the Dene Nation in the NWT or the Council for Yukon Indians in Yukon trust our words in our agreements with them if we are not prepared to proceed to be meeting our obligations to the Crees and the Mohawks and others.

I would like to spend just a little time this afternoon to talk about how we have been trying to resolve claims issues with Canadian Northern First Nations and to talk a little about what I perceive to be the differences between what we are trying to do in the North and what has occurred in southern Canada. First of all a little bit of the background.

Unlike what we saw in the James Bay Cree area, there were no court cases or imminent potential mass destruction to vast areas in the North when negotiations began on claims made against the federal government for lands taken and settled in Northern Canadian reaches. The situations are similar to the extent that our regional First Nations have never surrendered land to the government for the use and occupation of others. Meanwhile, others have used that land, sometimes profitably and sometimes badly. Traders took out vast quantities of furs; prospectors, goldrushers, and later mining companies took precious metals from the rock, the rivers, and the permafrost. Later, non-aboriginal populations settled to establish their own form of government and began a variety of non-aboriginal enterprises. And to a large extent, Northern aboriginal peoples benefited very little from all of this. Indeed, much of the non-indigenous acitivities left those who had been there all along the more poorly off.

Secondly, unlike when Chief Diamond was 21 and began his fight with the province of Quebec over the James Bay hydro development project, when we began negotiations with Northern First Nations there was no provincial jurisdiction which said "No" to aboriginal people, and we and the Northern First Nations had sufficient experience in dealing with the James Bay and Northern Quebec Agreement to know at least some of the pitfalls to avoid. But most importantly, we knew when we started out, and if not then, then soon afterwards, that major comprehensive claims settlements with Northern First Nations could not, and should not, and must not be simply a land and money deal. The agreements that we reached in the North had to be living documents, dynamic ones that would deal flexibly with future circumstances. Northern First Nations demanded full participation on broad-ranging decision-making boards governing the future use and disposition of Northern lands and resources, and they got it.

They also needed sufficient financial resources to participate actively in Northern business and cooperative sectors. The Inuvialuit which settled in 1984 have formed the largest, most powerful and best financed cooperation based in the Northwest areas. Northern First Nations groups also demanded greater control of their day-to-day community life. The two final agreements initialed in the past year provide guarantees for further self-government negotiations to take part on such wide-ranging topics as community health care, education, legal system, and community planning. Unlike the agreements signed earlier, here the federal government also received the full cooperation, support and assistance of the two territorial governments in the North. This was especially important in the NWT where the government there has a majority native aboriginal representation.

Finally we learned that any agreement is only as good as to the extent that it is implemented in a way that is acceptable and supported by all the signatories. I believe Chief Diamond's message this morning was, at least in part, that if his agreement had been implemented the way he and his people had anticipated it would be, there would be much fewer problems now.

For the agreements that we will achieve in the North, there have to be a further agreement by all the parties on the implementation planned that will specify the timing and the financial resources to be dedicated, and as sign the various responsibilities for each agreement provision. As many of you know, we have recently initialed two final agreements in the North: one with the Dene in the Mackenzie River Valley, and the other with the Yukon First Nations in Yukon. We have not finalized either of these, and they are not yet without their problems. The Dene want several changes made, and the Council for Yukon Indians are submitting theirs to an independent judicial board for its advice. Under the circumstances one cannot blame either of these for being cautious.

Finally, the people who attend this conference, who work in fields either in or touching the North, who love the North or some aspect of it, realize what a gift to all of us the North can be. It is first of all a gift to the native peoples indigenous to the North, who lived and created strikingly unique cultures over thousands of years, over some very tough and rough terrain. It was certainly a gift to the generations of European adventurers, traders, and miners, and perhaps its gift to my generation of people is that it will give us the opportunity to settle fairly and equitably with Canadas First Peoples residing there. Indeed, it could be a gift opportunity to do it right.

Indigenous Rights Achieved in Canada

John Bekale

Background

The story of aboriginal land rights in Canada is older than the nation itself. More than one hundred years before Canada became a nation, the British Government recognized that aboriginal people had rights to the land and that they deserved consideration before settlers moved in. King George III's *Royal Proclamation of 1763* stated that all lands not already granted to the Hudson's Bay Company (a British fur trading company) or already settled by early colonists were to be reserved "under our Sovereignty, Protection and Dominion for the Use of the Indians... and We do hereby strictly forbid on Pain of Our Displeasure, all Our loving Subjects from making any Purchases or Settlements whatever, or taking Possession of any of the Lands above reserved, without Our especial Leave and Licence for the Purpose first obtained." The British Crown unilaterally declared it had sovereignty and was to hold the land for use by the aboriginal people. It clearly recognized that aboriginal peoples had legal and original possession of their lands and that the proper process of acquisition was the surrender of title by them and a purchase by the Crown.

Treaties and Comprehensive Land Claims

As a result of this policy the British Crown and later the Canadian Government entered into a series of formal treaties with Indians to gain clear Crown title to aboriginal lands. Treaty making was based on the principle of obtaining the consent of aboriginal peoples. In turn for releasing their titles and interests to their lands the Indians were provided with reserve lands, cash, education and health services and hunting and fishing supplies and wildlife harvesting rights. The Metis (aboriginal descendants with mixed European blood) were dealt with by the granting of land or cash scrips. During the latter part of this treaty-making period two treaties were signed in the Northwest Territories: Treaty 8 in 1899-1900 and Treaty 11 in 1921.

It should be explained that Canada's first constitution, the *British North*

America Act, 1867, now the *Constitution Act, 1982,* created a division of powers between the national or federal government and the provincial governments. The constitution gave the Parliament of Canada exclusive Legislative Authority over Indians and Lands reserved for the Indians. The Supreme Court of Canada later ruled that this jurisdiction also encompassed the Inuit in arctic Canada. Canada implemented its responsibilities for Indians through the *Indian Act.*

Despite the fact that Canada did not make treaties to obtain a surrender of aboriginal interests and titles to large tracts of lands in Canada, successive federal governments were only prepared to resolve "lawful obligations," such as improper administration of Indian funds and breach of treaty rights. In 1969 the federal government introduced a White Paper Policy outlining this approach. It did not recognize aboriginal claims based on aboriginal rights. The policy called for the assimilation of aboriginal peoples into the mainstream society. This policy was resoundingly rejected by the aboriginal groups.

In 1973 the Supreme Court of Canada, in the *Calder* decision, ruled that aboriginal title existed in Canadian law. That fall the federal government issued a policy statement that it would negotiate settlements with aboriginal groups where rights of traditional use and occupancy had been neither extinguished by treaty nor superseded by law. This policy was later further defined to mean modern "comprehensive claims" and included a process to deal with "specific claims" arising from the Government's failure to live up to the terms of treaties.

Since the 1973 policy statement, three comprehensive claims agreements have been signed with aboriginal peoples: two in northern Quebec and one with the Inuvialuit in the Northwest Territories. The federal government is negotiating six more comprehensive claims in Canada including two more in the Northwest Territories with the Dene/Metis and with the Inuit. The claims being negotiated in the NWT include title to about 20% of lands in the territory, cash compensation, wildlife harvesting rights, non-renewable resource development royalties and participation on several land and resource management boards. I will further elaborate on the details of these negotiations in a moment.

The Emergence of Other Aboriginal Rights

First I would like to explain that these comprehensive claims negotiations are being affected by the emerging definition of aboriginal rights in court cases. When the Canadian constitution was proclaimed in 1982 it included a provision

106

that recognized and affirmed the existing aboriginal and treaty rights of the aboriginal peoples of Canada. In 1984 the Supreme Court, in *Guerin v. The Queen,* re-affirmed the existence of aboriginal title and underscored the duty of the federal government, as fiduciary, to protect such rights.

In the first amendment to the *Constitution Act, 1982* proclaimed in 1984, section 25 provided that the Charter of Rights and Freedoms would not abrogate or derogate from any aboriginal, treaty or other rights or freedoms that pertain to aboriginal peoples including those recognized by the *Royal Proclamation, 1763* and land claims agreements. The amended Act in section 35 also described aboriginal peoples to include Indian, Inuit and Metis and it guaranteed rights equally to male and female persons. In several constitutional conferences leading up to the Constitutional Accord forming the basis for this amendment the First Ministers could not agree on a provision to recognize an aboriginal right to self-government.

More recently, in the *Sparrow* decision, the Supreme Court made some important rulings and statements with respect to aboriginal rights. The decision sets out how the court will treat the relationship between aboriginal/treaty rights and legislation. Aboriginal peoples must first show that an aboriginal or treaty right claimed by them actually exists. Once accepted by the courts, the aboriginal party would then have to show *prima facie* that an infringement has occurred. Only then does the onus shift to government to show that the restriction on the aboriginal or treaty right is justified. The process of justifying restrictions though will be quite onerous for government.

The *Sioui* decision, also recent, indicates that in some cases the courts might be quite liberal in deciding what constitutes a treaty. Government will have to be cautious to only make promises to aboriginal peoples which it intends to keep, particularly during a treaty-making process such as the comprehensive claims negotiations.

The tone of these two recent cases suggest that the court intends to place more emphasis on Canada's *positive duty* to give meaning to aboriginal rights and treaty rights. In *Sparrow* the court said:

> Section 35 (1), at the least, provides a solid constitutional base upon which subsequent negotiations can take place. It also affords aboriginal peoples constitutional protection against provincial legislative power.

The statement appears to re-affirm the federal responsibility for aboriginal peoples and suggests that further negotiations will be necessary where Ottawa has made promises without delivering on them. The court stated that the affirmation of aboriginal rights contained in s. 35 (1) requires a "generous, liberal interpretation of the words in the constitutional provision." It is a solemn commitment that must be given meaningful content.

The Dene and Metis of the Northwest Territories have since decided to approach the Prime Minister and his Ministers in an attempt to seek a fundamental change to the policy of extinguishing aboriginal rights, titles and interests in exchange for specific rights and fee simple land title through the comprehensive claims process. Clearly the constitutional recognition of existing aboriginal and treaty rights is being given meaning by the Supreme Court and is inspiring aboriginal peoples across Canada to press the federal government to clarify and protect treaty and other rights, through negotiations or through litigation. There is a growing militancy amongst aboriginal peoples in Canada to exert what they consider their sovereign rights to land and to control their own lives.

Comprehensive Claims in the Northwest Territories

I mentioned earlier that one comprehensive claim has already been settled in the Northwest Territories, with the Inuvialuit of the Western Arctic, while two other claims are in the final stages of being negotiated, one with the Dene and Metis of the Mackenzie Valley and the other with the Inuit of the Eastern Arctic. These claims set out specific rights to land, resources and participation in resource management in great detail and, once ratified by the aboriginal organizations and the federal government, they are passed into law and receive the protection which the Constitution affords a modern-day treaty.

I will now outline briefly some of the main elements of these claims which pertain to the rights of each aboriginal group. The Western Arctic Final Settlement was enacted by parliament in 1984. Among the benefits which the settlement provides to the approximately four thousand Inuvialuit participants is title to 35,000 square miles of the land they traditionally used and occupied. Title to the land will be held by a land corporation on behalf of all of the Inuvialuit. Unimproved lands will not be subject to taxation.

A major section of the settlement concerns wildlife and environmental management and gives the Inuvialuit some exclusive rights to harvest certain wildlife on their own lands. They are also given preferential rights to harvest all other species of wildlife for their own use. They will have priority in harvesting marine mammals in their own areas, using quotas set in cooperation with government and will have a preferential right to harvest fish in their region. In addition, Inuvialuit will play an integral role with government in the management of wildlife and fisheries by holding membership on boards and agencies established to advise government on these matters.

The settlement legislation provided these rights in exchange for the extinguishment of all other aboriginal rights that might be claimed by the Inuvialuit. They will, however, be entitled to benefit from any rights that might be granted in the future through a process of constitutional amendment.

The Dene/Metis claim, which encompasses the Mackenzie Valley, saw a final agreement initialled by negotiators on April 9, 1990. It is due to be put to a ratification vote by participants in the spring of 1991. If the vote goes ahead as planned, participants will be voting on a package which will give them title to 70,000 square miles of land, approximately 19 % of the total settlement area of traditional use and occupancy. To put this into some perspective, this is an area a little more than half the size of Norway. 3,900 square miles of this land will include title to all oil and minerals beneath the surface. As a general rule this land will not be subject to expropriation by government and can not be sold or transferred by the Dene/Metis to any party other than government.

In regards to wildlife harvesting, the Dene/Metis will have the exclusive right to harvest wildlife on their own land and will have the exclusive right to trap furbearing animals on all land within the entire settlement area. They will also have preferential harvesting rights to all species in the settlement area subject only to quotas set for conservation purposes. When it comes to wildlife management, they will have a right to nominate 50 % of the members of the Wildlife Management Board which will make decisions and provide advice on wildlife management.

With respect to the management of land the Dene/Metis will be guaranteed half the membership on a land and water board which will permit uses of all land and water in the settlement area. They will participate similarly in a land use planning regime and on a board mandated to review and assess the environmental impact of major projects planned for the settlement area.

Finally, the Dene/Metis will receive a cash settlement of 500 million dollars amortized over 15 years.

The Inuit of the Eastern Arctic signed a detailed agreement - in - principle on April 30, 1990. This agreement, with adjustments for the differences in the size of their traditional land area and population, will contain elements comparable to the Dene/Metis agreement. For example, the Inuit will receive title to 136,000 square miles of land, 14,000 with subsurface title; a cash settlement of 580 million dollars amortized over 14 years; participation on similar wildlife and land management boards and exclusive and preferential wildlife harvesting rights. It is presently anticipated that the negotiation of this claim will be concluded by the fall of 1991.

In conclusion, these three northern claims, when settled, will be substantial, granting constitutionally protected wildlife harvesting rights and land and wildlife management rights to aboriginal peoples over an area comprising 1/3 of Canada. The constitutional protection afforded to these agreements means that all federal, provincial or territorial laws of general application can not conflict with the terms of each agreement.

However, as I stated earlier the Dene and Metis are now taking the position, based on the thrust of the recent court cases mentioned above, that the Federal Government has a fiduciary and legal responsibility to recognize and affirm the aboriginal rights.

They intend to seek a change to the federal policy of extinguishing aboriginal title, rights and interests through the claims process. The federal justice department has set up a task force to review the *Sparrow* case and may recommend an alternate process to resolve outstanding land claims.

The parameter for the process of reaching aboriginal land claims settlements in Canada are presently under review.

Sami Rights in Norway

Sven-Roald Nystø

Introduction

The territory inhabited by the Sami people is divided among Norway, Sweden, Finland and the Soviet Union. The Sami themselves call the land Sápmi. And the Samis consider themselves one people, one nation. The Nordic Sami-political programme states that "We, the Samis, are one people, and the boundaries of the national states shall not separate us." Estimating the total number of Samis is difficult. A credible figure for the present Sami population is 60,000, half of them living in Norway, 20,000 in Sweden, 8,000 in Finland and 2,000 in the Soviet Union. The number of Sami-speaking people is generally estimated at half the Sami population. This is partly due to the rather harsh assimilation policy towards the Sami and their culture in Nordic countries up to the 1960's.

Since then there has been a growing vitalization of Sami political and cultural activities. Sami organizations have been established and strengthened, and they have claimed political, cultural and land rights. As a result of these acitivies, the state authorities in the Nordic countries have taken steps to improve the status of the Sami people.

The Sami in Norway experienced the beginning of a new political era for the Sami people on 10 and 11 September 1989. For the first time in our history we had the opportunity to elect our own parliament - *the Sámediggi*.

The Sami Parliament was officially opened by His Majesty King Olav V on 9 October 1989, an act which represented the realization of an old dream for many Sami politicians in Norway. Finland has had a separate Sami Parliament since 1973, while the Swedish government is also examining a bill to establish a separate parliament for the Sami in Sweden. When this will eventually come before the Riksdag, the Swedish Parliament, is not easy to say. The bill for the Sami Act has produced very heated debate in the Swedish government.

Before the Sami Parliament was established in Norway, Sami politics were conducted through various Sami organizations. Two of the four major Sami organizations are members of the Nordic Sami Concil. The Nordic Sami

Council in turn is a member of the World Council of Indigenous Peoples (WCIP). The Sami in Sweden are organized into three main organizations, while there are only local and regional Sami associations in Finland. Such associations also exist in Norway and Sweden. The various Sami organizations will continue their activities in the future. How the establishment of Sami parliaments will affect these future activities in specific terms remains to be seen.

The Sami living in the Soviet Union formed their own Kolasami Association in 1989.

The Sami Act

The Act governing the Sami Parliament and other Sami legal conditions (the Sami Act) was passed on 12 June 1987. The purpose of the Act is:

> To establish the conditions which are necessary for the Sami minority in Norway to safeguard and develop its language, its culture and its community life.

The Sami Act lays down that the Sami population is to have its own nationwide Sami Parliament elected by and from the Sami.

The Sámediggi's area of competence, right to introduce initiatives, and power of authority are governed by § 2.1 of the Sami Act and are as follows:

> The Sámediggi's area of competence covers all matters which in the opinion of the Sámediggi are of particular concern to the Sami people.
>
> The Sámediggi can, under its own initiative, render its opinion on all matters in its own area of competence. Under its own initiative, it can also submit matters to public authorities and private institutions etc.
>
> The Sámediggi is empowered to pass measures where such authority is given by other provisions in the Act or is laid down in any other form.

In addition, § 2.2 of the Sami Act calls on other public bodies to give the Sámediggi the opportunity to voice its opinion before they take decisions in matters concerning the Sámediggi's area of competence. The provisions are directed to public bodies at national, regional and local levels.

The Sami Parliament consists of 39 representatives. These are elected from 13 electoral constituencies from all over the country, with three representatives from each constituency. The election of the Sami Parliament is held at the same time as the general election to Norway's national parliament, the Storting.

Very detailed rules have been worked out as to how the Sami Parliament is to be elected. In order to be eligible to vote in the election, and to be eligible to be elected to the Parliament, Samis must first be registrered on a separate electoral roll. Each individual Sami can choose whether he or she wishes to register on this Sami electoral roll and cast a vote.

The Sámediggi is the highest electoral authority for elections to the Sámediggi. Statutory provisions entitle everyone in the sessions of the Sámediggi to speak in either Sami or Norwegian as they choose. The Sámediggi also chooses its own order of business.

The Bodies of the Sami Parliament

The Sámediggi laid down its own order of business on 29 May 1990. Apart from the plenary session, the Sámediggi also has a Presidium, 6 principal committees, a Sámediggi Council and an administrative body.

The Presidium and the principal committees reflect the Sámediggi's political make-up. The Sámediggi Council is elected by majority vote.

The Presidium draws up the agenda for the Sámediggi, and convenes and chairs the plenary session of the Sámediggi.

The principal committees have the task of preparing all business the Sámediggi Council submits to the Sámediggi for final approval or which the plenary session of the Sámediggi refers to a committee. The committees are unable on their own initiative to raise matters in the committees or to pass resolutions. They are intended to function as political bodies for preparing matters and to submit reports to the plenary session.

The six committees are:
-- Principal committee for education and research
-- Principal committee for trade and industry, nature and the environment
-- Principal committee for rights
-- Principal committee for social affairs and health
-- Principal committee for culture and language
-- Principal committee for organizational and constitutional affairs.

The Sámedigge Council consists of a President, Vice President and three other members. It has the task of conducting and organizing the activity of the Sámediggi. This involves the initiation of business to be brought before the plenary session via the principal committees, the passing of its own final resolutions, and the implementation of the resolutions passed by the plenary session of the Sámediggi.

The President of the Sámediggi is permanently employed. The remaining delegates are remunerated according to the number of hours they attend the Sámediggi's meetings. The administrative body has authorization for 11 employees and is led by an administrative director.

The Activities of the Sami Parliament

The Sámediggi is a new constitutional creation in Norway. Today, the Sami Parliament in the main has only consultative powers. One of our greatest challenges in the future will be to have transferred to the Sami Parliament, as far as possible, the definitive authority in questions involving the Sami people.

In the future, the Sami Parliament will be the leading forum for the exercising of the Sami's right to self-determination and of harmonization. Many people have very positive expectations of the Sami Parliament. These expectations are linked, first and foremost, to the Parliament's ability to become engaged in politics. The Sami Parliament's future tasks will naturally fall into two distinctly different areas: on the one hand, the Sami Parliament's own *political initiatives,* and on the other, *administrative* tasks which will be delegated to the Parliament by higher national authorities.

As a political organ for the Samis, the Sami Parliament shall:
-- be the representative and most important organ for the Samis in Sami issues;
-- be the natural center for the debate concerning Sami politics;
-- be a center for ideas, a taker of initiatives and a prime mover in Sami issues;
-- be able to safeguard the rich variety of the Sami culture, economy and society;
-- be able to prevent and subdue inter-ethnic an intra-ethnic conflicts.

As an administrative organ, the Sami Parliament shall:
-- distribute economic subsidies for various Sami purposes on behalf of the state;
-- carry out other tasks pursuant to laws, royal decrees or ministerial measures;
-- submit an annual report to the King on its acitivities;
-- draw up proposals for Sami initiatives in the national budget.

We Samis naturally place the greatest emphasis on the Sami Parliament's role as an organ for Sami politics. And, using some key words, the following topics will be natural areas for the Parliament to work on:
-- formulation of goals for Sami politics;
-- economic issues and policies on employment;

-- use of land and protection of cultural heritage;

-- rights to natural resources.

This means that the Samis face great challenges in the future. I fully trust that we will succeed in these efforts.

The real validity of the Sami Parliament will, for the moment, depend on the Parliament's own ability to formulate a policy. Subsequently, it will depend on how seriously the Norwegian Parliament and the government will stand by their promise to listen to the Sami Parliament. All the political signals from most of the political parties represented in the Storting have been unambiguously positive: an elected Sami organ will be listened to by the central politicians. But the Sami Parliament's most important basis of all is that it is an organ elected among the Samis by the Samis. The authority of Sami politics requires in itself no more detailed regulation in terms of the law. It exists, and has validity in the eyes of everyone who has respect for democratically elected organs.

The Sami Language

The Norwegian Government sumbmitted a bill on 11 May 1990 for the Norwegian Parliament to anchor in law the right to use the Sami language. The bill encompasses regulations and measures directed at allowing the Sami language to be used to a greater extent in contact with public bodies. The bill takes the view that the Sami and Norwegian languages are of equal status and ought to enjoy equal rights. This principle of equal status and equal rights is advanced as a principal goal for all public services at local, regional and national levels.

According to the bill, most concrete regulations governing equality are to be implemented in a closely defined administrative district for the Sami language. This district will consist of five neighbouring municipalities in the county of Finnmark. Public bodies in this district will, amongst other things, be obliged to provide replies in Sami when enquiries are received in Sami. Employees shall be entitled to paid leave to learn Sami when the public body in question has an increased demand for Sami. Announcements made in these municipalities are to be in both Sami and Norwegian and forms are to be printed and be available in both languages. Regulations are also being proposed regarding the use of Sami in the legal sector, health and social institutions and the church.

It is also proposed that municipal councils be empowered to pass measures to introduce Sami as an administrative language in the municipality alongside Norwegian and that acts and regulations of particular interest for the Sami population be translated into Sami.

The bill proposes the establishment of a Sami Language Council whose members would be elected by the Sámediggi. The Language Council would work, amongst other things, with the development and protection of the Sami language, provide advice and assistance in language matters to both institutions and the public, and provide information on new language regulations. The Council will also submit an annual report to the Sámediggi on the status of the Sami language.

The bill also states that everyone will be entitled to instruction conducted in Sami, either at school or as part of adult education.

Certain changes are also proposed to the act governing primary and lower secondary schools in order to extend the law to allow Sami children to learn the Sami language and to receive instruction conducted in Sami. Municipalities will be also able to pass measures for Sami to be used as a compulsory medium for instruction.

The use of Sami place names is not dealt with in the Sami Act. This is regulated instead in a separate act governing place names in Norway which is expected to come into force on 1 July 1991.

Conclusion

In Sweden and Finland, Sami-speaking children are also entitled to learn Sami at school and to have Sami used as a medium of instruction.

The Sami people have no specified legal rights to land and water. In Sweden and Norway, only Sami can pursue reindeer husbandry. This is not the case in Finland, where more than half of the reindeer are owned by non-Samis.

On 21 April 1988, the Norwegian Parliament amended an article in the Constitution concerning the Sami population in Norway: "It is incumbent on the government authorities to take the necessary steps to enable the Sami population to safeguard and develop their language, their culture and their social life." The Finnish and Swedish constitutions do not have corresponding articles concerning the Sami population, but the Swedish constitution has an article concerning minorities in general.

Indigenous Rights Achieved in Greenland

Aqqaluk Lynge
with Frederik Harhoff

The extent and scope of indigenous peoples' right to self-determinaton depends on local conditions and history. In Denmark, for instance, the demand for local control on the Faroe Islands and in Greenland resulted in the introduction of "Home Rule" in 1948 and 1979 respectively.

The core of these arrangements is the transfer of legislative and administrative powers in particular fields from Denmark to the Home Rule authorities in each of the two overseas territories, with corresponding systems of financial support. What, then, are the constitutional relations between Denmark and the indigenous peoples of Greenland?

1 Greenland in the Danish Realm

Greenland was a Danish colony until 1953. Today it is a Danish overseas and autonomous territory enjoying widely extended self-determination through "Home Rule."

Greenland is the world's largest island and northernmost landpoint. It forms a geographical part of the North American continent and it is, for that reason, considered by the Americans to fall within the scope of the "Monroe Doctrine" as an area to be sheltered and embraced in the immediate defense of domestic American interests.

2 Greenland's Home Rule

2 a Background

When Greenland's colonial status was rescinded in 1953, the Danish policy aimed at turning Greenland into a modern society with living standards comparable to those of metropolitan Denmark. A highly ambitious development- and industrialization program was adopted by the Danish Government and supported institutionally by the creation in 1953 of a new Ministry of Greenland Affairs. The basic idea behind this comprehensive public modernization of Greenland was to attract private capital and industry from Denmark--and then leave it to the current market forces to develop a viable economy. Greenland was believed to be exceedingly rich in natural resources, especially fish, so it seemed to be an appealing suggestion. What the Danish State would have to provide for, thus, was mainly social health and welfare, sufficient labourforce and adequates conditions for plant constructions and transportation. And certainly, health-conditions improved significantly during this first period through Danish medical actions directed in particular against tuberculosis. It was the policy of assimilation--of much the same ideological character as the policies concurrently performed in both Alaska and Canada with regard to the integration of natives.

However, it never turned out quite the way it was expected. By the end of the 1950s, it became clear that private industry had failed to invest its resources in Greenland, despite the massive Danish State support in construction of harbors, store-houses, power-plants, housing-complexes, hospitals, etc. This development policy was even reinforced in a new comprehensive plan in 1964, which, i.a., called for an intensified concentration of the population in the industrializing towns on the Southwest coast. A number of settlements were subsequently closed, which generated or just added to the wellknown social problems in the towns to which these people were removed. By the end of the 1960s, the Danish State still found itself with the political and economic responsibility of transforming Greenland into a modern western society--without the anticipated support of private capital from outside Greenland.

A few determining events, however, began to take place at that time.

First of all, while most Greenlanders had been left behind in the wake of the modernization, an elite of well-educated Greenlanders now voiced the demand for political changes leading to decisive Greenlandic influence on the administration of their country. These were the people who later took the political leadership in Greenland.

Upon a Greenlandic proposal to introduce Self Government ad modum the Faroese Home Rule, a joint Danish-Greenlandic Commission, in its concluding report in 1978, recommended the introduction of a Greenlandic Home Rule, which went into force on May 1st the following year. After the first election to the new Greenland Home Rule Parliament in 1979, the social-democratic Siumut Party seized power and formed the first Home Rule Government. That party has remained in power ever since, together with changing coalition partners.

2 b   The Legal Structure of the Home Rule

The introduction of Home Rule in the Faroe Islands (in 1948) and in
Greenland (in 1979) raised complicated constitutional legal problems. In its present version, the 1953 Danish Constitution does not even refer to "Home Rule."

Section 1 of the Constitution rather stresses the unity of the realm--as a reflection of the immediate postwar aspiration to fully equate Greenland with Denmark in social and industrial terms.

The legal question is, therefore, whether "Home Rule" is just a unilaterally revokable delegation of powers from metropolitan Denmark, or whether it represents a permanent reallocation of the legislative and administrative powers in the Danish Constitution to the Faroese and Greenlandic Home Rule authorities.

In the end, this question refers to the overall political and financial balance between Denmark and the two Home Rule territories. This balance is reflected in the Home Rule Act of 1978.

The following five points will briefly outline the legal pattern of the Greenland Home Rule:

-- The essence of the Home Rule is the *transfer of jurisdictional (both legislative and executive) powers* from the Danish Parliament and Government to the new Greenland legislature (the 27 member "Landsting") and the Greenland Government (the 5-7 member "Landsstyre").

-- Powers are transferred *within certain, specified areas of jurisdiction*, which are listed in the Annex to the Home Rule Act. Such areas may be transferred only partly if so required by the Home Rule.

-- The Home Rule commission presumed that *certain powers or areas of jurisdiction could not--for constitutional reasons--be transferred to the Home Rule*. This was expressed directly in the Home Rule Act only with regard to foreign policy matters, but it was believed to be the case also for general constitutional matters (including national citizenship, human rights etc), for security/defense matters, for monetary and currency matters, for family and heritage law, property law, criminal law and for the judicial powers. In the Commission's Report, these areas were therefore declared exclusive Danish matters and have in principle remained so, even though the viability of these assertions has been questioned by the Home Rule.

-- In principle, *the financial responsibility in each of the areas is transferred by the Home Rule along with the jurisdictional power.* If assumption of the financial responsibility for a particular area is clearly incompatible with the Home Rule's economy, however, it may decline to assume the financial responsibility for that area. In such cases, Denmark will continue to defray the costs by granting annually the same sum of money to the Home Rule which Denmark expended at the time of the transfer. These various grants are then pooled into an annual "block grant" which is index-linked in the Danish State Budget and balanced with the Home Rule's own incomes (from taxation and exports). The principle behind this block grant "aid system" is that Denmark should neither gain nor lose by the

Home Rule assuming such fields of jurisdiction. This arrangement leaves the way open for Greenland to develop into an economically self-supporting society, at which time Denmark will gradually cease to transfer these block grants.

-- *The ownership of non-renewable resources in Greenland* is shared between the Danish Crown and the resident population in Greenland. According to Section eight of the Home Rule Act, "Greenland's resident population has fundamental rights in respect of Greenland's natural resources," but the legal character of these rights was never specified by the Home Rule Commission, lacking agreement on this issue. They are now believed to be collective rights (as opposed to individual rights) conferred upon all resident Danish, Faroese or Greenlandic citizens in Greenland--native or non-native. Individual proprietary rights to land or sub-surface resources in Greenland do not exist, and have never existed. The Home Rule Act stipulates that agreement has to be reached between the Danish Government and the Greenlandic Landsstyre (Government) prior to any decision on prospecting, exploration or exploitation of non-renewable resources in Greenland. Thus, each of the two governments has a right to veto any decision in this respect. Applications for resource operations in Greenland are considered in a joint Danish-Greenlandic Council for Mineral Resources, but it is still--formally-- left with the Danish Minister for Energy and Resources to issue the final concession in cases where prior agreement is reached between the two parties in the joint Council.

Revenues from resource operations in Greenland are now shared equally between the Greenland and Danish Purses.

3   Dynamic Development

When the Home Rule was established in Greenland, it was expected to take over the various possible areas of self-government within a period of 25 years. With the positive development of the Home Rule system it has been possible to transfer all areas that could be transferred according to the Home Rule Law within only ten years.

The latest subject to be transferred was environmental legislation, which was placed under the Home Rule Government by January 1989.

The health-sector was not anticipated to be transferred, but is now also under negotiation.

In 1985 Greenland left the European Communities, and formed an associate-relationship instead of full membership.

Even though the Home Rule has no foregin policy powers it has gained a position with the Danish state that enables the Home Rule to enter into cooperation with other regions and people outside the Danish realm. Greenland is a member of the Inuit Circumpolar Conference and also a member of the Nordic Council.

With the instalment of Home Rule in Greenland, there is no doubt that the relationship between the indigenous people of Greenland and the Danish state has improved and in many ways found a platform that is satisfactory to both parties. One of the main reasons for this it that both have seen the Home Rule Law as a dynamic concept and been willing to renegotiate areas along with the development of the Home Rule.

Besides having the Home Rule organisation, Greenland still holds 2 seats in the Danish Parliament.

Indigenous Peoples and the State: Some Basic Legal Principles Seen from a Nordic Point of View

Carsten Smith

Two Main Legal Approaches and a Synthesis

The task assigned to me is to expound generally, as a jurist, the present status of indigenous peoples in relation to the states where they live. This paper will thus deal primarily with rights of indigenous peoples according to *international law*, but will on this international background also make some remarks on the development of Sami rights in Norway. The status in Canadian law as well as in other national legal systems will be discussed by other panelists. The basis of the paper is my experience from the Norwegian Sami Rights Commission 1980-85 and subsequent studies regarding Sami law.

Indigenous peoples can, in order to protect their culture and their territories, invoke two main groups of legal norms. First, there are general sources of law pertaining to *minorities*, whose chief purpose is to provide *protection of culture*. Secondly, there are special sources of law relating *exclusively* to indigenous peoples, whose foremost aim is to provide *aboriginal territorial rights*.

The central legal norm on minorities is the provision on protection of culture in the United Nations Covenant on Civil and Political Rights Article 27. It says that in those states in which ethnic, religious or linguistic minorities exist, persons belonging to such minorities shall not be denied the right, in community with the other members of their group, to enjoy their own culture, to profess and practise their own religion, or to use their own language.

Special legal norms on indigenous peoples have their roots far back in history, and comprehensive positive legal material now exists, both in international instruments and in the domestic legislation and judicial decisions of many countries, the purpose of which is to give the indigenous peoples such a legal position in their traditional territories that they can safeguard and develop their form of life. This legal material covers a long period of time and large geographical areas.

In the Norwegian developments of the 1980s, as well as in a Swedish report, the Sami rights have been based on a kind of *synthesis* of these two main lines. This synthesis may thus be regarded as the Nordic doctrine--a Nordic contribution to the evolution of the international law on indigenous peoples.

A principal reason for forming such a synthesis is the dissimilarity as regards the *strength of the legal basis* provided by these two groups. Certainly, the UN Covenant is binding on the large number of states having ratified it, and its character is universal. The specific sources of law relating to indigenous peoples are less widespread internationally, and there may be some doubt as to the degree to which this material--apart from the treaties--can be said to have established customary law or general principles of law that are binding on the states. In this connection, the 1989 ILO Convention on Indigenous Peoples now represents a clarification and strengthening of their rights. But the protection of minorities following from Article 27 still on the whole rests on a more general and solid legal foundation than the particular legal protection of indigenous peoples.

The Norwegian reform efforts have therefore chosen this Article as starting point. When *interpreting* the provision, use has also been made of the legal sources on indigenous peoples. The result is a *differentiated* construction of Article 27, involving an *expansive* interpretation as regards the indigenous peoples. One may argue whether, in the course of this interpretation, regard can be had to circumstances relating only to *a group* of ethnic minorities, since the Article applies the term ethnic minorities as a uniform term. On this point, one must say that when a certain kind of ethnic minority is in need of a *special foundation for their culture*, and the group should lose this foundation, it would at the same time lose the real possibilities of enjoying their culture. In that case, the "right" to enjoy their own culture would be without substance. Like other provisions, Article 27 ought to be interpreted so as to make it effective.

At the present stage, until the international law of indigenous peoples has been further developed, an advantage of this synthesis is that there can be no doubt about the legal foundation per se, while there are, according to recognised principles of interpretation, strong reasons to undertake an expansive construction.

The Norwegian Development

The political and legal reform process commenced in 1980, during the conflict concerning the construction of a hydroelectric plant in the Kautokeino-Alta river, when the government set up a Sami Rights Commission and a Sami

Culture Commission. In 1984 the Sami Rights Commission submitted a report with considerable emphasis on international principles of law. The main legal milestones in the further process are the 1987 Sami Act, by which the Sami Parliament was established, and the 1988 amendment to the Constitution, Article 110 a, imposing on government authorities the obligation to provide the Sami people with adequate instruments for the safeguarding and development of their language, their culture and their social life. In June 1990, the new ILO Convention of 1989 on indigenous peoples in independent states was ratified. These events, together with a number of political statements, signify a breakthrough for a new Sami law and Sami policy in Norway.

The Material Basis of the Culture

Whether or not Article 27 also covers *territorial rights*--rights to land and water--depends on the understanding of the *concept of culture* contained in the provision. Obviously, it applies to ideal forms of expression, like books, theatre, visual arts, etc. The question is whether it also covers the *material foundation* --the economic and physical basis--of the culture of an ethnic minority. If so, the Article may cover the right to natural resources.

A report submitted at the request of the Sami Rights Commission, and incorporated in the Commission's own report, found that the best legal reasons favoured the inclusion of the material aspects of the culture. In short, the comprehensive reasoning was as follows: The wording, the travaux preparatoires, the legal theory and the practice of the UN Human Rights Committee provide certain, albeit not very strong, arguments for considering the material cultural foundation as protected. By its more detailed interpretation of Article 27, the report then makes use of the extensive legal material on protection of indigenous peoples. This indicates that each ethnic minority should have a right to demand the real basis that is decisive for just that minority's enjoyment of its culture. It is pointed out that there is increasing recognition of the fact that indigenous peoples are in great need of protection of their traditional use of land and water because the connection between the enjoyment of their culture and the exercise of their traditional trades is particularly strong. This expansive construction of the Article indicates that the use of natural resources and other economic circumstances should be covered "to the extent to which this is decisive for the group's maintenance and development of its own culture."

Thus, the conclusion is in principle positive as regards the material foundation of the culture, although somewhat uncertain as to the scope of the protection.

This conclusion of the Commission *was accepted* during the subsequent political process. The Ministry of Foreign Affairs expressed the opinion, it is true, that the report's construction of Article 27 was too extensive. But in the bill of 1987, the Ministry of Justice nevertheless adhered to the standpoint of the report. The Ministry of Justice stated directly that "it would agree to the Commission's principal interpretation of Article 27," that the concept of culture "must be understood also to cover the material conditions for the culture," and that "the state assumes an obligation to contribute positively to provide for the Sami people the preconditions for enjoying their culture and their language." This must be considered to be the Government's standpoint, seeing that it was the Ministry of Justice which presented the proposition and it was approved by the King in Council.

In the Parliament, the Justice Committee made certain that these views were even more firmly established as Norway's perception of international law on this question. The Committee agrees to the opinion that "the state has an obligation to provide for the Sami ethnic group the material conditions for the enjoyment of its culture and language, as well as enabling the group to influence the physical and economic foundation of their culture." During the parliamentary debate, the Minister of Justice emphasised that the concept of culture in the provision "must be understood as also covering the material foundation for enjoyment of the culture."

Under these circumstances, Article 27 must be recognised as an important source of law for Sami rights, both political, cultural and economic rights, also including rights to natural resources in the Sami areas of settlement and use. A chief objective must now be the concretization of this principle.

On Positive Discrimination

An interrelated issue is whether Article 27 provides for a preferential treatment of the minority compared to other citizens.

The Sami Rights Commission's report regarded it as "not at all doubtful" that the Article contains a demand for positive discrimination. The crux of the provision is that it affords special protection of minorities. Therefore, a state having an ethnic minority, does *not* fulfil its duty by only guaranteeing equal legal treatment of its citizens. The extent of the state's positive discrimination must depend on the actual situation in each state.

During the hearing, the Ministry of Foreign Affairs maintained that the report went too far. But the Ministry of Justice's agreement on the report's "principal interpretation of Article 27," and thus also the Government's adherence to the interpretation, must be presumed to include this question as well. And the opinion of the parliamentary Justice Committee is quite clear on this point, as it is emphasised that "it is in conformity with international developments of law" when Norwegian authorities "now clearly express willingness to contemplate positive special measures in relation to the Sami ethnic groups."

Therefore, according to Norwegian authorities' understanding of international law, the state is obliged to afford special rights to a minority insofar as is necessary to comply with the demand for cultural protection.

The Scope of the New Constitutional Provision

The constitutional amendment contains no general rule on minorities, but is directly aimed at the Sami, and it imposes a legal--and also a political and moral--obligation on the state in relation to the Sami. By this decision the Parliament has, according to the Committee on Foreign and Constitutional Affairs, "in the most solemn and binding manner known by our legal system, recognised and drawn conclusions from the fact, that throughout Norway's history there has existed a Sami ethnic group in our country." Implementation of the constitutional demands must take place by means of legislation, appropriations and other decisions by government authorities.

The constitutional protection should be considered to extend also to the material foundation of the culture. During the parliamentary debate, the chairman of the Justice Committee pointed out that "in its form" the constitutional article is not a rule on incorporation in relation to international law, "but its content corresponds to the international obligations to which the Norwegian state is already subjected according to Article 27." In this connection, express reference was made to the interpretation of Article 27 given during the debate on the Sami Act in 1987.

It should further be assumed that the constitutional protection authorizes positive discrimination when special measures are required to implement the safeguarding of the culture. Just this preferential treatment was one of the crucial points in the debate prior to the passing of the constitutional provision.

On this basis, the international and the constitutional law must be said to make the same demands. But the Constitution reinforces these international principles of law as they have now been given constitutional strength in Norwegian law.

The International Labour Organization Convention on Indigenous Peoples

What I have presented here is hopefully merely a present state picture, a 1990 picture which will fade away rather rapidly as treaties on indigenous peoples will establish a more solid general and legal foundation. In this regard I will add a few words about the International Labour Organization Convention on Indigenous Peoples which I briefly referred to above. This convention, which was signed in 1989, is a general treaty concerning indigenous peoples in independent countries. It contains provisions on general policy, on land rights of various kinds, among others of ownership and posession of the lands which indigenous peoples traditionally occupy. Furthermore, on recruitments and conditions of employment, on vocational training, handicrafts and rural industries, on social security and health, on education and means of communication and on contacts and cooperation across borders.

In the years to come this convention may hopefully obtain the status as *the* basic international instrument concerning indigenous rights, at least as an instrument establishing minimum rights. But unfortunately, we have not come that far yet. Norway was the very first country to ratify the convention in June this summer (1990), but the convention will not come into force for any state until 12 months after the date of its ratification, which means that today this convention is not binding upon any state, not even on my own country yet. Therefore, the discussion on international law in this field must still proceed on the basis of all the *other* sources of law, excluding so far this convention as a primary legal source.

Changing Political Loyalties in the Canadian North

Douglas C. Nord

As has been noted by several eminent scholars, "the idea of the north" has been intricately entwined with the economic, social and psychological development of the Canadian nation. With the possible exceptions of the peoples of the Nordic countries and the U.S.S.R., no other society has focused as much attention on its own "nordicity." The "true north strong and free" has become not only an oft-quoted line from the Canadian national anthem, but also a central defining element of the national mythos.[1]

Despite this apparent fixation on the "idea of the north"--and the accompanying physical reality that much of the national land mass clearly occupies northern territory--most Canadians have, surprisingly, little first-hand acquaintance or knowledge of the north. Few have travelled in the northern lands of the Yukon or Northwest Territories--or for that matter, in the northern stretches of their own provinces. For most Canadians, the north continues to be viewed from a distance--via television or newspaper or magazine accounts. The peoples and problems who inhabit these northern lands seem remote to the residents of Vancouver, Toronto and Montreal. More often their gaze is directed southward to the warmer and more inviting climes of the United States, Mexico and the Caribbean.[2]

When most Canadians do take the opportunity to focus their attention on northern issues or problems, they are motivated to do so by one or two overarching concerns. The first is a recurring interest in the economic potential of the northern regions of their country. The Canadian North has been viewed throughout the history of the nation as a vast treasure chest of natural resources ready to be exploited. Periodically, new proposals have been brought forth to access these resources as the natural wealth of southern lands has been exhausted.[3]

Alternatively, Canadians have become interested in their northern lands and waters whenever there has seemed to be a possibility that a portion of these territories might be alienated from them by some foreign power--most notably the United States. One has simply to recall the sudden upswing in Canadian interest regarding its northern extremities at the time of the Yukon Gold Rush, the passage of the *S.S. Manhattan* or the most recent maneuvers of American

129

and Soviet submarines in "Canadian" arctic waters.[4]

Unfortunately, widescale attention to the needs and aspirations of the residents of these northern territories has not been a regular concern of the Canadian public. Instead it has remained at the margins of the nation's consciousness, "a minor place in the national scheme of things."[5] Only in the past three decades has the Canadian North become an emerging focus for political debate and controversy.

The Nature of This Inquiry

This paper seeks to examine the manner in which political attitudes and behavior have altered in the Canadian North over the last three decades. It will focus its attention on a series of political developments in the area that have transformed the residents from non-participants in the political process to active players in the political arena of their region and nation. The paper seeks to chronicle the specific steps by which the peoples of northern Canada have sought to empower themselves to deal with the challenges of economic and social change in their homeland. The paper also endeavors to discuss the resistance they have encountered in this effort.

The paper begins with an overall discussion of the Canadian North as a political hinterland. It examines the traditional economic, social and political strategies which have been pursued by southern Canadian interests to maintain this virtual colonial status. It also considers the resulting sense of political impotence and alienation that has traditionally developed among the residents of this region.

The essay next moves to consider the specific political evolution of the two northern territories, the Yukon and the Northwest Territories, from Confederation to the decade of the 1960s. It discusses both the similarities and differences in their political status as well as their distinctive goals and aspirations. Efforts on the part of the national government of Canada to develop a comprehensive "Northern Policy" are also detailed.

The next section of the paper examines the specific events of the past two decades that have served to initiate greater political activism on the part of northern Canadians. It recounts issues related to resource development, native land claims, the creation of new northern provinces and the entrenchment of constitutional rights. Specifically, it examines the manner in which these political concerns were made manifest in the forms of political action and political change within the political institutions and processes of the region and nation.

130

The final section of the paper addresses the political challenges confronted by northern Canadians in the 1990s. Here specific reference is made to the recent debate over the Meech Lake Accord and its implications for the North's continued status as a political hinterland. The potentials of new political leadership and the possibilities of home rule are also outlined.

The Development of Colonialism in the Canadian North

Although the northern territories of Canada represent roughly forty-five percent of the nation's physical expanse, in population terms the Yukon and the Northwest Territories exist as extremely small communities. With populations of 27,000 and 53,000, respectively, the two territories have population density figures which are among the lowest in the world. These small human settlements seem to be almost swallowed up by the land that surrounds them.[6]

Because of their size--and relative remoteness from the main population centers of Canada--the Yukon and the Northwest Territories have rarely received the notice or careful attention of national leaders or the general public. Perceived as a vast wilderness--pretty much devoid of human settlement--most Canadians have been content to allow these northern lands to develop as hinterland societies, far from their collective consciousness and concern. Somewhat like distant overseas colonies, southern Canadians have known of their existence, but paid little heed to them.[7]

Like colonies, the northern territories have existed to serve the economic needs of the south virtually from the outset of the nation's founding. With vast reserves of furs, timber and minerals, the North has always represented a natural resource treasure house that has been repeatedly looted by enthusiastic exploiters from the South. With the subsequent discovery of significant energy resources in the area, this historical pattern has been further ingrained.[8]

Frances Abele has argued persuasively that this entire "colonial relationship" is reflective of the overall Canadian mode of development that is displayed in the National Policy. She notes that: "The northern territories were administered for decades as colonies of the South, at first lackadaisically and then, after World War II, with sudden energy. The National Policy Strategy, which had opened the West, was revived for the North, like a recurring dream, whenever it appeared that northern resource development was possible."[9] Inherent in this view is that the southern interest in the North was limited to the economic wealth that might be produced, and not focused at all on the needs or aspirations of the people who inhabited these resource producing areas. Political colonialism has accompanied economic colonialism in the Canadian

North. The northern territories have through much of their history been administered from a distance by politicians and civil servants who have been frequently ill-informed concerning the lands and people they directed. The territories, until recently, have not enjoyed representative government within their borders and still lack effective "home rule."[10]

In part, this style of colonial administration has been inspired by a sincere desire to provide efficient and effective "protection" to the lands and people who inhabit the North. However, more than often this approach has been motivated by a desire to keep "important decisions" regarding the exploitation of northern lands and natural resources out of the hands of local residents and within the "capable" grasp of southern decision-makers.

The consequence of this approach to policymaking in the Canadian north has been the creation of a hinterland system of politics. Within this system powerful political and administrative players in distant Ottawa interact with influential local elites to render decisions that are frequently not to the social or economic benefit of the local community. Instead such "wise public policy decisions" tend to benefit the metropolitan centers of power. Community members from the North are usually excluded from the entire process or "paid off" by the granting of insignificant or symbolic benefits.[11]

Over the long-term, the operation of this type of political colonialism results in a progressive increase in either political alienation or political protest (or both) among the local community. Both trends have been seen within the Yukon and the Northwest Territories over the past three decades. Some suggest that winning political and economic emancipation from such a colonial system has become the number one agenda item of both the white and native populations of the Canadian North.

The Political Development of the Yukon and the N.W.T 1870-1970

Canada's jurisdiction over its northern territories began shortly after Confederation. In 1870, Ottawa purchased Rupert's Land and the North-West from the Hudson's Bay Company. A decade later in 1880, the British government transferred to Canada control over the Arctic Islands of the Far North. The mostly native residents of these regions failed to distinguish a change in ownership partly because they considered the lands to be *their* homeland and partly because the new Canadian government did little to exercise any direct control over the region.

It was not until the Klondike gold rush of 1898 that Canadian officials in Ottawa were roused from their lethargy towards the North. Fearing possible civil disorder and potential annexation of the goldfields by the United States, the Canadian government created the Yukon Territory and established local government. Aided by detachments of the Royal North-West Mounted Police, this new civil administration maintained law and order in the region and oversaw the initial commercial development of the area. While the white population in the new territory remained large, there was some experimentation with various forms of responsible government. These steps toward creating a provincelike administration were abandoned in the 1920s, however, as the mining population in the area declined. In its place was established a contracted and less democratic territorial state structure with power and control emanating from Ottawa.[12]

The Northwest Territories was created as an administrative unit in 1905. Its boundaries were formed from the northern lands that were leftover after the creation of the Yukon Territory and the new provinces of Saskatchewan and Alberta. The Northwest Territories Act of 1905 established a broad grant of local self-government in the peoples of the NWT, but like the Yukon, these were quickly extinguished by administrative supervision from Ottawa.[13]

For much of the first five decades of this century, both northern territories were treated in an "absent-minded" fashion by responsible officials in Ottawa. The federal profile in the North was limited and expenditures for the benefit of white and native peoples in the area were scarce. The RCMP continued to administer law and order, but it was left to non-state institutions (chiefly the fur trading companies and churches) to provide social services.[14]

Throughout this era, the indigenous peoples were encouraged not to integrate themselves with the white settlements or economy. In contradistinction to the official government policy pursued in southern Canada, northern native peoples were not pressured to settle on reserves or to abandon traditional hunting patterns. Instead, "the human population of the territorial North was left largely in a 'state of nature.'"[15]

This overall policy of extended neglect was to come to an abrupt end in the late 1950s. Suddenly the federal government in Ottawa became conscious of the North both in economic and social terms. For the first time the North was seen as a true national asset that needed to be developed and fully incorporated into the nation.

With this in mind the Diefenbaker government unveiled a series of northern development schemes under the general heading of a "Northern Vision." These projects were directed at both promoting settlement in the northern territories and accessing the vast natural resources of the region. Abele notes in this regard that:

> The North was to be opened by means of a 'new National Policy.' The North, like the West fifty years earlier, would provide staple export commodities. Northern minerals, like western wheat in an earlier period, would fuel the engine of the national economy by providing export credits, jobs and investment opportunities. The role of the federal state would be to facilitate resource development.[16]

In the social arena, a similar frontal attack was made on the observed social welfare needs of the northern peoples. Inspired by a sudden awareness of the "disadvantaged condition" of many northern residents (especially the indigenous peoples) the Diefenbaker and Pearson governments launched a full-scale effort to provide improved health, housing, education and employment services for their "newly discovered" northern citizens. By the early 1960s virtually all native and non-native northerners were receiving the full panoply of social welfare payments enjoyed in southern Canada.[17]

While most residents of northern Canada welcomed these economic and social development initiatives, one notable weakness of both endeavors was their failure to involve the local residents (the supposed beneficiaries) in the decision-making process. Instead, these programs were launched with a distinct colonial mentality that suggested that central policy formulation in Ottawa was best and that local involvement was largely unnecessary.[18]

The above attitude was most prevalent within the central bureaucratic player in these economic and social development schemes--the Department of Northern Affairs and National Resources (DNANR). The DNANR (after 1965, the Department of Indian Affairs and Northern Development--DIAND) operated as "a kind of 'colonial office' for the North." [19] Its extensive administrative arms supervised most aspects of life in the Yukon and the Northwest Territories until well into the 1970s. It performed the functions that normally would devolve to a provincial government. In so doing, it effectively precluded the development of responsible self-government in the North.

The central role played by DIAND in the Yukon and Northwest Territories gave rise to two alternative political responses. One was an active system of brokerage politics between the local elites of the territories and the powerful bureaucrats of Ottawa. Under this system, influential locals became the spokespersons for the DIAND agenda and their faithful public defenders. In return, DIAND bestowed development resources upon these favored individuals and groups.

The alternative political response was one of increasing criticism and resentment toward DIAND. Throughout the late 1960s increasing numbers of white and native residents of the northern territories engaged in a series of protests demanding a voice in public policies affecting their lives and a devolution of authority from Ottawa to their local governments.

Their protests bore some initial results. The most significant of these was the establishment in 1965 of a federal commission of inquiry into the future development needs of the Northwest Territories. Among the eventual recommendations of the Carrothers Commission were several designed to increase public participation in the decision-making process. These included: the relocation of the seat of the NWT government from Ottawa to Yellowknife, the direct election of the Territorial Council, and the gradual transference of authority over local matters from the federal to the territorial government.[20]

Despite these concessions, Ottawa continued to exert major influence over the lives of northern residents through its continued supervisory oversight of the territorial administrations and its exclusive jurisdiction over natural resource development. It would take still another decade before these mechanisms of political control were to be directly challenged.

A Political Awakening in the Canadian North 1970-1990

The demands for public participation in decision-making that were first voiced in the late 1960s became more forceful in the 1970s. This new assertiveness was, in part, a response to renewed federal interest in "developing" the region. Plans aimed at "opening up the North" in terms of land use and resource development were to run into conflict with increased awareness on the part of Northern residents that their traditional ways of life were being sacrificed. Michael Whittington observes that:

> The 1970s witnessed an awakening of people's consciousness that the North, while a wilderness to southern Canadians, was in fact home to the Indians, Inuit and long-term white residents. . .The people of the North were committed to their land and felt a deep and justifiable resentment that their homeland was seen simply as a resource warehouse.[21]

During the decade a number of important development projects became the center of heated debate. One of the most wellpublicized related to a proposal to build a natural gas pipeline through the Mackenzie Valley of the Northwest Territories. Under significant pressure from northern opponents, the minority Liberal government of the day appointed Justice Thomas Berger of the Supreme Court of British Columbia to conduct an inquiry into the advisability

135

of the plan. Over the two year period of 1974-1976, the Berger Inquiry took testimony from hundreds of northern residents focusing on the potential social, economic, and environmental impact of the pipeline. Their views were to prove ultimately decisive in persuading the Berger Inquiry to recommend against the construction of the pipeline.[22]

Such concerted opposition to federal development schemes was also witnessed in the Yukon. Native and white organizations in the territory lobbied effectively against the construction of an Alaska Highway pipeline. They succeeded in forcing an official review of the plan--the Lysyk Inquiry--and eventually scuttled the project.[23]

This potent combination of grassroots political mobilization and administrative lobbying reached its zenith during the decade with the submission by various native groups of a series of land claims to the federal government. Rooted in long-standing resentment toward bureaucratic domination and high-handedness, the native land claims represented a direct frontal attack upon southern colonialism in the North. Abele notes that:

> The 'land claim proposals'...asked for more than real estate; each called for a fundamental readjustment in their relationship to the federal state, based upon native peoples' interpretation of their own situation and proposing new models of self-government that blended traditional governing forms with liberal democratic principles.[24]

While the settlement of such land claims became the central concern of many native groups in the Northwest Territories, white northerners--primarily in the Yukon--directed their political efforts toward other goals. These included securing greater representation in the territorial government; increased devolution of authority to local government; and, ultimately provincial status. By 1977 they had secured the first of these goals by forcing the inclusion of a majority of elected members on the Executive Council of the territorial government. A year later party politics formally arrived in the Yukon. By 1979, the first fully elected cabinet was sworn in under Government Leader Chris Pearson.

The new Progressive Conservative administration under Mr. Pearson lost little time in asserting the right of the popularly elected council to predominance over the Ottawa-appointed Commissioner of the territory. In a strong letter to Jake Epp, the then Minister of Indian Affairs and Northern Development, Pearson observed that:

> The growth of the Executive Committee concept and the advent of party politics for the

Yukon legislature have made it possible to entrust a large portion of the active, day-to-day administration of the Yukon government to elected officials directly accountable to the Yukon Legislative Assembly. In this context, it is our contention that the Commissioner need not and should not continue to play a prominent role in the day-to-day administration of the Yukon government.[25]

Mr. Epp's reply was that he agreed with Mr. Pearson's viewpoint and that he was instructing the new Commissioner, Ione Christensen, to undertake a more limited role. From that point forward, the commissioner would no longer sit on the Executive Committee of the Yukon government and would accept the advice of the elected council on all matters.[26]

This considerable step toward establishing responsible government in the Yukon was accompanied by a further devolution of powers from the federal government. Throughout the 1970s the territorial government acquired responsibility for delivering programs and services formerly undertaken by DIAND and other federal departments. These included: education; the administration of justice; the maintenance of public works and the Alaska Highway; the regulation of hunting and sports fishing; and the development of tourism and small business. These grants of authority endowed the territorial government with "province-like" powers with one notable exception--control over natural resources.

The movement for acquiring full provincial status for the Yukon was buoyed briefly in the late 1970s by Progressive Conservative leader Joe Clark's endorsement of home rule. Urged on by his close political supporter, Erik Nielsen (MP for the Yukon), Clark promised that the Yukon would move toward full provincial status during the Conservatives' first term of office.[27] This prospect was quickly dashed, however, due to the brief tenure of the Clark government and the return of the Liberal Party to power. Back in office in 1980, Prime Minister Trudeau scoffed at the idea of provincial status for the Yukon. "Not in my lifetime," was his estimation.[28] Further salt was added to the wound by Ottawa's decision not to invite the government leader of the Yukon to subsequent First Minister Conferences.

The path to "home rule" in the Northwest Territories has been similarly long and beset with an equal number of political successes and setbacks. Sensing an increasing level of political disaffection in the North, the federal parliament in Ottawa amended the NWT Act in 1974 to allow for a popularly elected territorial council. Elections took place in the subsequent year and yielded a council with a majority of native members. This new council let it be known that as a first priority it desired a full-scale review of the NWT's status in confederation.[29]

In an effort to mollify the NWT government, Ottawa announced in 1977 that it was appointing its own review commission to study the further constitutional development of the territory. Bud Drury, a former Liberal cabinet minister, headed the body. His commission held hearings over the next two years and submitted its final report in 1980.

Not surprisingly, the Drury Report discovered that there were major limitations to the existing political structures and processes in the territory. It suggested that Native concerns were not being well addressed within existing arrangements and that the potential of local responsible government had not been fully realized. Furthermore, it argued that additional grants of responsibility from the federal government to the territory were warranted.[30]

The NWT legislative assembly, however, did not wait for the eventual tabling of the Drury Report. Like the Yukon government before it, it unanimously passed a resolution in March of 1979 calling for immediate responsible government and the eventual granting of provincial status. It also called for the removal of all Ottawa-appointed officials, including the commissioner, and the devolution of additional authority to the NWT government.

Ottawa was to respond to these demands in piecemeal fashion. It accepted many of the recommendations of the Drury Report regarding the need to expand local government in the NWT and broaden its authority. It eventually supported the transference of responsibility for health, education, public works, social development and the administration of justice from federal authorities to local. It also moved substantially toward accepting the idea of responsible government in the territory. Whittington notes in this regard that:

> Unlike the case of the Yukon, there was no magical letter from Ottawa instructing the commissioner of the Northwest Territories to 'back off' and let the elected people take the initiative...However the position of the commissioner in the territory has evolved to a role virtually identical to that of the commissioner of the Yukon.[31]

What the federal government proved to be unwilling to accept with regard to either the NWT or the Yukon was the quick conferring of provincial status. Ottawa's objections were threefold. It argued that populations of both territories were too small and too widely dispersed. It contended that the economic bases of the communities were too limited to provide the tax revenues necessary for a provincial government. It has also argued that the peoples of the North have yet to provide a clear sign of their unified desire for such status.[32]

The latter contention is somewhat hard to defend given recent history. In the early 1980s when the Trudeau government was involved in efforts to patriate the Canadian Constitution, the legislative assemblies of both the Yukon and the Northwest Territories lobbied hard to secure constitutional language affording a quick transition from territorial to provincial status. In November of 1981 the entire NWT Legislative Assembly travelled to Ottawa to argue on behalf of this cause and the entrenchment of native and aboriginal rights. In both areas, they were effectively rebuffed by federal representatives and sent back to the North disillusioned as to whether federal officials would ever recognize their aspirations to equal status within the nation.[33]

The struggle for effective "home rule" in the North during the 1970s and 1980s were concurrent with two other major political developments in the North during the same period. One was the gradual replacement of the old system of brokerage politics between local elites and administrative bureaucracies in Ottawa. With the development of popularly elected legislative assemblies in the Yukon and the NWT one saw the decline in clout of "traditional insiders" and their replacement by leaders of political protest movements and native organizations. A new generation of leadership grounded in grassroots political mobilization has come forward. A prime example of this trend has been the replacement of Erik Nielsen by Audrey McLaughlin as member of parliament from the Yukon. In similar fashion, the 'establishment' Progressive Conservative Party has become increasingly ineffective in winning elections at either the local or federal level. Presently they are a minority in the Yukon Legislative Assembly and hold none of the three northern seats in the House of Commons.[34]

The other major political development in the North during the past decade has been the effort to subdivide the Northwest Territories into two separate political communities--Nunavut and Denendeh. Space does not permit a full discussion of this endeavor here, but it is interesting to note that this initiative is sustained, in part, by the concern of residents in the territory that the federal government has no interest in ever granting the NWT, as a unit, full provincial status.[35] Furthermore, like northerners in the Yukon, they argue that they have been repeatedly excluded from decision-making circles in Ottawa and are no longer willing to wait patiently for a delayed invitation. The time has come to assert their own right to popular sovereignty.

Political Challenges Confronting the Canadian North in the 1990s

The agenda for home rule and popular sovereignty in the Canadian North remains full at the outset of the 1990s. While important strides have been made over the past two decades toward securing greater social and political development in the region, the process is still unfinished. Moreover, there remains serious obstacles to overcome. The most significant of these has been the failure of the federal government to accept the concept of early provincial status for the Yukon and the Northwest Territories.

This reluctance has been graphically illustrated in the manner in which the Meech Lake Accord was negotiated and supported by Ottawa. When Prime Minister Mulroney met with the ten provincial premiers in 1987 to seek amendments to the Constitution Act of 1982, the leaders of the territories were not invited. In so doing, Ottawa signaled that it was not interested in listening to their concerns or having them as full partners at the table. Ottawa clearly desired to give the perceived constitutional needs of Quebec its top priority and did not want to be side-tracked by northern and native demands for home rule.[36]

There is a significant irony here in that the Meech Lake Agreement came hard on the heels of the constitutionally mandated First Ministers Conference on Aboriginal Treaty Rights. At that meeting, Ottawa and the provinces proved unable to focus their attention on the constitutional needs and aspirations of the peoples of the North. Yet within a month, they were able to come forth with a supposedly acceptable package recognizing a special status for Quebec.[37]

Besides being excluded from the Meech Lake talks, the leaders of the Yukon and Northwest Territories found several specific elements of the agreement to be inimicable to future northern political development. Perhaps the most serious was the new requirement of unanimity with respect to the creation of new provinces. Prior to 1982, this matter was exclusively a prerogative of the federal government. The Constitution Act of that year mandated consultation with the provinces and a two-thirds vote of agreement among them. The Meech Lake Accord raised the ante to full concurrence on the part of all provinces. Most observers in both northern and southern Canada concluded that such a requirement would result in the Yukon and the Northwest Territories remaining as "forever colonies."[38]

Equally troubling to proponents of popular sovereignty and responsible government in the North, was the fact that Meech Lake did nothing to facilitate the inclusion of northern government representatives in First Minister Conferences or allow for their territorial legislatures to participate in the process of Senate and Supreme Court appointments that were to be afforded the ten existing provinces. Such exclusionary provisions have led many northerners to begin speaking of "being second class citizens or of being consciously discriminated against simply because of their place of residence."[39]

Perhaps most galling of all to the peoples of the North has been the "distinct society" language of the Meech Lake Accord. Northerners have not opposed Quebec's aspirations for safeguarding its own cultural and linguistic identity. What they complain about is the failure of the agreement to recognize equally sound claims for constitutional protection on the part of Canada's native peoples. The attitude has been similar to that of Inuit leader John Amagoalik who commented in a television interview: "If Quebec is a distinct society, what are we? Chopped liver?"[40]

These and other perceived flaws and inequities in the Meech Lake Accord led most northern politicians to oppose the agreement soon after its negotiation. The electorate was of a similar disposition as witnessed in a series of federal and territorial elections during the late 1980s. The 1987 by-election necessitated by the sudden resignation of Erik Nielsen from the Mulroney government was fought precisely on the issue of Meech Lake. Despite the Tories having held the seat for over thirty years--and Nielsen's considerable success in securing federal expenditures in the riding--the electorate voted in NDP candidate Audrey McLaughlin primarily because of her strongly voiced opposition to the constitutional accord. In the 1988 federal elections, northern anger toward the Meech Lake Accord and its sponsor, Brian Mulroney, was sufficient to break a nation-wide trend in favor of the Progressive Conservative. Two Liberal members were elected in the Northwest Territories and Audrey McLaughlin was returned in the Yukon.[41] Finally, in February of 1989, the NDP government of the Yukon was returned to power in territorial elections that focused on the party's steadfast opposition to the Meech Lake Accord.

Rejection of Meech Lake which began in the North, was to spread more broadly through the nation as a whole during 1989-90. Ultimately the agreement was rejected in May 1990, in part through the steadfast opposition of northern and native citizens who organized themselves effectively in protest. Their efforts to secure political and constitutional recognition of their distinct status and rights was perhaps best represented by MLA Elijah Harper's persistent blockage of Manitoba's consideration of the Meech Lake Accord. In quiet, but determined fashion, Harper and the people he represented made it clear that they would no longer be excluded from the councils and considerations of the nation.[42]

At the outset of a new decade, residents of Canada's northern territories remain wary regarding the continued process of political development in their region. No longer trusting Ottawa to deal fairly with their concerns and aspirations for home rule, they are increasingly looking to their own leaders to articulate and implement their visions of popular sovereignty. A new generation of leaders like Audrey McLaughlin, Tony Penikett and John Amagoalik are emerging that are willing to take up this challenge and carry the message to the rest of the nation.

Clearly it is time for the issue of home rule in the northern territories to be directly addressed by Parliament and the provinces either as part of a new constitutional amendment package or on its own merits. The process of political development that has taken place in the territories over the past two decades deserves recognition and support. As Michael Whittington notes:

> There are fully equipped governments in place in the Yukon and the Northwest Territories, governments that pass laws, deliver services, pay taxes, and in general act much like governments elsewhere in Canada. When the territories feel they are ready for it, the leap to provincehood should be a small one.[43]

Increasingly the people of the North are saying that they *are* ready and now is the time to act.

In the latter days of this century, it is clear that the North has become an increasingly more important component of the Canadian nation. Not only does it continue to perform its historical role of providing natural resources for national economic development, but its peoples and their cultures provide the country with a unique contribution to the nation's overall social and political development. Several scholars have argued that the manner in which Canada receives the second of these two gifts is, perhaps, more critical than its routine acceptance of the first.[44] Canada must see to it that all of its peoples, *northern* and southern, feel included in an equitable fashion in important public policy decision-making. Recent events associated with the Meech Lake Accord show how difficult a process this can become. However, the degree of difficulty should not be interpreted as an absolute barrier to such attempts. Only by actively pursuing policies of equity and justice are the political loyalties of a people toward its government maintained.

Notes

1   See for instance: L.E. Hamelin, "Images of the North" in Kenneth S . Coates and William R. Morrison, *Interpreting Canada's North,* (Toronto: Copp Clark Pitman, Ltd., 1989), pp.7-17 and Thomas G . Barnes, " 'Canada, True North' A 'Here There' or a Boreal Myth?" *The American Review of Canadian Studies* 19 (Winter 1989), 369-380.

2   Andrew Malcolm has written that: 'Many Canadians are uncomfortable paying attention to or celebrating their unique northerness or hearing others do so. Every time I was planning a northern trip, I ran an unscientific test. I would describe my plans to friends. Inevitably, Americans bombarded me with jealous protestations and offers to serve as luggage bearers while my Canadian friends and neighbors would simply say, "Whyever would you want to go up there." *The Canadians* (New York: Times Books, 1985), p. 35.

3   Kenneth Rea, *The Political Economy of Northern Development* (Toronto: University of Toronto Press, 1976).

4   Janet Morchain, *Sharing a Continent* (Toronto: McGraw-Hill, 1973), pp. 105-124.

5   Kenneth Coates and Judith Powell, *The Modern North* (Toronto: James Lorimer and Company, 1989), p.58.

6   Sam Hall, *The Fourth World: The Heritage of the Arctic and Its Destruction* (New York: Vintage Books, 1987), pp. 157-163.

7   Michael Whittington, ed., *The North* (Toronto: University of Toronto Press, 1985), pp. 8-12.

8   Morris Zaslow, *The Northward Expansion of Canada, 1914-1967* (Toronto: McClelland and Stewart, 1988), pp. 234-250.

9   Frances Abele, "Canadian Contradictions: Forty Years of Northern Political Development," in Coates and Morrison, op. cit., p. 312.

10   Both territories have had representation in the federal House of Commons for some time, the Yukon since 1901 and the NWT since 1952. However, as Coates and Powel indicate: "The region's representatives have enjoyed only limited success in raising the profile of territorial concerns. Like the region they represented, most northern MPs faded into the background." *op. cit.,* p. 59.

11   Douglas Nord, "The Politics and Politicians of Northern Hinterlands: Canada Scandinavia and the United States," in Jørn Carlsen and Bengt Streijffert, eds., *Canada and the Nordic Countries* (Lund: Lund University Press, 1988), pp. 247-262.

12   Ken S. Coates and William R. Morrison, *Land of the Midnight Sun: A History of the Yukon* (Edmonton: Hurtig Publishers, 1988), pp. 185-190.

13   Abele, p. 313.

14   Zaslow, pp. 151 - 173 .

15   Abele, p. 313.

16   Abele, p. 312.

17   Zaslow, pp. 332-366.

18   Abele comments that: "In retrospect, the striking thing about the new approach was the extent to which it was developed without consulting with the people to whom it was directed." *op.cit.,* p. 315.

19   Michael Whittington, "Canada's North in the 1990s," in Michael Whittington and Glen Williams, eds., *Canadian Politics in the 1990s* (Scarborough, Ont.: Nelson Canada, 1990), p. 33.

20   Coates and Powell, p. 90.

21   Whittington, p. 23.

22   Thomas R. Berger, *Northern Frontier, Northern Homeland* (Vancouver: Douglas and McIntyre Ltd., 1988), pp. 3-4.

23   Kenneth Lysyk, E. Bohmer and W. Phelps, *Alaska Highway Pipeline Inquiry* (Ottawa: Supply and Services, 1977).

24   Abele, pp. 320-321. See also: Bruce Alden Cox, ed., *Native People, Native Lands* (Ottawa: Carleton University Press, 1988).

25   Coates and Powell, p. 64.

26   Coates and Powell note that: "Christensen was not comfortable with the diminished status, and resigned her office in 'protest against the Territory's pell mell dash towards democracy.' She ran unsuccessfully against Erik Nielsen in the federal election campaign." p. 64.

27   Coates and Morrison, p. 294.

28   Coates and Powell, p. 65.

29   Coates and Powell, pp. 72-73.

30   *Ibid.*

31   Whittington, p. 72.

32   The conflict over native land claims in the NWT has been interpreted by some Ottawa officials as a sign that the northern territories have not reached sufficient "politica maturity" to warrant increased self-government. See William Wonders "Overlappin Native Land Claims in the Northwest Territories," *American Review of Canadian Studies* 18 (Autumn 1988) 359-367.

33   Michael Mandel, *The Charter of Rights and the Legalization Politics in Canada* (Toronto: Wall and Thompson, 1989), pp. 249-251.

34   Coates and Powell, pp. 60-62.

35   Geoffrey R. Weller, "Self-Government for Canada's Inuit: The Nunavut Proposal," *The American Review of Canadian Studies* 18 (Autumn 1988), pp. 341-358.

36   Yukon Government Leader Tony Penikett observed at the time: "Our fates were as much or more at stake as Quebec's or any other province's. It was not necessary to sacrifice the North in order to save Quebec." Coates and Powell, p. 78.

37   George Erasmus of the Assembly of First Nations noted: "We were told for five years

that governments are reluctant to entrench undefined self-government of aboriginal peoples in the constitution. Yet, here is an equally vague idea of a 'distinct society' unanimously agreed to and allowed to the courts for interpretation." Mandel, p. 252.

38   Coates and Powell, p. 77.

39   Whittington, p. 43.

40   Abele, p. 235.

41   Alan Frizzell, Jon H. Pammett and Anthony Westell, *The Canadian Federal Election of 1988* (Ottawa: Carleton University Press, 1989), pp. 168-169.

42   John Howse,"A New Native Hero," *Macleans* 103(July16,1990),13.

43   Whittington, p. 41.

44   Michael Whittington notes that: "The manner in which the world and future generations of Canadians judge Canada's worth as a nation may well come to rest upon the manner in which the present generation of political leaders resolves the poignantly human dilemmas of northern development in the last decade of the twentieth century." p. 43.

Comparing Government Administrations in Fennoscandia and Canada on Aboriginal Land Title

Lennart Sillanpää

The Sami of Fennoscandia (Finland, Sweden and Norway), like the aboriginal peoples of Canada, are an indigenous minority with a recognized territorial base and distinct languages. As is often the case with Canada's aboriginal minorities, Sami communities can be vulnerable to pressures on their lands caused by outside interests.

There are numerous points of comparison on the issue of aboriginal rights to land between the Sami of Norway, Sweden and Finland and the aboriginal peoples of the Canadian North. The Sami have a clear concept of territory that compares with similar aboriginal claims in other parts of the Arctic North. It would be useful for policy makers in Canada and in Fennoscandia to examine each other's jurisdictions in dealing with aboriginal rights issues; these are comparable in many significant ways.

There have been a number of recent developments among the Nordic Sami over the recognition of their historic rights as an indigenous people. The Sami began to organize themselves only after the Second World War. Over the past twenty years, Nordic Sami have been demanding and receiving greater public recognition of their rights to be consulted/represented on any land-use decisions affecting their homeland areas.

Aboriginal organizations in Canada over the past twenty years have enjoyed a kind of renaissance as they have begun to assert their claims to a unique legal status within the Canadian confederation based on the historical fact of being the first inhabitants of the homeland they share with the colonizers. These demands have gained recognition from the wider Canadian public.

This paper will briefly discuss the appropriateness of such comparisons. It will then examine the historical legal roots of aboriginal rights in both Fennoscandia and North America. The paper will then examine recent developments in Norway, Sweden and Finland on the issue of indigenous rights as well as on the international legal scene and make some comparisons with the situation in Canada.

1. Appropriateness of This Comparison

Before proceeding with comparisons of the legal status of the Nordic Sami and Canada's aboriginal inhabitants, one should note that there are profound differences. In the course of interviewing numerous public officials and Sami representatives in Finland, Sweden and Norway over the past year, this writer has noted that some Nordic citizens feel sensitive that one would want to compare Canadian Indians with their Sami. They point out that the Sami do not live on reservations and that Sami reindeer breeders can practice their livelihood over a wide area and even cross international borders. They also emphasize that the Sami are entitled to the same services in education and health as other citizens and that these are among the best in the world. There is no jurisdictional dispute in the Nordic countries between two levels of governments as there has been in Canada over, for example, the delivery of schooling to Indians (a federal responsibility) while education is otherwise, under the Canadian constitution, a provincial responsibility.

Also, while recognizing the validity of the term "colonization" as applicable to the settlement of the Sami homeland areas by non-Sami, Nordic specialists emphasize that this colonization differs greatly from the North American experience.[1] There has been co-existence for hundreds if not thousands of years. Archaeological evidence, for example, shows that the Vikings have sailed along the northern coast of Norway to Murmansk for more than one thousand years and have shared the coast with Sami fishermen.

The ongoing Norwegian royal commission has also questioned the use of the term "aboriginal" and "indigenous."[2] Whether the Sami are aboriginals (i.e., the first inhabitants) in the Nordic context as Canada's Indians and Inuit truly are, is open to some question; however, the Commission felt that this was immaterial with respect to their human rights. The Sami are clearly recognized as an indigenous people within the national boundaries of Norway and this would require some kind of special policies by the state.

In September 1989, Kaisa Korpijaakko, a legal researcher for the Nordic Sami Institute, presented her dissertation entitled: Saamelaisten oikeusasemasta Ruotsi-Suomessa (Legal Rights of the Sami in Finland during the period of Swedish Rule)[3] to the Faculty of Law, University of Lapland, Rovaniemi, Finland. Her dissertation received wide coverage on Finnish radio and television on the day it was presented as well as in newspapers. This extensive media coverage certainly indicates that an historic issue such as Sami claims to land title remains a lively national issue in Finland.

Based on research into the Swedish and Finnish state archives for the period when Finland was a part of the Kingdom of Sweden, her study demonstrates that the Sami peoples had title to the lands they ocuppied and that this title was recognized in the laws of that time and through special taxes such as a Lapp tax. Her dissertation effectively refutes the myth of the Sami as a nomadic people and demonstrates that Sami title to lands had at one time been integrated into the national land tenure system.

The question that her study raises is whether national governments in Finland and Sweden are prepared to restore some form of land title to the Sami.

The Nordic Sami clearly identify their cause with that of other indigenous minorities in the world who base their culture on a traditional livelihood derived from the land. In 1975, Canada's National Indian Brotherhood (the forerunner of the present Assembly of First Nations) and the Nordic Sami were among the founders of the World Council of Indigenous Peoples, an international organization which enjoys non-governmental organization status with the United Nations.[4] The third WCIP General Assembly held in Canberra, Australia in 1981, adopted a resolution calling on nation states to respect the land title claims of their indigenous inhabitants.[5] The sixth General Assembly is being held in Tromsö (Samiland), Norway on the same weekend as this Conference (August 1990).

2. Historical Basis of Indigenous Rights

The border between Norway and Sweden (which then included Finland) was established in its entirety by the Border Treaty of 1751.[6] This Treaty, which drew a clear undisputed border between Denmark-Norway and Sweden (Finland), cut through the Sami areas of settlement and use. During the negotiations, the two states recognized that the new border traversed territory of vital importance for the Sami and tried to protect this by an international treaty. The result was a codicil to the border treaty that was worked out during the same negotiations--the Lapp Codicil. Article 8 of the Treaty made the Codicil equal in validity to the text of the Border Treaty itself.

The object of the Lapp Codicil was to regulate "the customary migration of the Lapps" so that in the future there should be "no cause for quarrel or misunderstanding" concerning the crossing of the border or the citizenship of the pastoral Sami.[7] The Lapp Codicil contains detailed rules on citizenship (section 3-9), the right to land and water (10-11), internal administration (15-21), and on a limited internal administration of justice (22-27). The legal order of the Codicil could be described as a mutual gurantee whereby the states assumed the mutual responsibility for securing the basis for the survival of the Sami.

On four occasions, Sweden and Norway have negotiated changes to the operations of the Lapp Codicil but the Codicil itself has never been revoked:[8]

(a) the "Joint Legislation" of 1883 adopted by both the Norwegian and Swedish parliaments; the Codicil was replaced and suspended for the period of the validity of this legislation;

(b) the Karlstad Convention of 1905 when the Norwegian-Swedish union was dissolved; the continued validity of the Lapp Codicil was expressly confirmed and the codicil was secured against unilateral abrogation;

(c) the Reindeer Grazing Convention of February 5, 1919; the Codicil and Art. 1 of the Karlstad Convention were suspended for the duration of the validity of the 1919 Convention but were not abolished;

(d) the current Reindeer Grazing Convention of February 9, 1972; the Lapp Codicil continued to be suspended but not abolished; the Karlstad Convention was abolished.

Decisions of the Norwegian and Swedish Supreme Courts indicate that, while the Codicil does not grant the right of ownership to the Sami in either Norway or Sweden, Sami claims to ownership of land and water in their homeland areas may be based on other considerations such as immemorial usage.[9] These Supreme Court decisions also maintained that the Codicil provides for firmly protected rights of use based on their use of lands for traditional occupations long before the Codicil was enacted. This places an obligation on the states to continue protecting these rights.

Two observations can be made about the Lapp Codicil and the subsequent bilateral agreements:

(1) no Sami have ever participated in the negotiations of either the Lapp Codicil of 1751 or in the negotiations on any of the subsequent agreements; the fate of the Sami nations rested in the good offices of outsiders;

(2) each of the negotiations have "refined" (i.e., placed restrictions, often considerable ones) the possibilities for the Sami to pursue their livelihood; the 1919 Agreement was particularly onerous on many of the Swedish Sami who were forced to relocate to more southerly regions outside their recognized homeland. [10]

A dependence on outside forces for determining the extent of their rights in their recognized homeland areas has also affected aboriginal groups in other parts of the world. For some two hundred years Canada's aboriginal inhabitants have gradually lost their position within their homeland areas to European colonizers. At the time of the Royal Proclamation of 1763, Canada's Indian peoples were recognized as an important ally to the British Crown. This was to prove the case during some of the battles of the American Revolution and escpecially during the War of 1812.

After peace was declared between Britain and the United States following the War of 1812, the Indian peoples in Canada have undergone a long extended period of retreat on their rights and their ability to administer their homeland areas in a meaningful way. Through a number of treaties and surrenders concluded with the British colonial administration and, after Confederation in 1867, with the government of Canada, Indian groups ceded their title to lands in what is today Ontario and the western provinces of Manitoba, Saskatchewan and Alberta in exchange for small reserves and some guarantees to the use of lands for traditional purposes.

In 1876, the Canadian government enacted the Indian Act whereby the Federal government assumed what has been characterized as a paternalistic responsibility for its "Indian subjects." This system continues to this day although in the past twenty years, aboriginal groups have begun to challenge this process and demand greater control of their destinies.

Unlike the case with aboriginal peoples in different areas of Canada, there has never been a surrender or treaty between any group of Sami with any of the three states concerned. The encroachment of non-Sami into the homeland areas of the Sami was accompanied by an assurance by the Crown that the Sami were to continue to occupy their traditional area along with practising their accustomed means of livelihood. The State has asserted its right to administer the lands of the Sami homeland. On no occasion were the Sami required to "hereby cede, release, surrender and yield up. . .all their rights, titles and privileges whatsoever, to the lands included within the following limits" as was the case of the post-Confederation numbered treaties (or for that matter, in the wording of the James Bay and Northern Quebec Agreement of 1975 and the Inuvialuit Final Agreement of 1983).

Unfortunately for the Sami, the administrative procedures devised by the respective States were, in many ways, as frustrating as the Treaty procedures devised by the Canadian government in the nineteenth century.

3. Recent Developments on Indigenous Rights in Fennoscandia

The work of royal commissions and various committees in the three Nordic countries has had a significant impact in developing a heightened public apprecation of the legal situation of the Sami minority within each nation's territorial boundaries and in recommending changes to legislation. In a similar, way in Canada, Justice Thomas Berger's royal commission inquiry[11] into the feasibility of constructing an oil pipeline down the Mackenzie Valley of the Northwest Territories had a profound impact on public consciousness on the issue of aboriginal rights and land title. International law and jurisprudence has also come to have an increasing impact on the governments of the Nordic countries in the development of policies and legislation for dealing with indigenous minorities; Canada has adopted these same international conventions.

This section will examine recent developments in Norway, Sweden and Finland on the legal status of the Sami and on the impact of international jurisprudence on these three Nordic countries.

3.1 Norway

There have been a number of recent developments in Norway that have consolidated the legal position of the Sami as an indigenous minority. These are directly related to the recommendations contained in the first report of the Norwegian Royal Commission on Sami Rights published in 1984.

This Royal Commission was established in 1980 in the aftermath of the demonstrations by the Sami and environmentalists against the construction of the Alta-Kautokeino hydroelectric project.[12] For the first time in history, the Sami had confronted the Norwegian Government stating that it did not have the right to make decisions unilaterally on water development in the Sami homeland region. The Norwegian government reacted by establishing a royal commission with a wide mandate to determine the legal status of its Sami population. In developing the recommendations contained in its first report, the Commission acted on the basis that it was dealing with an urgent national issue.

In 1987, the Norwegian Storting (Parliament) implemented one of the major recommendations of the Royal Commission when it enacted the Sami Act.[13] This legislation created the "Sameting"--a repesentative assembly elected by the Sami people of Norway to represent their collective interests. The first elections to the Sameting were held on September 11, 1989, the same day as elections for the national Parliament. The King of Norway, in a nationally televised ceremony, officially opened this assembly on October 9, 1989.

Another recommendation of the Sami Rights Commission was enacted in 1988 when the Norwegian Parliament amended the Norwegian Constitution[14] to include a clause respecting Sami rights.

The Norwegian government and Parliament has also accepted the Commission's recommendation that, at least once in the four-year term of a

Norwegian Parliament, a period of debate and consideration would be dedicated to the situation of the Sami in Norway. The King would present proposals to the Storting; the Sameting would assist in preparing these proposals.

The Norwegian Sami Rights Commission, now with its third chairman, is examining Sami land title in the northern most Norwegian province of Finnmark. A second report is not expected to be ready for at least two or three years.[15] A third report will deal with Sami land title in other areas of Norway.

3.2 Sweden

In 1983, the Swedish Government established a Royal Commission to clarify the rights of the Sami as recognized by the 1981 Supreme Court of Sweden decision in the Skattefjäll ("Taxed Mountains") case.[16] In its decision, the Supreme Court had dismissed Sami claims to ownership based on rights of usage since time immemorial to certain areas of the Swedish province of Jämtland. However, the Court did recognize that: (1) that right of usage since time immemorial was a valid means of acquiring land title under Swedish law; (2) such a legal interpretation, while not applicable to Jämtland, might be successful in the more northern areas of Sweden; and (3) the traditional Sami practice of reindeer herding is a strongly protected user right of a special kind based on immemorial use and this form of title was safeguarded against expropriation without compensation.

In its first report published in 1986, the Royal Commission discussed the general situation of the Sami people and Sweden's obligations to the Sami under international law.[17] The second report of Sweden's Sami Rights Commission, published in 1989, entitled: Samerätt och sameting (Sami Rights and a Sami Assembly)[18] recommended:

(a) that the special status of the Sami as an ethnic minority and an indigenous people be codified in the Swedish Constitution;

(b) the enactment of a Sami Act with provisions concerning the promotion of Sami cultural and social life and the establishment of an elected "Sameting" capable of representing all of the Sami in Sweden;

(c) that certain safeguards found in international law that can apply to reindeer herding be incorporated into the Reindeer Herding Act and the Expropriation Act.

Consultations on these two reports are taking place among various departments of the Swedish government, regional and local governments, as well as with Sami representatives themselves.[19] Two Swedish ministries,

Agriculture and Forestry, have registered strong objections to some of the recommendations saying they go too far.[20] On the other hand, Sweden's Ombudsman for Ethnic Minorities has stated that the recommendations of the Commission do not go far enough.[21]

None of the national Sami associations in Sweden are very happy with the recommendations. Representatives of the major Sami associations that, participated in the work of this Commission registered minority reports.[22] (Interestingly, Hans-Åke Wångberg, the Chairman of this Commission, also wrote a minority report.) The general consensus among the Sami leadership is that the Commission's recommendations are the minimum acceptable to the Sami and they want to have at least these legislated.[23]

Legislation is being drafted for a Sami Act that would deal with the creation of a Sameting, amendments to the Reindeer Herding and Expropriation Acts, and for an amendment to the Swedish Constitution.

This Commission on Sami Rights does not have a mandate to examine the question of Sami land rights.[24] It is empowered to examine other special needs concerning the Sami as an indigenous people in Sweden which might be interpreted broadly to mean their rights to traditional lands but this is less than the mandate that the Norwegian Cabinet has given to its Sami Rights Commission.

3.3 Finland

The Sami in Finland have had en elected representative assembly since 1973 when the President of Finland signed a law creating what Sami refer to as the "Sami Parliament."[25] The creation of this assembly was the result of a recommendation by a Finnish state committee examining the legal rights of the Sami. This Sami Parliament has focused attention on a number of issues of direct concern to the Sami.[26]

Sami rights in Finland are presently focused on a single issue: land title. On June 18,1990, the Standing Advisory Committee on Sami Affairs (composed of Sami representatives and senior Finnish bureaucrats) presented the Finnish Government with its proposal for a Sami Act and amendments to other Finnish legislation touching on Sami issues (Ehdotus saamelaislaiksi--Proposal for a Sami Act).[27]

The goal of this proposed legislation is to return to the Sami people those land and water rights they used to enjoy for their livelihood.[28] It also proposes to secure the Sami language and culture as well as preserve Sami occupations and commerce that have been traditionally considered a part of this culture.

This proposed legislation is to apply specifically to the Sami homeland area in the northernmost communes of Finland. This proposal is not intended to take away any existing rights of other citizens to private property nor to continue in their established occupations and rights of trade. The Committee states that this proposal is not intended to give any new rights to the Sami people in Finland. Rather it seeks a restoration of their previous legal status.[29]

This Committee had first been charged by the Finnish Parliament (Eduskunta) in 1978 with the responsibility of drafting a Sami Act.[30] One of the items listed in its terms of reference was to clarify the land title situation in Lapland with regard to the historic claims of the Sami. The Standing Committee on the Constitution of the Finnish Parliament had examined this question and had given the opinion that the Sami claim to land and water title in the Lapland area of Finland based on immemorial usage needed to be clarified.

This is considered a very radical proposal in Finland so it will be interesting to see how the various Finnish Ministries within the Finnish state as well as the political decisionmakers respond.

3.4 International Law

Of particular note in the work of commissions that have studied the legal status of the Sami people in Norway, Sweden and Finland, is their meticulous examination of the potential impact of international agreements that have been adopted by the Parliaments of their respective countries on domestic legislation and administration. Both the ongoing Norwegian and Swedish royal commissions regard Article 27 of the UN Covenant on Civil and Political Rights as the key provision concerning the protection of ethnic minorities under current international law:

> In those States in which ethnic, religious or linguistic minorities exist, persons belonging to such minorities shall not be denied the right, in community with the other members of their group, to enjoy their own culture, to profess and practice their own religion, or to use their own language.

The Norwegian Royal Commission believes that Article 27 authorizes a claim to what it terms as "positive discrimination" and elevated this to be one of the fundamental human rights. How far a state has to go in the direction of such positive discrimination would depend on the actual conditions in the state in question; the minority is entitled to "enjoy their own culture."[31] The Commission also stated that Article 27 also imposes an obligation on the various states to provide economic support to enable the minority groups to use their own language and other aspects of their culture.

The Norwegian Commission concluded that the interpretation of Article 27 could be expanded to allow an individual ethnic minority to demand the material basis necessary for it to enjoy its own culture.

> The Sami people are unquestionably an ethnic group whose culture is protected according to Article 27. Therefore, they are entitled to the support of the Norwegian State in their enjoyment of their own culture. At the same time, the Sami people comprise an ethnic group whose cultural basis lies largely in a traditional utilization of natural resources. Therefore, it is highly likely that their traditional forms of economic activity are also protected to a certain extent by Article 27.[32]

This interpretation was accepted by the Norwegian Ministry of Justice and was published in the working papers that accompanied the Sami Act when it was tabled in the Norwegian Parliament in 1976.[33]

The first report of Sweden's Sami Rights Commission (1986) also concluded that the term "culture" in Article 27 should be broadly interpreted in this context so as also to include the material foundations of culture, e.g., the reindeer-herding acitivities of the Sami.[34] The Commission found that Article 27 also could be construed as entitling the minority to a certain measure of cultural autonomy.

The International Labour Organization has been concerned with indigenous rights since 1921, particularly questions dealing with the exploitation of indigenous labourers. On June 27, 1989, the International Labour Organization adopted Convention No. 169, the Indigenous and Tribal Peoples Convention.[35] Part II of this Convention--articles 13 to 19--deals with land title of indigenous minorities and recognizes a clear material basis for cultures particularly with respect to indigenous peoples that live off the land. The Canadian, Norwegian, Swedish and Finnish goverments took part in the negotiations leading up to the adoption of this Convention; Canadian Indians and Inuit as well as Nordic Sami also participated in the prepatory sessions.[36]

On June 20, 1990, the Norwegian Parliament adopted this convention--the first nation to do so. The official background material prepared by the Norwegian government in support of this legislative proposal indicated that the Norwegian state recognizes that the Sami are an indigenous people covered by this Convention.[37]

Sweden and Finland (as well as Canada) are presently considering whether they should adopt this new ILO Convention. The Nordic Sami Council has endorsed adoption of this Convention[38] as have national Sami associations in Finland, Sweden and Norway.

4. Comparisons with the Canadian Situation

This section will discuss two aspects of the Canadian experience that compare directly to the situation of the Sami indigenous minority of the three Nordic countries:
(a) the crisis of legitimacy of political system, and
(b) self-government vs. land claims.

4.1. Crisis of Legitimacy

The political systems of the Western democracies are based on a recognition of a plurality of political views and competing ideologies that recognize the legitimacy of the established political process. When one group refuses to recognize the existing socio-political order as being effectively able to serve its needs, governments can face a crisis of legitimacy. One traditional means for responding to such a crisis is for government to develop new policies and legislation to meet the basic demands of an excluded group and, as needed, to establish new institutions.

In the late 1960's, Canada's aboriginal inhabitants began to openly question many of the policies of the Canadian government and their underlying assumptions. The first instance was the introduction by the Canadian government in 1969 of its White Paper where the Canadian government proposed transferring many Indian programs to the provinces, the scrapping of the Indian Act and declaring the treaties to be redundant. For the first time, Indian groups united in opposition and their position was widely supported by key groups in the wider Canadian public such as unions and church groups as well as key opinion leaders. The Canadian government withdrew its proposals.[39]

Other events during the early 1970's included the defiance of the James Bay Cree against the unilateral decision of the Quebec government to proceed with the construction of the massive James Bay hydroelectric project and the inquiry by Justice Thomas Berger into the feasibility of constructing a pipeline down the Mackenzie Valley in the Northwest Territories. Both of these had a major impact in increasing the awareness of the Canadian public of the legitimacy in the concept of aboriginal land title. The long process whereby the Canadian government sought to repatriate the Canadian constitution from the British

Parliament (1978-82) was highlighted by the aggressive--and eventually successful--efforts of Canada's aboriginal inhabitants to ensure constitutional recognition for their rights.[40]

Within the subject Nordic countries, there is only one instance of a crisis of confidence in the institutions of state: namely, the Alta-Kautokeino demonstrations of 1979 and 1981.[41] These demonstrations awakened the Norwegian national consciousness to the fact that there existed an indigenous national minority which had been ignored--and at times even legally repressed--by the Norwegian state. Many Norwegians were particularly distressed that every sixth policeman in Norway was in the small northern community of Alta (population about 5,000) in 1981; this was considered "not a Norwegian way of doing things"[42] and opinion leaders urged the Norwegian government to rectify this situations.

There has been no crisis of confidence in either Finland or Sweden. This may explain why the institutional and official attitudinal changes in Norway towards its Sami minority have been so far-reaching as compared to its two Nordic neighbours. While the Sami directly challenged the Swedish state in the Skattefjäll from 1966 to 1981, a unanimous decision of the Supreme Court ruled in favour of the Swedish state. The work of the royal commission in Sweden established by the government after the Skattefjäll decision did not have the sense of urgency that was characterstic of the early work of the Sami Rights Commission established by the Norwegian government after the Alta demonstrations.[43]

In Finland, it has been national institutions such as the Constitutional Committee of the Finnish Parliament and a doctoral dissertation by Kaisa Korpijaakko that have crystallized the public debate on Sami rights.

4.2 Self-Government vs. Land Claims

The three Nordic countries, in dealing with their Sami minorities, have emphasized some form of self-government. Both Finland and Norway have established Sami assemblies, democratically elected by all eligible Sami to represent the collective interest of the Sami minority within their respective national boundaries. The royal commission established by the Swedish government has made a similar recommendation. These assemblies have the right to appoint Sami representatives to official state bodies and to make recommendations on such issues as education, curriculum and culture. These assemblies may eventually turn to the issue of indigenous land title. This is on the agenda in both Finland and Norway.

Canada has not been successful in addressing the self-government issue in a comprehensive manner. Four constitutional conferences were held (1983, 1984, 1985 and 1987) where the Canadian Prime Minister and ten provincial premiers met with representatives of Canada's Indians, Metis and Inuit to discuss the issue of amending the Canadian Constitution to recognize the issue of aboriginal self-government. This amending process came close to success in 1985 but broke down in 1987. The Canadian government today is undertaking a number of major incremental measures to address the issue of aboriginal self-government. The Department of Indian Affairs and Northern Development (DIAND) is working at devolving provincial type powers to the territorial governments which could involve special rights for aboriginal groups in the North.[44]

The major thrust of the Canadian government, on the other hand, has been in resolving the issue of land claims by Canada's aboriginal peoples. This has especially been the case in the northern territories where the Federal government retains jurisdiction.[45] The Federal government has enjoyed a number of major aboriginal land claim negotiation successes in northern Canada recently: the Inuvialuit of the Western Arctic (a legislated settlement in 1984); the Dene Nation and Metis Association of the Mackenzie Valley (final agreement in 1990); the Council for Yukon Indians (final agreement in 1990); and the Tungavik Federation of Nunavut (agreement in principle in 1990).

The Sami of the three Nordic countries are aware of the land claims option as practised in Canada but have not indicated that they intend to pursue this course of action in the foreseeable future.[46] The Sami have made their views known on a number of issues through resolutions passed at national and Nordic Sami conferences but there is no established formal mechanism for direct negotiations with any of the three States on these issues.

The Sami in the three countries emphasize a strengthening of their usufructuary rights to the land they occupy.[47] They are concerned at the impact on their livelihood and culture of major economic development projects such as the hydro dams being proposed in northern Norway, Sweden and Finland and the huge mines located in northern Sweden. They have also voiced concern at the increasing numbers of tourists visiting their homeland. The Sami have demanded to be consulted on any land-use decisions affecting their homeland areas. In many instances, the Sami are examining valid Canadian examples (such as James Bay and Inuvialuit settlements) as models.

5. Conclusion

A number of useful comparisons can be made between the situation of the Sami of Fennoscandia and that of aboriginal peoples in Canada. There has been little research in which the rights of Europe's peripheral minorities have been compared with those in North America. The comparative approach can bring substantially new perspectives to the study of indigenous minorities in the Arctic north. The Sami of Fennoscandia and the aboriginal inhabitants (Indians, Metis and Inuit) of the Canadian North represent minorities with a recognized territorial base. Both in Western Europe and in North America, there have been new and renewed claims by indigenous minorities occupying a recognized traditional homeland for greater self-determination over their livelihood and over the lands they use and occupy.

Recognizing that there are major differences between the regions being studied, a comparative analysis of indigenous peoples on the peripheral regions of Western Europe and northern Canada is important for both the indigenous minorities concerned and for developing a greater recognition by social scientists and the international legal community of the special nature of the issues involved. This research can also be useful to the public administrations in both Canada and the three Nordic countries on an important human rights issue of common historic significance.

Notes

1   *Om samenes rettsstilling* (Report of Sami Rights Committee). Oslo:Norges Offentlige Utredninger 1984:18. English: Summary of the First Report from the Norwegian Sami Rights Committee; Oslo, 1984. The author has also been able to obtain a translation of Chapter 6 of this report entitled: "International and Foreign National Law" prepared by the Faculty of Civil Law, University of Oslo, from which I will cite references.

2   Ibid. Chapter 6; section 1.6 of report.

3   Kaisa Korpijaakko, *Saamelaisten oikeusasemasta Ruotsi-Suomessa* (Legal Rights of the Sami in Finland during the Period of Swedish Rule). Helsinki, Lakimiesliiton kustannus, 1989.

4   Douglas Sanders, *The Formation of the World Council of Indigenous Peoples,* IWGIA Document No. 29. Copenhagen, 1977.

5   Resolution of Third General Assembly of WCIP held at Canberra, Australia, January 1981.

6   An extensive analysis (in English translation) can be found in Chapter 6; section 2 of the

Norwegian Sami Rights Commission report.

7   Ibid. Chapter 6; section 2.4 of report.

8   Ibid. Chapter 6; sections 2.11 to 2.16 of report.

9   Ibid. Decisions of the Norwegian and Swedish courts are examined in great detail in Chapter 6.

10   Johannes Marainen (1982), "The Swedish-Norwegian Convention on the Right of the Migratory Sami to Reindeer Grazing Lands: General Background Conditions and Consequences of the Convention" in *The Sami National Minority in Sweden* (ed. Birgitta Jahreskog) Uppsala: Rättsfonden.

11   Thomas R. Berger (1977), *Northern Frontier, Northern Homeland: The Report of the Mackenzie Valley Pipeline Inquiry.* Two Volumes. Ottawa: Supply and Services Canada.

12   Robert Paine (1985), "Ethnodrama and the 'Fourth World': The Sami Action Group in Norway," in *Indigenous Peoples and the Nation-State: "Fourth World" Politics in Canada, Australia and Norway,* edited by Noel Dyck; St. John's, Nfld.: Memorial University; 242-259.

13   Ot prp nr 33 (1986-87), *Om lov om Sametinget og andre samiske rettsforhold* (sameloven). English translation prepared by Norwegian Ministry of Foregin Affairs: Act concerning the Sami Assembly and other Sami legal matters (Sami Act); 12 June 1987.

14   English translation of this amendment in English Summary of Norwegian Royal Commission report; section 1.10.5, p. 46.

15   Interviews with several members of the Norwegian Sami Rights Commission conducted during February and May, 1990.

16   An English translation of this decision by the Supreme Court of Sweden can be found in *The Sami National Minority in Sweden,* (Jahreskog, 1982).

17   *Samernas folkrättsliga ställning* (Legal Rights of the Sami People) SOU 1986:36.English-language summary.

18   *Samerätt och sameting* (Sami Rights and Sami Assembly)--SOU 1989:41. English-language summary.

19   Many of these comments were published in the Justice Department report: Remissyttranden över samerättsutredningens betänkanden (no English-language summary available).

20   Ibid.

21   Ibid.

22   *Samerätt och sameting;* pp. 347-57.

23   Interviews with Jörgen Bohlin and Lars Anders Baer of the SSR, 13 June 1990; Arjeplog, Sweden.

24   Kommittedirektiv (Swedish Cabinet Directive). Vissa frågor om samernas ställning i Sverige, 1982-09-02. Also, Tilläggsdirektiv till kommitten med uppgift att utreda vissa

frågor om samernas ställning i Sverige, 1983-02-03.

25   Asetus saamelaisvaltuuskunnasta (Cabinet Decree on a Sami Assembly) No. 824, 9 November 1973.

26   *Saamelaiskomitean mielinto* (Report of the Sami Rights Committee). Helsinki: Komiteanmietinto 1973:46.

27   *Ehdotus saamelaislaiksi* (Proposal for a Sami Act). Saamelaisassiain neuvottelukunta. Rovaniemi, Finland: 1990.

28   Ibid. From summary "Esityksen paaasiallinen sisalto."

29   This theme of restoring rights to the Sami was especially emphasized by Asko Oinas, Governor of Lapland Province, when he presented this proposal to the Finnish government in a ceremony in Rovaniemi; 18 June 1990.

30   Op. cit.

31   English Summary of report of Norwegian Sami Rights Commission; op. cit.

32   Ibid.; p. 20.

33   Norwegian Sami Act; op. cit.; section 4.14 of the working papers: "Remarks of the Department concering international law and foreign law." Translation of this working paper arranged by author.

34   *Samernas folkrättsliga ställning*. English-language summary. op. cit.

35   Convention 169. Convention Concerning Indigenous and Tribal Peoples in Independent Countries. 76th Session International Labour Organization Conference, Geneva, 27 June 1989.

36   A critical analysis of the process leading up to adoption of ILO Convention No. 169 by a Canadian Cree Indian is by Sharon Vene, "The New Language of Assimilation: A Brief Analysis of ILO Convention 169," in *Without Prejudice*, the EAFORD International Review of Racial Discrimination; II(2); 53-67.

37   St. prp. nr. 102 (1989-90). Om den 76. internasjonale arbeidskonferanse i Geneve 1989.

38   Resolution of Nordic Sami Council Conference; August 1989.

39   A thorough study of the White Paper legacy was written by Sally M. Weaver (1981), *Making Canadian Indian Policy. The Hidden Agenda 1968-70*. Toronto: University of Toronto Press.

40   A good description can be found in Douglas Sanders (1982), "The Indian Lobby," in *And No One Cheered. Federalism, Democracy and the Constitutional Act*. Edited by Keith Banting and Richard Simeon; Toronto: Methuen; 301-332.

41   Paine (1985), op. cit.

42   Interview with Gudmund Sandvik, member of Norwegian Sami Rights Commission; 31 January 1990.

43   Interview with Carsten Smith, Chairman of Sami Rights Commission (1981-85); 18 May 1990. Professor Smith felt that the Commission had to issue its report at the earliest opportunity to meet this serious social problem.

44   *A Northern Political and Economic Framework.* Ottawa: Indian and Northern Affairs Canada, 1988.

45   *Comprehensive Land Claims Policy.* Ottawa: Indian and Northern Affairs Canada, 1987.

46   Interviews with Pekka Aikio of Finland; Lars Anders Baer of Sweden and others.

47   Tom G. Svensson (1986), "Ethnopolitics among the Sami in Scandinavia: A Basic Strategy toward Local Autonomy" in *Arctic, 39:3* (September 1986), 208-215.

Canadian Government Inuit Policy in the Interwar Years

Richard J. Diubaldo

The years between the First and Second World Wars saw the Canadian Government establish rules of conduct for its Inuit inhabitants in the high North. These policies would determine relationships between Canada and the Inuit well into the 1950s, and in many ways hindered the government in applying new solutions to old problems after 1945. Policies that have been seen as uncaring, and sometimes scandalous can only be understood by examining the roots of such programmes, and the attitudes and perceptions of the bureaucrats who formulated and carried them out.

One major stumbling block throughout the 1920s and 1930 was the vexing question of the legal status of the Inuit: were they wards of the state, like Indians, or were they ordinary Canadian citizens. In 1939, the Supreme Court of Canada declared Inuit to be Indians (!), and hence the responsibility of Ottawa. Needless to say, federal officials were not pleased with this decision.[1] The Canadian government demonstrated its reticence to tackle the problems in other than the old-style colonial approach with its attendant racism. This was due in part to the prevailing laissez-faire convictions of Canadian policy-makers, the vastness of the territory, but also to the low priority given to native matters in general. This is somewhat surprising, given the advances made in Greenland and even Alaska before and during the same period. Concern for the welfare of the Inuit was always present but never paramount. Priority was given only to the wider aspects of sovereignty and to ensuring that the Inuit conform to the law of the whites. Yet in a number of areas, Canadian government officials, struggling with the fuzzy precepts of Inuit status, managed to address themselves, officially and unofficially, to a series of questions during the 1920s and 1930s: conservation, the economic condition of the Inuit (including their relationship to various trading concerns), health and welfare, and even education. One can argue that, in doing so, the government of Canada never totally abandoned the Inuit, although a cynic might suggest that if more had been done--even in an enlightened paternalistic fashion--the Inuit would have at least avoided some of the hardships and traumas that beset them in these years; this may well be true, but the fact remains that Canada chose otherwise and steered a course that differed from the Alaskan and

165

Greenland experiments.

At the centre of much of government policy from 1921 to 1931 was the Northwest Territories and Yukon branch of the Department of the Interior, until the Depression forced its closure. During the 1920s, the Northwest Territories branch, under O.S. Finnie, pursued an enlightened Inuit policy, as enlightened as circumstances would allow and squaring with what was thought best for Inuit survival and protection. In essence, this would mean not direct intervention, except in upholding the king's law, but encouragement to remain self-sufficient hunters and trappers--a policy that would ring through four decades.

Finnie's had, in truth, no mandate to deal *directly* with the Inuit; nevertheless, empowered to advance the interests of the territory as a whole, he could in ingenious ways construct a number of measures which touched on the Inuit and their way of life. Finnie himself possessed a genuine concern and was not of the usual mould. To him, the Inuit should come ahead of sovereignty as "the welfare of the Eskimos should be considered of first importance in any scheme of future development."[2] Much of his mandate came from the findings and recommendations of the "Royal Commission to Investigate the Possibilities of the Reindeer and Musk-Ox Industries in the Arctic and Sub-Arctic Regions of Canada" established in 1919 by the efforts of the arctic explorer Vilhjalmur Stefansson.[3] In 1922, the commission made some fifteen recommendations, a number of which could be acted upon by Finnie : continuing conservation and protection of musk-oxen; establishment of small experimental reindeer herds, with the natives encouraged to learn reindeer husbandry; research and information gathering on the numbers and movements of wild caribou, and prevention of their "wasteful or useless slaughter" either by natives or others.[4]

Civil servants, especially Finnie, wanted more government intervention, arguing that the game preserves should have the necessary "schools and trading posts. . .under the care and supervision of the Government itself," the practice followed in Greenland and northern Alaska.[5] A conservation programme aimed at protecting caribou and musk-oxen was begun in 1924, the Inuit being warned that overkill would make the government "very angry" and that the "Eskimos should do as [the Police] say because it is right."[6] The year before, two huge game preserves were established exclusively for Inuit, Indians and half-breeds, one in the Back and Thelon River basins and the other on Victoria and Banks Islands. In 1926, the latter reserve was extended to cover all the Arctic Islands and became known as the Arctic Islands Game Preserve.

Much of government perception and policy regarding the Inuit had its origin in the early to mid-1920s. The bulk of information came from the police,

166

whose observations were limited to their immediate post areas, their patrols, and quick visits to Inuit locations. Explorers, missionaries, and traders also played their part in this information-gathering. No one, it was thought, was better suited to inform Ottawa on a comprehensive and current scale than the explorer, Knud Rasmussen, as "his recommendations should go a long way to suggesting the course of action we should follow in our administration."[7] Like his contemporary, Vilhjalmur Stefansson, this native Greenlander never tired in his fascination with, and scholarly interest in, the Inuit. Under his pioneering command, the Danish Fifth Thule Expedition (1921-1924) provided more than a passing glimpse of the natives of arctic North America.[8] After headquartering one and one-half years at Danish Island, at the top of Hudson Bay, Rasmussen set out in the spring of 1923 on a stupendous journey. Until then, he and his party had studied the surrounding Inuit from Baffin Island to Baker Lake. In August 1924, he completed his trek by crossing the Bering Strait to Siberia, travelling some 20 000 miles by sledge. In that time he traversed the coastline of the Northwest Passage, and was able to investigate every major Inuit group which inhabited the Central and Western Arctic of North America. For Ottawa, Rasmussen's comprehensive travels and observations were of considerable import.

Traders

When queried about the ill-effects of traders and their posts, Rasmussen's response was that the clock could not be turned back. With few exceptions, he said, all the Inuit in Canada were dependent on white men's goods. In most areas the young were familiar with firearms and had lost their ability to hunt with bows and arrows, kayaks and spears. But this was not totally bad: as long as only the necessary, as opposed to luxury, articles were imported, any harm trading stations could do would be "compensated for by the great aid the importation of firearms gives a hunting tribe in their battle for existence." Once the traders "are informed of their responsibilities, they will be able to bring the milder customs of the white man out among the native people."[9]

As for the alleged ruthless exploitation of Inuit by the traders, Rasmussen saw none of it. True, the Inuit had to pay high prices for their goods, but one had to take into account that "the risk in trading in these different sections is very great and that expenses necessarily must be in proportion to the great distances. . ." Moreover, he could not recommend that the government involve itself in trading, as it would incur considerable losses, given the nature of government enterprises. "Private trading--private initiative--seems to me to be the healthiest and most modern way of furnishing the Eskimo with their necessities." Further, white trappers should not be entirely kept away from the arctic coast because "as a rule competition with these has a stimulating and educating effect on the Eskimo." Besides, the country was so large both white and native could trap without the Inuit experiencing any adverse effects.[10]

Rasmussen's information and opinions became crucial to Canada's southern administrators of northern lands, but in many respects they were at variance with Ottawa's northern agents whose sympathies towards the Inuit went just as deep, and whose northern experience in Canada may not have been as far-ranging but certainly derived from longer periods of contact; their experience was not of the whirlwind variety. In many respects their ambitions coincided with Rasmussen's, but they were more pointed in their worry about widespread starvation and the lack of game. The most critical remarks were reserved for the traders, including the Hudson's Bay Company. Unlike Rasmussen, who was more charitable in his remarks about the Hudson's Bay Company, the R.C.M.P were always suspicious of the Company's trading practices, and they may have had good reason. The police considered the majority of fur traders, managers and assistants in the Central and Western Arctic "a poor class of men . . . the beachcombers of Nome and the coast."[11] In the Eastern Arctic, one of Finnie's field men, exploratory engineer L.T. Burwash, pulled no punches and provided a gloomy and depressing report on fur trade activities practice on Baffin Island:

> For many years trapping was conducted chiefly by the women and in no way influenced either the selection of camp sites, or indirectly, the food and clothing supply.
>
> . . . concurrent with the increase in value of the arctic furs, and the practical closing of the whaling operations, the traders commenced to organize both the natives and the territories with a view of increasing the fur production. With the business assuming greater proportions the traders in many cases considered it to their advantage to keep large numbers of natives either at, or in the close proximity of the Post where they have been used as labourers, stevedores, etc., only leaving the post late in the summer to take up winter quarters at a site selected by the company agent as a good fox area and which might or might not supply either caribou or seal.
>
> Traders will, it is true, issue a weekly dole of biscuits, tea and molasses which possibly keeps body and soul together, but which in no way compensates for the lack of meat, seal and caribou skins. During the past winter an Eskimo settlement was seen, containing forty-five natives, who were without meat or blubber.
>
> The inside of the tupeks were dark and festooned with frost, and the people, more especially the women and children, existing in misery almost beyond belief. These people

had been sent to this area not only without their consent but in the face of as strenuous a protest as an Eskimo, with his fear of the trader, dared make.[12]

In Greenland, as Burwash noted, Danish authorities had had success with state monopoly of trade. The year 1924 represented the one-hundred and fiftieth anniversary of that monopoly, and Danish authorities had no hesitation in asserting that the practice would and should continue, as it was "an absolute necessity. . .for the single reason that the native population should be exterminated if it came into unrestricted connection with the great world."[13] Whether Canada could adopt such a practice was a moot point. Greenland's coastal settlements were much more accessible than Canada's far-flung arctic counterparts. The Hudson's Bay Company had, for all intents and purposes, entrenched rights and powerful connections; for any government to stray from the path of laissez-faire capitalism ran the danger, in those days, of strong criticisms from the Canadian business community.

Nevertheless, Canadian officials were in a quandary. Something had to be done. The unscrupulous practices of the venerable Company appeared quite widespread, to the detriment of the Inuit. But the exploitation was patent, and went beyond what a fair and reasonable profit meant--even in northern climes:

> Avanna, a south Victoria Land native, made a catch of one hundred white foxes and purchased from the Hudson's Bay Company at Bernard Harbour a second Land canoe for which he had to pay fifty fox skins, the market value of the skins would, at the time, be around $41.00 each and the canoe was of the type sold to Mackenzie Delta natives at $75.00.[14]

The government was also of the opinion that Baffin land Inuit had been "reduced to a state of peonage" by the Company and cited a number of unsavoury practices, including questionable hiring procedures and contracts for indentured servitude between Inuit and the trading operations.[15]

The Company always had its version of any alleged charges and acquitted itself well in defending its practices. Obviously, it was irate that its integrity had been questioned, adding that "the company's strongest argument is the history of its dealings with them [native races] through more than 250 years and it would be strange indeed if the Company should prove false to its history, traditions, and principles."[16] Not really concerned by this display of outrage, Canadian officials remained wary of the Company and its practices, and their communiqués and incessant inquiries served notice on the Hudson's Bay Company that its practices and dealings with the Inuit were being watched closely. Now and then, government officials would raise the spectre of the government of Canada entering the trading arena, on a monopoly basis in the Arctic much like the case in Greenland, or like the limited government intervention in Alaska.[17] How serious the Canadian government may have been is debatable, but it was determined to influence the Company's activities, even if it had to drag out from time to time this veiled threat or bogey man.

The government had more on its mind regarding the Inuit than the alleged practices of the H.B.C. Equal, perhaps more pressing for Canada's northern policy, were other problems confronting the Inuit during the interwar years. Yet even on other fronts, government officials were handicapped, partly by the uncertain status of the Inuit, and partly by the onset of the Depression, which consumed Ottawa's attention further south.

Relief

Of immediate concern as the 1920s gave way to the Depression was the problem of relief for destitute Inuit. Traditionally, relief to Inuit was extended to widows, the old and orphans. In the Eastern Arctic the situation appeared very severe. The problem arose not so much out of responsibility but out of a standardization of relief issue. Suggestions had been made regarding a set scale for relief items,[18] but it was found that each case required discretionary action by the person in charge. While accounting procedures might be simplified, individual circumstances had to be taken into account.[19] Whether equity was guaranteed was another matter, as there were many instances when destitute Inuit, having the same circumstances, were supplied with differing quantities and articles.[20]

It has been the established policy of the Northwest Territories branch since mid-1928 to encourage Inuit "to rely upon native foods rather than those of the white man."[21] Such rations as milk, butter, bacon and patent medicines were considered luxuries and were not issued as relief items, except for infants. All who were responsible for the distribution of relief were informed that the greatest economy was to be practiced and, whenever possible, ammunition was to be handed out in lieu of food and clothing. Congregating or loitering at the trading posts was absolutely prohibited. Trading post officials were instructed by their district managers to encourage and teach the natives to provide for themselves and families and not to depend upon the trade stores for support.

In 1937, mission "industrial homes" were opened at Chesterfield and Pangnirtung to take care of the aged, infirm, or chronic cripples. It was a humanitarian gesture welcomed and supported financially by Ottawa at $200 per inmate; in addition, the homes were designed to allow physically fit Inuit to carry on their hunting and thus "the issue of relief would be reduced to a minimum." Thought was given to the establishment of similar homes in the Northwest Territories, in the Coronation and Queen Maud Gulf areas, but the government demurred in this instance until the Supreme Court decided on the status of the Inuit.[22] Nevertheless, the government was anxious for others to take on the burden. Certainly, both missions and traders received compensation for the activity of relief, but the government, as the evidence suggests, wished to keep costs to the minimum. The drain on the public purse and the "spoiling" of the Inuit, according to the government officials, was attributed partly to the uncertain fur cycle, but also to the centralization of relief at mission and trading posts. In the eyes of "old timers" in the North, missionaries encouraged the Inuit to come to the posts rather than going out among them, the result being that the natives abandoned fur trapping and hunting; this, in turn, made them dependent on relief and raised the costs of hospitalization.[23] Once the H.B.C. had absorbed its Eastern Arctic rival, Révillon Frères, there was some comfort gained in Ottawa that relief costs for the government had fallen off "as competition in 'charity' disappeared."[24]

In the Western Arctic, which had an ailing economic base, less effort and expense was put into actual relief, as faith was placed in an experiment more positive in nature. The Mackenzie delta, in particular, was endowed with richer food resources, including muskrats, fish, white whales, ducks and geese in the summer, and seals off shore; even the caribou appeared to be returning. This region would have appeared an absolute paradise to the suffering Inuit of the Central and Eastern Arctic. In the Western Arctic, one of the central recommendations of the Reindeer and Musk-Ox Commission was implemented to "reduce further dependence by the natives upon the white man for a living."[25] The Royal Commission had recommended in 1922 the establishment of reindeer herds in northern regions which could support such an enterprise. In the spring of 1929 the Canadian government purchased a herd in Alaska; by 1935, the animals finally reached a newly constructed reindeer station in the eastern Mackenzie delta.[26] It was hoped that under expert tutelage, the Inuit would eventually take over the operation, but it was considered politic to retain government supervision for the time being; otherwise the Inuit would deplete the herd "and expect that more animals would be obtained in the same way. . . The idea of always having fresh meat available and also for clothing, appeals strongly to the Eskimos, but he is like the Indian in that he does not see the need for providing for his future."[27]

Despite experiments like this, Inuit relief and widespread starvation continued to dog government officials throughout the 1930s and 1940s. The government was convinced that the best type of relief for the Inuit in the Eastern Arctic was regular rations of ammunition.[28] Such a policy might have worked were it not for the vagaries and caprice of weather conditions from year to year and the cyclical nature of the game. Traders and bureaucrats tended to hope that "next year" would always be better,[29] but much was left to providence rather planning. The H.B.C. instructed its post managers, "by all means at their disposal," to encourage a credit or banking system "so that excess prosperity. . .may be carried over, thereby preventing unnecessary suffering. . .next year."[30] No plan existed, however, to cope with a succession of bad hunting seasons or hard winters.

By the end of 1942, with war raging in Europe and in the Pacific, the Bureau of Northwest Territories and Yukon Affairs could claim some control over relief expenditures, aside from the policy of parsimony. Separate cards were kept for each individual who received a relief. "It will be noted that in the N.W.T. where relief issues are controlled by medical officers and R.C.M. Police the costs average 73 cents per head for destitute whites, Inuit and half-breeds whereas in Eskimo territory of northern Quebec where there is no supervision the costs run to $13.17 per head."[31] The costs were higher in northern Quebec partly because there were no hospitals, residential schools or industrial homes, except at Fort George where an Indian population predominated.[32] Total relief expenditures for Quebec Inuit took a nose dive by mid-1943, from $22,510 (1941-42) to $5287.93 (1942-43). The decline was due mainly to a high fur cycle and high fur prices, the transfer of natives to more productive areas, and, most important, but nevertheless a mixed blessing for the future of the Inuit, their employment on joint defence projects carried out mainly by the United States Army.[33]

The war was a period of opening up for the North and, for the government and especially the H.B.C., the onset of severe criticism by U.S. Army personnel and newspaper reporters over deplorable conditions amongst the Inuit. The H.B.C. reacted in a cavalier fashion, dismissing American charges of exploitation as

a weakness of many temporary visitors to the North [who] make sweeping and general criticism and comments, which do not hold water when they are put up against the test of plain facts. . .I think we all recognize that the present defence activities in the North will have some repercussions upon the Eskimos, and not many to their advantage, and no matter how well intentioned these critics may be, most of whom are seeing the North for the first time, it would be too much to expect them to understand the Eskimos and their characteristics, and govern themselves accordingly.

. . .May I say that we are probably just as qualified to express opinions upon the conditions and circumstances of negroes and sharecroppers in the Southern States as are these casual visitors in expressing their opinions concerning the Eskimos in the North.[34]

The government was under pressure from the U.S. Army, and looked critically at the H.B.C. relief practices, which appear to have kept the Inuit scandalously on the edge of subsistence. In response, the H.B.C. directed its district and post managers in July, 1944, to ease up:

In regard to relief measures nothing should be done which could in any way undermine the natives' self-reliance and initiative. However, a too literal interpretation of this objective has, I know, often resulted in a procedure being followed which merely amounted to supplying such meagre ration that it was all the native could do to keep body and soul together. Such a parsimonious and short-sighted attitude can only defeat the main objective, namely that of maintaining the native's self-reliance and initiative, because anybody so undernourished suffers in health to such an extent that they lose initiative and ability to make a living for themselves. Doubtless a great deal of sickness and epidemics which result from under-nourishment could be avoided if a more humane and common-sense attitude was used in looking after the native basic life necessities during poor times.[35]

One problem which seemed to plague both the government and the Company during the 1940s was that of the so-called "Non-Producers," those able-bodied Inuit who were not hunters. This category of male Inuit was considered as "lazy" and any relief given to them "should be of a character, while nourishing, does not encourage them to get along on relief rations...these lazy people should be required to do menial tasks in return for the allowance."[36] The term "lazy" was a charitable one when compared to their also being called "flunkies" and "bum boys."[37] Later they would be referred to, politely and for official reasons obviously, as "camp assistants" and "inefficient trappers." The Company argued that it should not be responsible for their well-being, and chided the government for being too generous in its relief policy:

We believe that the government, in its present policy of giving the natives what they themselves cannot afford, is undermining their morale. The natives are being forced to accustom themselves to a standard of living that their economic system cannot support. Natives in this locality are becoming more concerned with the question: "How can I get relief?," rather than working harder to make their own way. We believe that the present policy is making "bums" out of the majority of theses natives. No person can keep his self-respect when the attitude is: "The more I get for nothing, the better."

We hope that our criticisms will be taken in the spirit with which they are given. Our concern is for the natives. We would like to see them the strong, upright, hard-working, independent and prideful people they were before the white man brought his "blessings of civilization" to them. To approach that goal, the native must be made to stand on his own feet, and it is our personal idea that the present policy of too much help is killing him with kindness.[38]

Noble sentiments, perhaps. But H.B.C. was just as guilty in bringing the "blessings of civilization" to them. Were it not for government "generosity"-- if it could ever be called that--the Inuit would have even been more dependent on the Company. A cynic might suggest that this was exactly what the trading company wanted.

The old policy of keeping the native had not worked. Several factors made it impossible to encourage all male Inuit to be hunters and trappers. The relief scheme was one but there were others: the encouragement of trapping for profit did not go hand in hand with, for instance, hunting for meat; traditional skills were lost by many who had no recourse but to remain close to camps and posts. Neither white traders nor government officials were happy with the situation, and the Inuit, who may have had other ideas and aspirations, were at the mercy of forces beyond their control. Besides, no one bothered to ask them if they wished to change, or to subsist in the old native tradition, merely hoping for better days.

Early Educational Policies

An enlightened attitude, coupled with a deeper sense of responsibility and the ever-present issue of sovereignty, was to influence government education policy. A growing awareness of a need emerged in the 1940s, but caution, reticence and parsimony were still active ingredients. Before World War II, lip service was paid to educating--or rather, providing education for--the Inuit. It was simpler to let others do it; in this case Anglican and Roman Catholic missions, which had been expanding in the west and north from the 1840s onwards.

Early in the twentieth century it was recognized that the Inuit had the potential to become excellent workers, but there had to be something "in sight in that far northern country to justify expenditure" beyond relief measures and the prevention of starvation.[39] When the Reverend E.J. Peck requested support for his mission school on Blacklead Island in Baffinland in 1909, he was informed that "for the time being it is not the intention of the government to assist in educational work amongst these people."[40] The foremost concern of the missionary, generally speaking, was the teaching of Christianity and the conversion of the "pagan" Inuit. In the Eastern Arctic, the New Testament, along with other hymn and prayer books, was translated into *Inuktitut* by Reverend Peck,[41] who adapted the syllabic form of writing first devised for the Plains Cree by James Evans in the 1830s. In the Western Arctic, Roman script would be used.

Continued missionary requests for financial aid in education did bear some fruit. By 1915-1916 the Department of Indian Affairs was providing a grant of $400 per year for a teacher's salary and $100 a year towards the renting of a building at Herschel Island for the Inuit there.[42] Between 1918 and 1923 the department had spent about $4000 per year for the education of Inuit children in mission schools.[43] Throughout the 1920s monies were devoted to Inuit education (through Finnie's proddings), but scarcely enough. In 1930-31 $12787.50 was divided among eight mission schools in the North. Observed Diamond Jenness, Canada's most eminent anthropologist, such subsidies "could hardly be termed manifest, especially when the churches were operating their arctic missions on shoestrings and possessed no funds of their own for educational purposes. Their first task. . .was to teach the Eskimos Christianity, not to instruct them in regular school subjects. . . Inevitably, then, the secular education that the missionaries imparted to the Eskimo children was commensurate with the funds that the government expended on it. In other words, it was negligible."[44] From the government's point of view, there seemed little reason to do more. Again, it was a question of keeping the native native. Why give Inuit children a white-oriented education when, for the foreseeable future, they would just be fur-trappers. Besides, bureaucrats believed that Inuit "mental capacity to assimilate academic training is limited."[45]

When two Inuit lads were brought south by missionaries in 1928 to an exclusive private school, the government appeared displeased with the scheme and the surrounding "cute" publicity.[46] The experiment ended in failure as both youngsters, although academically promising, succumbed to repeated bouts of colds, flu and head infections and were forced to return to the North.[47] The government agreed with A.L. Fleming, the influential Anglican archdeacon of the Arctic, that Inuit should be left to lead a natural life and not be confined or sent to boarding schools of any sort:

My [Fleming's] feeling about the boarding school question is simply this. For a period of years at any rate the Eskimo in the Far North are not likely, as far as I can judge, to suddenly change their nomadic habits. . .If this be the case, then as far as I can judge the boarding schools would serve to make him a less successful hunter. . .and therefore would be less able to earn his livelihood in the winter. Further as a result of these years in a boarding school, he would adopt the white man's ways, and become used to the white man's food. When therefore his school years were over, he would have a strong hankering after the white man's ways and food, and I believe would tend to become inefficient from the point of view of a citizen dwelling in the far North.

How can the Eskimo children be educated without destroying those habits so necessary to them as nomads? Either they can be taken into boarding schools and speedily educated, but in the process they will become less fit to continue the nomadic life of today; or if the nomadic life is not seriously interfered with, the education of the children must be of necessity somewhat slower.[48]

This position was certainly in startling contrast to Alaska and Greenland where, although caution had not been thrown to the wind, there were distinct and enlightened government educational policies. In Alaska, all schools were operated by the United States Bureau of Education. Missions, apparently, were no longer permitted to operate private schools for natives. All villages of a "certain minimum number" of children were provided with a teacher, usually white, and a schoolhouse. In Greenland, all schools were operated by the government. There, following public school, native students of exceptional ability, or those unsuited for the life of hunters and fishermen, were encouraged to go to high school or normal school; all teachers were natives. Canadian government officials were well aware of these successes but felt that the Inuit of the N.W.T. "are not yet sufficiently advanced for the white man's system of education."[49] This view seems to beg the question of when they would ever be ready, unless some concerted action were initiated. The time never seemed right. Education was left to the missionary, with some government financial support.[50]

In effect, very little would change in educational policy until World War II, and some of the prods came from outside Canada. Before long, the Canadian government faced severe and embarrassing criticism from the United States forces and civilians involved in the various defence projects in the Eastern Arctic: "Why has nothing been done to educate the Eskimos. . .Why have the traders been allowed to exploit the Eskimos?"[51] For Americans to criticize their Canadian host was considered breach of diplomatic protocol. The U.S. military attaché in Ottawa, was given a polite and unofficial warning by R.A.

Gibson, Deputy Minister of the Northwest Territories Branch, who explained the problems in northern native education as a factor of the Depression followed by the exigencies of war. Nevertheless, to avert future criticisms, Gibson privately told his right-hand man, the Administrator of the Arctics, W.L. McKeand, that Canada should pick up the pace of "any arrangements that could be consummated even under existing conditions.[52]

The problem went deeper, however. Fundamentally, the view that it would take generations to educate the "primitive" Inuit had to change. Political masters in Ottawa had to realize that the stereotype of Canada's Inuit, their mental capabilities, and their lack of place in the fabric of Canada, could not stand up to close examination. Nowhere was this truer than in the Mackenzie delta area, where many Inuit in the early 1940s were chafing, near seething, under restrictions and regulations which retarded their education and advancement. In terms of conspicuous wealth, portions of the Western Arctic were a veritable paradise compared to its eastern counterpart.

These [Western Inuit] have actually achieved the material success and adjustment in the modern world towards which we are supposed to be leading all Eskimos. The attainment of success might well be expected to bring social rewards over and above worldly goods just as it does with the white man, and it is the desires that their money cannot gratify that are at the root of their complaints. One of the most universal desires of prosperous people everywhere is that their children should have the cultural opportunities that they themselves were unable to have. Some of the older Eskimos who had no formal education see with dismay that their children are learning no more or even less at school than they themselves were able to pick up in their youth. . .Many well-to-do Eskimos would readily abandon the present free [mission] schooling available to their children if they could obtain better at their own expense.[53]

This demand for education was to be paralleled in the Eastern Arctic a few years later[54] and anticipated a wide-ranging evaluation of education prepared in late 1948 for the Northwest Territories administration.[55] The "Report on Educational Facilities in the Eastern Arctic" cited the general inadequacies of the present system--including the spotty and ineffectual education imparted by the missions, the acknowledged intelligence of the Inuit, and the growing pace of change in a region entering the Cold War era--and recommended a sound educational policy under federal auspise: experimental day schools, operating year round and in addition to seasonal day schools, were seen as the most satisfactory answer to the Inuit nomadic way of life; instruction in the English language; the eradication of syllabic writing, considered then as a psychological

177

impediment to learning English; health instruction, elementary science, and most important, first class teachers who would be both teacher and social worker.[56] By the late 1940s the federal government embarked upon a long-range programme to provide northern education for both whites and natives, with eight federal schools being established in the north between 1948 and 1951.[57]

Still the debate existed as to just how and to what degree the Inuit should be educated. The government's official policy--getting them back to the land to hunt, remain self-sufficent and independent--was still in force in the early 1950s;[58] but the idea of keeping the native native would lead to cross-purposes, confusion and a painful period of adjustment for both parties.

Health Care Policy Before and After World War II

The interwar years also witnessed scandalous medical neglect. In the fall of 1938, the *Canadian Resources Bulletin*, a government publication, proudly announced that the Eskimos of Canada were in good health, as a result of years of care provided by government doctors and nurses who were part of the annual Eastern Arctic Patrol. "Instances of heart disease, and various forms of tubercular disease among the natives. . .are less frequent than among whites."[59] The basis of this official report was a general medical survey of Eastern Arctic Inuit conducted by Dr. Keith F. Rogers during the summer of 1938. Yet, if one examines Rogers' internal confidential reports, one discerns a gap between what he actually reported and what the government wished to convey. As this was Rogers' first trip to the Artctic, he made clear in his report that his observations were opinion only and based largely on conjecture, especially his views on the prevalence of tuberculosis. In fact, he acknowledged in his report to Ottawa that:

(a) In order to make an accurate diagnosis of early pulmonary tuberculosis, an X-Ray is an essential--this must be taken properly, and must be interpreted by one who has had special training, and experience, in disease of the lungs.

(b) Neither the hospital at Chesterfield, nor the one at Pangnirtung, are at present equipped to make a proper survey of lung conditions among the Eskimos, or to do so in a manner which would enable one to decide definitely just how prevalent pulmonary tuberculosis is among the natives.

(c) No X-Ray study of the lungs of Eskimos is available at present.[60]

In fact, throughout the 1930's Canadian doctors conjectured that the Inuit just had bad colds, not T.B. The government wanted to believe this. Despite the glowing medical reports that emanated from the North during the 1920s and 1930s and found their way to departmental annual reports and bulletins,[61] the health and care of the Inuit, particularly in the Eastern Arctic, was in shambles; Ottawa would do its utmost to keep the truth from the public. Policy was virtually non-existent, and a band-aid approach had been adopted. D.L. McKeand, R.A. Gibson's right hand man in policy matters and who had been in charge of the Eastern Arctic patrol since 1932, considered in 1933 that northern medical services were very unsatisfactory: "Since the patrol was inaugurated in 1922. . .there have been no less than thirteen different Doctors serving as Medical Officers with the patrol. Consequently, there have been wide differences of opinion on medical questions, glaring evidences of inexperience, no continuity of service, no research, and, therefore, the cause of at least seventy deaths in Southern Baffin Island alone remains unsolved." Lack of continuity made it impossible to establish a coherent medical programme. Doctors were unwilling to serve in the north on a long-term basis, and in 1936 McKeand's office had been reduced to telephoning boys' summer camps desperately searching for a doctor--any doctor--for the Patrol.[62]

In terms of general treatment of ailments, it was very difficult to convince the Inuit of the advantages of the white man's healing powers. According to Dr. J.E. Bildfell, who reported on the medical conditions in the Eastern Arctic in 1934, trying to convince the Inuit of the efficiencies of southern health techniques was a "herculanean task from a white man's perspective."[63] Bildfell described his futile efforts to win over the Inuit. His views reveal as much about himself as about the Inuit:

> The practice of Medicine among the "Inuit" is as interesting as it is difficult. . .Medical benefits like Christian benefits, are largely invisible. As is known, Medical results are seldom dramatic and startling. The natives expect them to be. The only way to convince the native is by way of eyes. Hence the Doctor, is early compelled to throw off his scientific cloak, and disguise himself as salesman, and missionary. . .the natives seldom present themselves for treatment, until disease processes are well advanced. The only exceptions to this are such minor ailments, as constipation which they know the white man can remedy intelligently, minor wounds and abrasions. . . The above are obviously abnormal and are to be taken to the doctor. This of course for two reasons; one being that they are by duty supposed to and the other it encourages the doctor's "good will". . .A cut finger should be good for a mug up or perhaps a cigarette. Such ailments as the annual Conjunctivitis or other periodic complications arising out of conditions of climate, are merely tolerated as something which occurs naturally. Sickness is not understood.

Pain an discomfort are merely something to be tolerated along with other hardships which they bear without a grumble. Since there is no appeal to reason in these matters, disease advances considerably and is usually not regarded as such until some particular function is disturbed.

In the native mind, surgical advantages are extremely doubtful. They feel sure that whosoever undergoes an operation necessarily dies. They have mentioned this. Perhaps this is in part a return of the powers they enjoyed in the past, of being able to die whenever they seemed to desire. Their lives are intimately wrapped up with a fatalistic outlook and death is relatively a simple matter. But the fact that they are poor surgical risks constitutionally, is not to bedenied; this largely because of the prevalence of Tuberculosis among them, and it appears to me that natives although they are up and around, are taxing every bit of energy and resistance they possess; hence they are unable to tolerate any added stress which is necessary for surgical recovery.[64]

The Eastern Arctic Inuit were also suffering from other maladies. At Fort Chimo in 1935, approximately 50 per cent had badly decayed teeth, with a number of cases of pyorrhea; there were numerous cases of eye problems, ranging from conjunctivitis to partial and total blindness.[65] Although the internal medical reports--written for government eyes only--are illuminating, they make sad reading. The organization of health services, if one can call it that, needed not only an overhaul, but direction, expertise and the continuing presence of qualified personnel. On the eve of World War II, government reliance on others to do the job, though coldly cost-efficient, had not ameliorated the suffering of the Inuit in Canada's Eastern Arctic:

In various posts there are two or three individuals more or less attempting to attend to the health needs of the native. To cite the case of Lake Harbour as being fairly representative we have the following state of affairs: The Anglican missionary receives the Government Medical supplies; but according to his own words is not in any way trained nor gifted in the matter of treatment of illnesses, as a consequence our supplies accumulate from year to year in his cupboards. The Hudson's Bay factor administers whatever relief he can with the medical supplies that are issued by his company. The most logical men, the R.C.M.P., to do this work, are not supplied in any form with medical equipment. It has been the experience at this post that whenever surgery has been necessary the R.C.M.P. have been called.

Other posts such as Sugluk, Wolstenholme, Southampton and Dorset have no problem as far as the decision as to who will be responsible for medical aid to the natives in as much as there are no R.C.M.P. or missionaries resident. On the other hand natives at these places are being given whatever attention the post manager can with the

Company's supplies that are issued to him. In some cases the work done is excellent, in others, it is grossly inadequate.[66]

Canadian northern health policy in these years may have been a deliberate stall; it was also just the usual, slow-paced way, penny-pinching, doing things. World War II, and its attendant opening up of the Eastern Arctic to a host of American defence schemes, would change this.

The reports during the war contained tales of human suffering and tragedies under the guise of a smile on the part of the Inuit.[67] According to the Reverend A. Steinmann, in charge of the Roman Catholic mission at Wakeham Bay, the false impressions given to visiting members of the Eastern Arctic Patrol regarding the condition of the Inuit bordered on the theatrical. In September, 1943, Steinmann charged that the real physical conditions were being covered up. Instead, "the Chief of the Eastern Arctic Patrol makes a picnic of his inspection. He is installed on a trading ship, and when he arrives at the different posts he sees everything shipshape. The traders must give a good impression to the visitors. Everything is in order; painted, polished, and the Eskimos dressed in the cleanest they can find, even buying new clothing, or, as I have seen with my own eyes, borrowing from the more fortunate some garments that will make them appear less miserable. Why blame them when it is the instruction they have received from the traders? They do what they are told, and what they have seen. At ship time all must be well-ordered; 'we must save our face,' said the Chief of the Eastern Arctic Patrol."[68]

While such observations were being made, a series of epidemics was sweeping the Eastern Arctic; not unusual, perhaps, as government authorities "had known for twenty years that epidemics of more or less severity followed the visits of ships to government stations and trading posts."[69] In 1941-42 there were three serious epidemics which were partially checked by immediate action on the part of the medical officers using local radio communications. Still, the tragedies continued. During the fall and winter of 1941-42 there were two epidemics running concurrently in and around Pangnirtung--respiratory diseases with a high percentage of lobar pneumonia and influenza or paratyphoid fever. Of the eighty individuals treated, forty-three died; thirty-five of the latter died in camp.[70] The following year an epidemic of cerebro-spinal meningitis plagued the Eastern Arctic from Southampton Island to Lake Harbour. The death toll was high; at Cape Dorset alone the Inuit mortality rate was 25 per cent.[71]

By this time the region was being invaded by U.S. military personnel and doctors who, in their valiant attempts to help, expressed shock and outrage at

181

the health conditions of the Inuit, and the medical care extended to them by the government of Canada. D.L. McKeand, Gibson's principal advisor in such matters, dismissed the U.S. medical officers as "itinerant, inexperienced doctors" with no previous experience with Inuit and no idea of the financial constraints.[72] When an incredulous Gibson--who should have known better-- asked, "Am I to understand. . .that [Canadian] medical officers at either Pangnirtung or Chesterfield have refused admission to any Eskimos requiring medical treatment because they believe funds were not available to take care of the hospital bills?"[73] McKeand replied in a matter of fact manner: "Certainly. Incurable tubercular Eskimo patients have never been admitted, except under exceptional circumstances. Moreover, when death was imminent from any cause, (Inuit) patients were removed from the hospital to die in tents or snow houses. I doubt if...the U.S. army doctors temporarily stationed in the Arctic are familiar with these well-known departmental regulations and practices."[74] Regulations and procedures took precedence over humanitarianism and proper hospital care. It was no wonder that American doctors reacted so; if the whole truth had been made public, the Canadian government, already stinging from embarrassment, would have had much to answer for.

For decades the government wished to keep out of the hospital business. Simply put, it was not just a matter of funding but the prevailing notion that government had no business in socialized medicine or anything that smacked of it. But the experiences of the Depression, and the war itself, were fostering a new mood in the country. Canadians would soon expect their government to involve itself more in the daily lives of its citizens.

Public aid in the North to hospitals was based on the Hospital Ordinance of the Northwest Territories and subsequent amendments. The commissioner of the Territories had the discretionary authority to determine the nature and extent of public aid to be given. There were no government hospitals. By 1943 there were eleven private hospitals in all the vast Northwest Territories, nine operated and owned by the missions and two by mining companies. Aklavik had two mission hospitals, with a total of seventy-three beds to treat the Inuit, and served an area stretching from the Yukon-Alaska boundary to the Gulf of Boothia; there were 1777 Inuit in the district, according to the 1941 census. Chesterfield had a thirty-bed hospital and served 1632 Inuit north of 60°, along the coastal area, the islands in northern Hudson Bay and a section of northwestern Quebec. Baffin Island and the north coast of Quebec including Ungava Bay, with an Inuit population of 1993, was serviced by an eighteen-bed hospital at Pangnirtung. Aid to these private hospitals in 1943 included a 40 per cent grant toward the initial costs of construction, (exclusive of furnishings), and thereafter a $2.50 per diem rate for the care of indigent whites, half-breeds and Inuit, a portion of the drugs and medicines, and the services of doctors and registered nurses. Also, $200 per year was allotted for the maintenance of the tiny industrial homes at Chesterfield and Pangnirtung which cared for the aged and infirm. The government would not, however, contribute towards the purchase of X-ray or other medical equipment.[75] The inadequacy of such arrangements took its toll among the Inuit. Surveys conducted for the years 1937 to 1941 indicated that 85 per cent of Inuit in the Eastern Arctic who had died did so without a doctor in attendance; of the white and Indian population in the region, 37 per cent and 48 per cent respectively. The death rate from tuberculosis, the big killer among the Indian and Inuit population, was placed at 761 and 314 per 100,000 respectively--compared to 50 per 100,000 for Canada as a whole. The general death rate from all causes for the Inuit was a staggering 1100 per 100 000.[76]

There was still sentiment in government circles to let the missions continue their healing: their staffs, it was argued, worked without remuneration; the missions received large donations from a wide variety of organizations to continue their work; the missionaries were themselves in intimate contact with the native population; "hospitalization is synonymous with the advancement of civilization and Christianity"; federal ownership of hospitals, bureaucrats shuddered, would cost approximately a half million dollars. On the other hand, there were compelling reasons for the government to enter the field vigorously:

(1) There are two hospitals at Aklavik--one operated by the Anglican and the other by the R.C. Mission. One hospital would suffice for a settlement of this kind but the policy of erecting separate institutions in places where both dominations are represented will probably be continued as long as the hospitals are owned by the Missions.

(2) The doctors do not have the same jurisdiction over the operation of the hospitals as they would if the institutions were Federally owned.

(3) Up to recent years the Missionaries have selected the sites for the hospitals, and also determined the type of building to be erected, the Department having no say as to location, type of construction, design, etc.[77]

One compelling reason for change went unspoken: things were a mess.

Prodded by a series of exposés, epidemics and a newer and far-sighted breed of bureaucrats replacing the old guard, the government realized that "it is now clear that more radical and fundamental steps will be taken."[78] Throughout 1944, medical officers and others were asked not only to look after the sick, but to comment on the condition of the Inuit--which was really already known and had not changed for the better in two decades of observation--and to proffer suggestions as to how the system should be improved. In many ways, these efforts resulted in the first hard look at what had to be done. Epidemics continued, the most serious being at Eskimo Point-Padlei where diphtheria carried off 25 per cent of the Inuit population in 1943-44.[79] The reports received all suggested a revamping of the medical system under government auspices, and the improvement of emergency transportation facilities, particularly by air.[80] In the light of such reports, though the Northwest Territories administration was jealous of its prerogatives, responsibility for the health of the Inuit (as well as of Indians) was transferred to the newly created Department of National Health and Welfare on 1 November 1945.[81] The Department of National Health and Welfare, its budget bolstered, immediately embarked on far-ranging services. As many Inuit as possible, in both sections of the Arctic, were x-rayed and immunized, while those Inuit who desperately needed outside hospital care were removed to the south by boat and plane. Dental, eye, and nutritional surveys were intensified.

The war against all the ailments which had plagued the Inuit had begun in earnest. Southern hospitals in western and eastern Canada were filled with Inuit --T.B. patients especially--in the late 1940s and throughout the 1950s. It is true that for decades northern administrators, including medical officers, R.C.M.P., missionaries and traders, had argued against removing the Inuit from their environs and continued to do so. But the Department of National Health and Welfare felt otherwise, pointing out that it was better and most cost effective (i.e. cheaper) to accommodate Inuit in southern hospitals under expert care than to embark on massive spending to duplicate facilities; moreover, it was particularly difficult to persuade medical experts to move north. In this, they were correct, for T.B. was battled successfully in the south in the 1950s. There were social costs, however, as Inuit patients, dropped into a strange and bewildering environment, unable to speak the language and cut off from their families, found the change difficult and traumatic. A 1962 memo of the Department of Northern Affairs and National Resources

boasted--and lamented at the same time--that in 1956, 1,600 Eskimos were in hospitals in southern Canada. Now there are only about 350. Many of the 3,000 Eskimos who have been hospitalized over the past six years and who have returned to the north cannot return to their life on the land; many have been unable to adapt to a wage economy and culture (where such an economy and culture existed). Because all could not be absorbed by existing rehabilitation programs, the inevitable alternative has been relief. Better health services have saved more lives than before, but many of these persons have been left handicapped and depend to a greater or lesser extent on relief for their subsistence.[82]

At least, by war's end, the Inuit and their plight were receiving serious attention, and the pace of government concern and policy quickened appropriately in the next decade. But this attention and attitude, sometimes naive and misguided, would create a set of new problems and dislocations. As late as 1959, Inuit policies were made exclusively in the south, thousands of miles away, and made by whites who up until then had argued that they knew best; it had become clear even to them, however, that their paternalism had failed. In that year, 1959, Inuit representatives met with the government of Canada--for the first time; this landmark meeting began a process, which continues to this day, whereby the Inuit viewpoint could no longer be ignored.

Notes

1   See: Richard J. Diubaldo. "The Absurd Little Mouse: When Eskimos Became Indians." *Journal of Canadian Studies* XVI (Summer1981).

2   Public Archives of Canada (PAC), Record Group (RG)/85/Vol.1667/File 4069/Pt.2, O.S. Finnie to C.E. Whittaker, 4 December 1926.

3.   Richard J. Diubaldo, *Stefansson and the Canadian Arctic* (Montreal: McGill-Queen's University Press, 1978), pp.135-60; also, Canada, *Report of the Royal Commission to Investigate the Possibilities of the Reindeer and Musk-Ox Industries in the Arctic and Sub-Arctic Regions of Canada* (Ottawa, 1922), pp. 36-38.

4.   PAC, RG85/1667/4069/2, Finnie to Whittaker, 4 December 1926.

5   PAC, RG85/1127/251-1-1/1A, Finnie to W.W. Cory, 22 September 1924.

6   PAC, RG85/883/9104, "A Letter from the Government to the Eskimo People," 1 April 1924.

7   PAC, RG85/1127/251-1-1/1A, Finnie to W.W. Cory, 16 April 1925.

8   See: Denmark; Ministry of Education, *Report of the Fifth Thule Expedition. The Danish Expedition to Arctic North America in Charge of Knud Rasmussen.* 12 vols. (Copenhagen, 1927-19-). Vols. 3,4,5,11, and 12 not published; also, Knud Rasmussen, *Across Arctic America* (New York: Putman, 1927),

9   Those in attendance in Finnie's office for the meetings with Rasmussen varied from meeting to meeting, but included R.M. Anderson, J.B. Harkin, Arthur Gibson, Diamond Jenness, Henry Toke Munn, and Colonel C. Starnes. For a complete list and detailed discussion see: PAC, RG85/145/400-6/2, Meetings of the Advisory Board on Wild Life Protection, 29 and 30 April, and 1 and 5 May 1925. See also: Ibid., Queries put to Dr. Rasmussen, n.d., received 20 July 1925.

10   Ibid., Testimony of Knud Rasmussen before Advisory Board on Wild Life Protection, 1 May 1925.

11   PAC, RG85/1069/251-1/1, Inspector S.T. Wood to Finnie, 22 August 1924.

12   Ibid., Burwash to Finnie, 30 October 1924.

13   "Greenland Trade State Monopoly," Danish Foreign Office Journal, Danish *Commercial Review*, no. 41 (June, 1924), p. 63.

14   PAC, RG85/1069/251-1/1, Synopsis of reports during 1924-25 concerning certain members of the Hudson's Bay Company, July 1925.

15   Ibid. See also Ibid., Report of Sergeant A.H. Joy, 11 February 1925, Hiring contract between H.B.C. and the native "OO-took-oo too."

16   Ibid., Reply of Edmund Fitzgerald, Deputy Chairman, Canadian Committee, H.B.C., 10 April 1925.

17   For example, see ibid., W.W. Cory, Deputy Minister and Commissioner, N.W.T., to Fitzgerald, 16 October 1925.

18   PAC, RG85/1129/253-1/1, J.H. MacBrien, Commissioner, R.C.M.P., to H.E. Hume, Chairman, Dominion Lands Board, 4 January 1933.

19   Ibid., Minutes, Special Meeting of Interdepartmental Representatives--Department of the Interior, Pensions and National Health, Indian Affairs, R.C.M.P., 3 April 1933.

20   PAC, RG85/1129/253-1/1, Return of Reverend Father J. Easton, Povungnituk, 1931; see ibid., for returns from other posts.

21   PAC, RG85/1130/253-1/2, MacBrien to Hume, 4 January 1933.

22   PAC, RG85/1129/253-1/1A, A.L. Cumming to R.A. Gibson, 12 September 1938.

23   Ibid., Gibson to Cumming, 14 April 1938.

24   Ibid., D.L. McKeand to Gibson, 27 June 1939.

25   PAC, RG85/1132/270-1/1, Reasons for the Purchase of the Reindeer Herd, n.d., probably mid-1930s.

26   PAC, RG85/1132/270-1/1, Extracts, Interdepartmental Reindeer Committee, 18 June 1935.

27   PAC, RG85/1132/270-1/1A. Report of M. Meikle, Agent and Superintendent, Wood Buffalo Park, on Mackenzie River Reindeer Herd, [1935]. Also: PAC, RG85/1132/270-1/1, Minutes, Interdepartmental Reindeer Committee, 23 February 1937; PAC, RG85/1132/270-1/2, Minutes, 25 October 1937.

28   PAC, RG85/1130/253-1/1B, Extracts of Report by Dr. Bildfell, 15 July 1941 to Northern Advisory Board; also D.L. McKeand to Gibson, 27 October 1941.

29   For example see ibid., McKeand to Gibson, 18 November 1941.

30   Ibid., R.H. Chesshire, Assistant Manager, Fur Trade Department, H.B.C. to Gibson, 7 November 1941.

31   PAC, RG85/1130/253-1/2, G. Doyle to Cumming, 5 November 1942.

32   Ibid.

33   Ibid., Doyle to Cumming, 31 July 1943.

34 PAC, RG85/1069/251-1/1, R.H. Chesshire, Manager, Fur Trade Department, H.B.C. to Gibson, 10 June 1943.

35 Ibid., Memorandum of Instructions to [H.B.C.] District Managers Commercial, from Chesshire, 13 July 1944.

36 PAC, RG85/1130/251-1/2, Gibson to Wright, 28 June 1948.

37 PAC, RG85/1130/253-1/1B, Extracts of Report by Dr. Bildfell, 15 July 1941, to Northern Advisory Board.

38 Ibid., W.A. Buhr, Post Manager, H.B.C., Sugluk, to J.W. Anderson, Manager, Ungava Section, H.B.C., 11 October 1948.

39 PAC, RG85/1130/254-1/1, F.W. White, R.C.M.P., to Frank Pedley, Deputy Superintendent General of Indian Affairs, 19 February 1906.

40 Ibid., J.D. McLean to Reverend E.J. Peck, 18 February 1909.

41 Ibid., Peck to D.C. Scott (?), 13 May 1909.

42 Ibid., Martin Russell to D.C. Scott, 24 June 1919.

43 Diamond Jenness, Eskimo Administration: Canada (Montreal: The Arctic Institute of North America, 1964), p.32.

44 Ibid., pp.32-42.

45 W.C. Methune, "Canada's Eastern Arctic, its history, resources, population and administration." (Ottawa: Department of the Interior, 1935), p.55.

46 See: Toronto *Star*, October 1928.

47 Ibid., Toronto *Star*, 21 June 1929.

48 PAC, RG85/1130/254-1/1, A.L. Fleming to Finnie, 6 January 1928. See also: G.P. MacKenzie to Finnie, 13 January 1928; Finnie to W.W. Cory, 16 January 1928.

49 Ibid., A.E. Porsild to J. Lorne Turner, 22 May 1934.

50 Ibid., D.L. McKeand to J.L. Turner, 28 June 1934.

51 PAC, RG85/1130/254-1/1, Extract of notes compiled by Lieutenant T.H. Manning re. "Conditions in the Eastern Arctic. . .being criticized severely by U.S. Officers," April 1943.

52 Ibid., Gibson to McKeand, 7 May 1943.

53 Ibid., C.H.D. Clarke to Cumming, 19 April 1943.

54 Ibid., Report of S.J. Bailey, Eastern Arctic Patrol, 27 July - 13 August 1948.

55 Ibid., "Report on Education Facilities in the Eastern Arctic" by H.R. Lamberton, 1 November 1948.

56 Ibid.

57 Ibid., "Education for the Eskimos" [1952]; c.f. Ibid., "Classification of Pupils in Schools of the MacKenzie District . . .as of March 31, 1951, including summary of attendance in the Eastern Arctic and Northern Quebec."

58 Ibid., Report of A. Stevenson, Eastern Arctic Patrol, 1950; "Education for the Eskimos" [1952]; E.M. Hinds, Welfare Teacher, Port Harrison to the Director of Northern Administration, 3 March 1952.

59   *Canadian Resources Bulletin.* no. 82 (22 October 1938).

60   PAC, RG85/836/2876/1, Report of Dr. K.F. Rogers, "General Medical Survey of Conditions of Eastern Arctic Eskimo as seen during the summer of 1938," Part "B", 14 October 1938.

61   See Jenness, p. 46, for a sampling.

62   PAC, RG85/892/9436, McKeand to Gibson, 26 October 1938.

63   PAC, RG85/815/6954/1, Medical Report of Dr. J. Bildfell, 1934.

64   Ibid.

65   Ibid., Report of Dr. A.L. Richards, Special Medical Investigator, Eastern Arctic Patrol, 1 October 1935.

66   Ibid., Summary Report on Natives Health, Eastern Arctic Patrol, 1939.

67   See ibid., Report of Dr. John McCrombe, March, 1944, "Survey of Medical Conditions Among the Eskimo People of the Eastern Arctic and More Particularly Those of Hudson Strait."

68   Ibid., Reverend A. Steinmann to T. Manning (?), September, 1943.

69   PAC, RG85/815/6954/3, McKeand to Gibson, 5 February 1942.

70   Ibid.

71   Ibid., Dr. Ross Millar, Medical Assistant to Deputy Minister of Pensions and National Health, to Under-Secretary of State for External Affairs, 8 April 1943.

72   PAC, RG85/1871/550-1/1A, McKeand to Gibson, 25 October 1943.

73   Ibid., Gibson to McKeand, 26 October 1943.

74   Ibid., McKeand to Gibson, 28 October 1943.

75   Ibid., "Policy respecting the operation of hospitals in the N.W.T., Precis for N.W.T. Council, 1 March 1943; see also, ibid., A.L. Cumming to Gibson, 16 March 1937.

76   PAC, RG85/863/8276/2, Meeting re. Eastern Arctic Medical Service (draft), 13 November 1944, pp. 22-23.

77   PAC, RG85/1871/550-1/1A, "Policy respecting. . . N.W.T.," March 1943.

78   Ibid., Minutes, N.W.T. Council, January - February,1944.

79   PAC, RG85/863/8276/2, Report by J.L. Robinson concerning Diphtheria ("Septic Throat") Epidemics, 1944, 20 September 1944.

80   See: ibid., Preliminary Report of 1944 and Recommendations for the Administration of the Canadian Eastern Arctic, by J.L. Robinson, 20 September 1944; Recommendations of Major P.D. Paird, Second in Command, Eastern Arctic Patrol (1944), [n.d., received 14 November 1944]. PAC, RG85/863/8276/3, Medical Report of Dr. Dennis Jordan, Eastern Arctic Patrol, 20 September 1944; Report of Dr. George Hooper, Eastern Arctic Patrol (1944), 8 November 1944,

81   PAC, RG85/1871/550-1/2, Privy Council decision, P.C. 6495, 12 October 1945.

82   Memorandum from Welfare Division, Department of Northern Affairs and National Resources, 31 October 1962, as cited in Jenness, p. 89.

Health Care Devolution to Canada's Territorial North

Geoffrey R. Weller

1 Introduction

The concept of devolution in the Canadian context involves processes of both constitutional and administrative development for the 45% of Canada's total land area that remains in federal hands, namely the Yukon and the Northwest Territories. However, the term "devolution" conjures up the wrong imagery in most minds. It is often thought of as implying a greater regional control or influence within a fully established state structure. In fact, the process taking place in Canada might be more appropriately thought of as one of "decolonization" for Canada's northern territories have long been internal colonies.[1] In short, Canada is a country still in the process of completion and not in the process of decentralizing to a northern "region."

Devolution in the Canadian context has a constitutional aspect. This is the effort to increase the span of control possessed by the governments of the two territories and to give them greater freedom from the control of the political centre, that is, Ottawa. It was often assumed that this process of constitutional development would eventually lead to the formation of two additional provinces. It was only a question of time before the population levels and the degree of economic development would lead to two additional units in the confederation much like the ones already part of it. However, the existence of large numbers of Native peoples in the two northern territories and their affinity for operating not as isolated individuals in the liberal-democratic context but as part of social collectivities led to the possibility that the additional political units might not be like the ones already a part of Confederation. Moreover, the relative cultural homogeneity of the Inuit north and east of the treeline in the Northwest Territories has meant that there is the possibility that it might be divided into two.[2]

Devolution in the Canadian context also has an administrative aspect. The process of devolution, or decolonization, involves the need for institution building to ensure that there is something to replace the central authority when it withdraws. Administrative units have to be established with the necessary financial resources, facilities and personnel. These units have to have control

189

over both the level and the type of services that they deliver and the operations they conduct. The process of decolonization could not take place, or certainly could not take place smoothly, if adequate consideration is not given to such administrative concerns. In Canada's northern territories the finances, personnel and physical facilities all belonged to an "outside" power, namely the federal government, and could have been unavailable to any new administrative unit within the territories.

This paper analyses one of the largest and most critical elements of administrative devolution or decolonization, namely that of the health care delivery system. It was one of the largest elements simply in terms of the number of people involved, the amount of money dealt with, and the number and dispersal of the physical facilities used. Certainly if the two territories were to eventually develop into provinces their health departments would account for nearly one-third of all expenditures and be the single biggest administrative units within their provincial bureaucracies. It was one of the most critical because health is a field of public policy which not only touches a vast proportion of any given population, but it is one about which most people have strongly held views. It was also one of the most critical because the institutions in place had clearly very nearly reached the limits of their effectiveness and yet were not bringing about the results desired in terms of morbidity and mortality statistics.[3] While there had been vast improvements in some areas the pattern of illness and death in Canada's northern territories resembled that of a third world nation.[4]

The chapter begins by discussing the likely advantages and disadvantages of the devolution of health care. This is followed by an examination of the policy context in which the issue was discussed and, in the case of the Northwest Territories, effected. The actual process of devolving health care in the case of the Northwest Territories is then analyzed in detail. This is followed by a discussion of the content of the health care devolution process in terms of finances, facilities, personnel, and structures. An examination is then made of whether or not the anticipated advantages or disadvantages can be detected in the policy outcomes of the devolution of health care. The chapter concludes with a discussion of the likely future for health and health care services in the Territorial north.

2 Health Care Devolution: Advantages and Disadvantages

The advantages and disadvantages of any devolution process relate to both political matters and to matters specific to the policy field in question, in this case health. The emphasis here is upon the second category of advantages and disadvantages, namely those related to the health policy field. The possible advantages will be discussed first followed by the possible disadvantages.

The major advantage of devolving health care services from the federal government to the Territorial governments would be that the system should be closer to the people served and be more likely to be sensitive and responsive to their wishes. The system established by the Medical Services Branch of the Department of National Health and Welfare to deliver health care to Native people was certainly not established to serve the specific interests of the territories either singly or jointly. The system was established to cover the whole nation and was indeed operated on a uniform system nation-wide that paid little or no attention to political boundaries or the varying needs of different ethnic groups. This is revealed in the consistency of its units across the nation, both in the territories and the provinces, and in the north-south system of connectors.[5] Clearly, the system was established with administrative convenience uppermost in mind not consumer satisfaction or participation.

The system that was established across the entire nation, both territories and provinces, developed largely in the 1950's and 1960's. The Department of National Health and Welfare, which had been established in 1944, had the responsibility for Native health transferred to it in 1945. In 1954 the Department created the Medical Services Branch (MSB) to oversee this responsibility and this marked the true beginning of what became an extensive network of health care facilities and services across the nation.[6] The MSB divided Canada into several major regions and established a system of north to south corridors. Within each three levels of care were linked. The first level of care was a network of nursing stations that had basic medical supplies and drugs, x-ray and basic laboratory equipment, an examining room and a few beds. They were staffed by from one to six nurses depending upon their size, which was itself dependent upon the size of the community they served. The secondary level of care consisted of small "zone" hospitals serving a number of communities with nursing stations. Typically they had 20-30 beds, more elaborate equipment, a more extensive nursing staff and 4 or 5 general practioners. They dealt with minor surgical matters, more complicated childbirth and more elaborate diagnosis than the nursing stations. The third or tertiary level of care was provided by major hospitals in the southern cities of Montreal, Toronto, Winnipeg, Edmonton and Vancouver. The MSB also came to arrangements with the Health Science centres at the major universities in these cities to provide some visiting staff to the zone hospitals and nursing stations. In addition the MSB developed an increasingly sophisticated system of communications between the elements in its system including an air evacuation system.[7]

At one level this system was markedly successful. When it was established the health care status of Canada's indigenous and northern peoples was appalling.[8] The system was the curatively oriented southern system adapted to northern conditions. It was clearly intended to have as rapid and dramatic an effect as possible on health status. The incidence of infectious diseases and infant mortality rates did rapidly decline. The situation now, while by no means as good as it is for southern Canadians, is a vast improvement. However, the system was very costly. Moreover, it was not one that was particularly sensitive to the needs of its clientele. It's imperative was really one dictated by the criteria of one group being applied to that of another.

A second major advantage of devolving health care services, at least in theory, is that the services would be delivered by people who are less likely to be "outsiders" and, therefore, were likely to be a reflection of either the population make up of the northern territories or, at least, of the values of northern residents. One of the major criticisms of the health system established by the Medical Services Branch was that it was delivered by the people of one race to the people of another. Moreover, the federal authorities were criticized for putting relatively little effort into training health care workers among the aboriginal peoples, except at the very lowest levels. In addition there was a high turnover rate among those who did serve in the north (among nurses in some regions it was more than 100% per annum)[9] and clearly the motivation for service in the north was in most cases either monetary or a search for adventure, not a long-term commitment to either the north or to Native peoples.

It is certainly the case that the aboriginal organizations in the Northwest Territories were motivated to support the idea of health care devolution because they believed it would allow them to have more direct control or influence over the health care system. They wanted a health care system that would be responsible, both organizationally and programmatically, to the needs of Native peoples. This is why they were so concerned to have Native groups directly involved in the transfer process.[10]

A third advantage is an essentially administrative one, namely that a single administrative region would replace a dual one. This should result in a greater consistency of approach and efficiency of operation. The dual system was the consequence of some services being delivered to territorial residents by the MSB and others by the territorial governments. After the creation of the MSB, territorial health systems developed steadily. In 1960 the Yukon Hospital

Insurance Services and the Northwest Territories Hospital Insurance Service Board were founded. At that time both of the two territories delivered insured services in some hospitals of their own. The YTG then slowly transferred its hospitals to federal control but the GNWT continued to operate its own facilities and in 1988 it operated four hospitals (Yellowknife, Hay River, Fort Smith and Iqualuit), the Inuvik long term care facility, 12 nursing stations and 1 public health centre. In 1970 the NWT joined the national medical insurance plan which ensured that all residents, both Native and non-Natives, could receive doctors services without direct cost to the patients or their families. The Yukon followed in 1972.

The desire to avoid a split administrative regime was evident when the federal authorities argued for a consolidation of services to their system in the Yukon in the late 1950's.[11] It was also evident when the GNWT argued for a health transfer to itself in the 1980's. The GNWT was motivated to push for such a transfer because they believed a single system would administer financial matters more effectively, would eliminate the effects of federal policies being imposed in the north such as hiring freezes, and would allow for the introduction of programs that would be more specifically suited to the needs of the NWT and not all of Canada. The GNWT also thought a single administrative regime would be able to respond more speedily to new health issues as they arose.

Fourthly, devolution, from the point of view of the federal Department of National Health and Welfare, had the advantage of allowing them to easily meet downsizing targets imposed by the federal government without significantly affecting the number of jobs available. Moreover, devolution also fitted in not only with downsizing, which was partly the effect of the Nielsen Task Force,[12] but also to the principle espoused by that Task Force in relation to the territories, namely that there should be increased delegation to the territorial administrations if only to simplify and rationalize the administrative structure.

A fifth and truly major advantage is often held to be that devolution would increase the likelihood of there being a reorientation of health care services away from the curative, high technology approach favoured by the federal authorities, and which many agree has nearly reached the limit of its effectiveness, to a more preventive low technology approach likely to produce better health outcomes, especially among the aboriginal peoples. While the MSB's operations did succeed in markedly reducing the rate of infectious diseases and improving health care status on the usual indicators of morbidity and mortality the rate of improvement has slowed markedly in recent years and doubt has arisen as to the utility of pouring additional amounts of money into a system that is experiencing diminishing marginal returns. In addition, it is argued that the pattern of illness and death has changed significantly and in a way that the current system is not equipped to deal with.[13] Infectious diseases have been replaced as the major killers by suicide, accidents and violence, many of which are alcohol or drug related and all of which are a reflection of a life of poverty, hopelessness and, indeed, desperation. A curatively biased, highly technological, doctor dominated system is not well equipped to deal with such problems. In fact, no health care system is likely to be as these are not "health" problems but problems (or more accurately symptoms) of social and economic disorder. However, a preventively-oriented health system, involving its clientele and well linked to social services as well conducting extensive educational programs directed at affecting lifestyles, is likely to have somewhat greater success.

Associated with the possible reorientation of the health care system from a curative to a preventative emphasis was the additional hoped for advantage that local control would lead to a greater integration of health care services with other local agencies such as those that dealt with housing and welfare. The new pattern of illness in the north indicated that such linkages were increasingly necessary as it reflected generalized social problems rather than health problems per se. Experience in the NWT and elsewhere has been that such linkages tend not to occur in the higher reaches of the various systems and that, therefore, a better approach might be to try and link them at the community level. As far as the GNWT was concerned this also fitted in well with its concept that each local community constituted what it called the "Prime Public Authority."

One of the disadvantages of health care devolution might be that it would result in a health care system that would be too small to be efficient. It would have to cover a very small, very widely scattered and very variegated population and would be unable to achieve economies of scale or achieve a significant research capacity. It must always be remembered when discussing the territories that they have very small populations. The Yukon only has 30,000 and the Northwest Territories only 50,000, far smaller than even the smallest of the provinces. These populations are scattered over vast tracts of land (the Northwest Territories is as big as Europe from Lisbon to the Ural Mountains) in very small communities sometimes only numbering a few hundred. Moreover, the population is very variegated and each segment tends to have widely differing health care needs and expectations. However, this having been said, it should be noted that this is not a condition that is specific to health care services, it is true of nearly all areas. But the fact remains that

194

being part of a nation-wide system had economies of scale unlikely to be achieved with either one of the territories.

A second disadvantage of health care devolution could flow from the first. That is, the system's small size would make it easier for it to become controlled by a dominant professional group such as physicians or the administrators. It might then become responsive to their wishes and not those of the clients thus detracting from one of the possible advantages, namely greater responsiveness to the population served. All areas of public policy are liable to penetration and control by a professional group rather than by a client group or by politicians. Very clearly health care systems in most of the world, and certainly in Canada, have been dominated by physicians. The structure of the system and the kind of services it concentrates upon are a clear reflection of this. Even if the physicians do not have predominant influence it could well be exercised by the health administrators who, even in the south, seem to be achieving greater relative prominence. The likelihood of real control being exercised by lay clients is slight as they have, by definition, little expertise and little direct control and, even if they did, are likely to be influenced by others because of their lack of expertise.

A third potential disadvantage of health care devolution is that the resulting system might be less able to reorient itself from a curative to a preventive approach even if it is more responsive to the client population. This is because the client population has yet to be convinced that it needs a more preventive approach. There are clear indications that, as elsewhere in the nation, high quality care, which is what is wanted (but may not be needed) is associated with curative not preventive approaches to health care. Thus it is quite likely that the client group will pressure for what they want, namely more of the curative services they see southerners getting in greater abundance than themselves.[14]

A fourth possible disadvantage of the devolution of health care is that it would be a devolution of authority to only a partial government and one without full constitutional powers. Thus there would not be what might be termed full "back-up" services from a complete civil service as is the case with federally delivered programs. For example, it would be unlikely to have much of a research capability.

3 The Policy Context of Health Care Devolution

The policy context in which the idea of health care devolution is discussed can determine whether or not it actually takes place, and if it does, the speed of the process and the precise content of what is devolved. Clearly, the policy contexts were quite different between the two federal territories as health care devolution has already taken place in the Northwest Territories and has not yet done so in the Yukon. This reflects very different situations and policy agendas. In this section the different policy contexts will be discussed beginning with a brief discussion of the differential experience in the two territories with areas of authority previously devolved. This will be followed by analyses of the other devolutions going on at the same time in each territory, the different nature of approaches to provincial status and to the concept of regional government, and the different nature of the land claims process. Finally, there will be an analysis of another important contextual factor, namely the belief among many observers that the largely federal health care delivery system had reached the limit of its effectiveness.

The devolution of health care services should be briefly placed in historical context. Firstly, it should be noted that there had been changes in the federal system after its establishment in 1954 which, while not devolution as such, set the stage for it. In 1974 the northern region of the MSB was divided into the Yukon Region and the Northwest Territories Region. Then, in 1980, the headquarters of the Northwest Territories Region was relocated to Yellowknife from Edmonton. Secondly, experiments in partial transfer did occur in the NWT before the full transfer in 1988. These preliminary stages will be discussed in greater detail later. Here it will just be noted, firstly, that in 1982 the federal hospital in Iqualuit was transferred to the GNWT, which created a regionally representative Board of Management to operate the hospital and, secondly, that in 1986 all the nursing stations and regional public health were transferred to the GNWT, which created a Regional Board to deal with these issues. These preliminary transfers were followed on April 1st, 1988 with the full transfer which involved two more hospitals (Inuvik and the cottage hospital in Fort Simpson) and the remaining nursing stations in the Central and Western Arctic.

Administrative devolution has been ongoing over the past several decades in both the Yukon and the Northwest Territories . There have been periods when the number of devolutions or transfers have been more numerous than at others. The periods of most rapid expansion have been between 1959 and 1962 and between 1975 and 1979. However, the tendency towards devolution received a boost in 1985 with the election of a Progressive Conservative government. The new government was more sympathetic than previous ones to the granting of more province-like powers to the territories, perhaps as compensation for the territories relative loss of constitutional status and potential greater loss in the future, and perhaps because of a genuine interest in

196

moving the territories to provincehood. The GNWT no doubt thought it had a four year opportunity to move through several devolutions and if the government should change thereafter a new government would have difficulty reversing the trend. The GNWT thus gave priority to devolution[15] and had discussions with a sympathetic new DIAND Minister, David Crombie, which resulted in a method of jointly identifying eligible areas for transfer, a manner of negotiating the transfers, and central coordinators within DIAND and within the GNWT. In 1985 the GNWT set up a Devolution Office as part of the Executive Council Secretariat to coordinate its side of the devolution process. The GNWT gave assurances to the Native organizations by preparing a Memorandum of Understanding which stated that no agreement would be concluded in an area likely to affect land claims without their consent and which offered the Native organizations a role in the transfer process itself.[16] This led to the transfer of all remaining health care services (after the Baffin transfer) in 1988.

The attitude of the Yukon Territorial Government to devolution in general was and is different from that of the Government of the Northwest Territories. Both constitutionally and politically, the Yukon considers itself to be in advance of the Northwest Territories and has, therefore, paid less attention to specific program transfers. The current attitude of the Yukon Territorial Government to health care devolution is also very different from that of the Government of the Northwest Territories. This is because there was an abortive attempt at health care devolution in the Yukon in 1978. Throughout the 1970's the YTG grew increasingly critical of the federal government's handling of health care. It argued that a chronic shortage of public health nurses had developed, that there had been too much attention paid to the health of Indians and that the YTG had little influence over the nature of the health care system. By the mid 1970's the federal authorities came around to agreeing to organize a transfer of all health care services on the condition that the Yukon Native Brotherhood was a party to the agreement. In October, 1977 the YTG gave approval in principle to a transfer and the target date was established as April 1st, 1978.

It should be noted that this call for devolution on the part of YTG came after it had previously transferred some responsibilities in the other direction, that is, to the federal government. The population of the Yukon expanded rapidly during World War II and for a time thereafter. This led to an expansion of territorially delivered health care services. In the 1950's the federal government made the point that it would be more rational to have a single health care delivery system for such a small total population rather than a federal one for the Native population and a separate territorial one for the non-Native population.[17] Resources could be pooled and overlap eliminated. A polio epidemic in 1953 revealed the weaknesses of the dual system and in 1954 the Yukon Territorial Council gave approval for a unified health service under federal control.[18] On April 1st, 1957 some territorial services were transferred to the federal government. In 1959 the federal government largely financed a new hospital in Mayo. In 1962 all remaining territorial services were transferred and in 1970 both the Mayo and the Dawson hospitals became federally administered.

The reverse transfer scheduled for April 1st, 1978 began unravelling in February of that year. This was because the Yukon Native Brotherhood indicated to the federal government that it would no longer agree to the transfer. The YNB gave several reasons for its change in position. They stated that there was not widespread support for the transfer in the Indian communities. They argued that the YTG was not a sufficiently mature government and might not be able to fairly administer a health care system.[19] They also feared that most health care personnel would not want to join a territorial public service and would leave the Yukon, thereby leading to a deterioration rather than an improvement in health care services. The YTG argued that it would offer certain guarantees to the Natives and design programs specifically for Native communities, but to no avail. Because the YNB would not agree to a transfer the federal government withdrew from any further discussions on the matter.

The policy context between the Yukon and the Northwest Territories was also different in terms of the way in which provincial status was being pursued. The Yukon was clearly politically more advanced than the Northwest Territories and did not suffer from the possibility of division. Thus the YTG had no reason to push the devolution process. In the Northwest Territories there was a possibility that attempts to divide the Territory between Denendeh and Nunavut might be revived. This possibility was a clear motive for the GNWT to push for the rapid devolution of areas such as health which affected many people. The GNWT wanted to be seen as a unit that could efficiently provide useful services to the population. It wanted to enhance its legitimacy in the eyes of the population in case the issue of division again came to the forefront. In fact, many of the Native groups regarded the push for devolution on the part of the GNWT as precisely a rush to get responsibilities in the hope that it would help stave off the possibility of division.

A further complication affected the policy context in the NWT which it did not in the Yukon. This was the move to enhance regional government in the NWT. This had a direct effect on health devolution because it affected to whom powers would be devolved. Would they largely be devolved to the GNWT in Yellowknife or to regional bodies? The Native organizations saw regionalization as a mechanism by which money and responsibility would be channelled through the GNWT to the regional bodies where the Native organizations would have a great deal of influence. Thus they were suspicious of the GNWT's development of the concept of the "prime public authority" because it implied a direct dealing between the GNWT and each community thus by-passing the regional organizations.

At the time that health care devolution reached the policy agenda in the Northwest Territories and was being mooted in the Yukon there were a number of other policy areas also being devolved. Thus although health was a large transfer it was only one of many going on at the same time. However it, along with the forestry transfer, was so time consuming that it did detract from the others. The GNWT, in fact, was able to complete fewer transfers than originally anticipated because of this.[20]

Another element in the policy context at the time of health care devolution was the prominence, if not pre-eminence, of land claims issues. Certainly in the Yukon land claims issues were preeminent and that is the reason that the health transfer has not yet occurred. The YTG has said clearly that it is more concerned with settling land claims issues and dealing with economic development than it is with the whole process of devolution. The attitude of the Council of Yukon Indians (CYI) matches that of the YTG. They have simply been too busy with land claims issues to pay a great deal of attention to devolution. Moreover, they seem to be more concerned with natural resource issues in general than with health care issues. Even though the attitude of the GNWT and the aboriginal groups there was somewhat different, neither really wanted the devolution of health care to detract from on-going land claims discussions but they were able to come to an accommodation.

4 The Process of Health Care Devolution

The health care devolution process in the NWT worked relatively smoothly. Unlike the earlier abortive attempt in the Yukon it enjoyed the support and participation of aboriginal groups (though at varying levels of enthusiasm) throughout. The process was relatively slow and was carefully staged in three parts over the better part of a decade with each of the first two stages being evaluated before the next stage was proceeded with. Thus the process was participatory, piecemeal and prolonged. Steering committees were formed in the final stage which worked deliberately and with care. The central devolution offices of both levels of government offered these committees and others useful assistance. This having been said, the role of personalities should not be forgotten. Key individuals in the GNWT, the aboriginal groups and the federal government thought that a devolved health system would produce not only a more efficient and responsive health care system for all northern residents but better health outcomes as measured by the usual indicators.

It should be noted at the outset that the process of health care devolution was performed within the context of purely administrative change. There was no legal change of status between the federal and the territorial authorities nor were there any legal changes specific to the health policy area. In view of the fact that the territorial governments are themselves emanations of federal legal authority the federal government was essentially shifting administrative responsibility for health from one element of its administrative structure to another. This observation is not to make light of the difficulties of such a switch or to deny the significance of the action but merely to place the parameters of the change in context.

It should also be noted early on that the process of health care devolution and, indeed, of devolution in general was piecemeal and evolutionary. There was no detailed overall agreement between either or both territorial governments and the federal government. Moreover, there was no timetable agreed upon between the parties. This was acceptable to all the parties. None showed any signs of wanting to establish a detailed plan for devolution with a similarly detailed timetable. It was also clear that although all of the interested parties in the GNWT were in favour of the devolution of responsibility for health care they wanted to "feel" their way towards the goal.

This having been said, both levels of governments did establish devolution offices. However, these were not offices that were in charge of the process, they were essentially advisory to the various units at each level of government that were involved in, or were likely to be involved in devolution. Moreover, they had responsibility for all of the devolutions and not just health. The GNWT Devolution Office, established in 1985, was technically advisory to the Assembly and Cabinet but it also provided detailed advice and some administrative support to individual Departments, such as Health. The GNWT Devolution Office even produced a fairly detailed guide or handbook for GNWT staff involved in transfers.[21] While opinions differ as to the value of the handbook there seemed to be general agreement that the role of the Devolution Office was a valuable one, especially with regard to generalizable matters that affected all Departments to some degree. Matters pertaining to a specific policy area such as health had to be dealt with in greater detail by members of the line Departments. Much the same can be said of the federal officials who advised the various federal government departments involved.

It was critical to the process of devolution that it have the support of aboriginal groups. Not only was this a common-sense requirement given the policy context, but it was also something the federal government erected as a stipulation given that it had the responsibility for non-insured benefits for Inuit and status Indians in perpetuity and given the prior experience of the abortive devolution of health in the Yukon. In the case of the Northwest Territories the support of the aboriginal groups was forthcoming and was largely maintained throughout, despite some reservations at times on the part of the aboriginal groups. Indeed, the initial support for the health transfer in the NWT came from the Inuit Tapirisat of Canada in 1980. That year the organization passed a motion calling for each community to have its health services provided by the GNWT. The GNWT was certainly not averse to this idea and approached the federal authorities concerning the matter.

The ITC's desire to have authority for health devolved led to the process of transferring just one small part of the system to the Baffin Regional Hospital in Iqaluit (Frobisher Bay) to the GNWT. The detailed negotiations for this transfer began in January 1981 and then, in the summer of the same year, the GNWT established a Board of Management that would assume responsibility for the hospital after the transfer. The Board of Management would operate the hospital on behalf of the GNWT and ensure a great deal of local input thus, hopefully, ensuring responsiveness to local needs. By December, 1982 the transfer was complete. The hospital then operated for two years and was evaluated. The evaluation was a positive one and stated that the transfer and the Board style of management was successful.[22] As a result of this positive evaluation the next stage was implemented by September 1986, namely the transfer of the nursing stations in the Baffin Region. These two stages were known as Baffin Phase I and Baffin Phase II. Although Phase II was a much larger operation the principle of maximum participation by aboriginal groups and those affected was preserved. This was done in the form of creating a broadly representative steering committee and three broadly representative working committees that practised wide-ranging consultation.

The Steering Committee was the key organization and it had a large membership that included the ITC, the Native Women's Organization, the Baffin Regional Council and the Baffin Regional Hospital Board as well as representatives of the GNWT and the federal Department of National Health and Welfare. This ensured that the Native groups felt that they had involvement and, indeed, ownership of the process and the outcome. The three working committees reported to the Steering Committee and dealt with the nuts and bolts issues of Personnel, Operation and Finance and Capital. Various Departments of the GNWT advised these working committees on their specialized areas and all were helped by the GNWT Devolution Office.

Another important aspect of obtaining and preserving the support of aboriginal organizations for health care devolution was agreement ahead of time on a regionally representative organizational structure to which authority for health would be passed by the GNWT when health care was devolved. In short, the aboriginal organizations had to be convinced that local and regional control was a real possibility. It became clear that the concept of regional control was the main reason that aboriginal organizations supported health care devolution at a time when they were also deeply involved in land claims and other issues. They gave their support at a difficult time as they believed they would benefit directly.

The experience of the Baffin Phase I and Phase II exercises led aboriginal organizations across the NWT to, by and large, give support to the transfer of health care throughout the NWT. The primary reason for their support was that the Baffin experience led them to believe that the Regional Boards that the GNWT was to set up in each region following the Baffin model and the broadly participating nature of the Steering Committee would give reasonable assurance that they and regional residents would have a large say in the fully devolved health care system. This idea of local or regional control over health care services also fitted in well with their concepts of self-government. The ITC gave full support to the transfer as did the Keewatin and Kitikmeot Inuit Associations and the Committee for Original People's Entitlement (OPE). The Dene Nation and the Metis Association of the Northwest Territories wanted guarantees concerning the process and the outcome in writing and argued for a formal Participation Agreement. The Dene Nation signed a Participation Agreement[23] on February 13th, 1987 but the Metis withdrew from discussions concerning the agreement and never did sign.

The Dene insisted on a Participation Agreement largely because they did not trust the GNWT. They wanted to ensure not only that they would be consulted and that responsibility would be further devolved to Regional Boards but also that the health devolution came within the Memorandum of Understanding on Devolution that they had signed with the GNWT and that it would not interfere with or prejudice the on-going discussions concerning self-government and land claims. The Metis did not agree with health devolution but they were unable to halt the process because of their legal and constitutional status, or, more accurately, lack of status. Thus after Baffin Phase II most of the aboriginal groups in the NWT gave their support either warmly or with reservations to the third stage of health care devolution, namely full transfer.

It was a critical factor in the health care devolution process in the NWT that it was a staged operation. Everyone of the participants in the process were nervous of the intentions of the others and the staging allowed each to observe both the nature of the transfer process and the result of that process. It allowed the Native organization to gauge whether or not the GNWT would allow significant Native participation in the process and give the hospital Board of Management and the Regional Board significant powers. It also allowed the GNWT and the federal authorities an opportunity to observe and evaluate whether or not a highly representative transfer process and management approach would lead to a reasonable degree of efficiency of operation. The demonstration effect of the successful smaller transfers in one region also enabled interested parties in other regions to see how it could be adopted or adapted elsewhere.

Another critical factor in the health devolution process was the interest and participation of individuals within a decentralized system. Such a system was dependent upon there being reasonably active and expert Community Health Committees in each community. The CHC's would not only be important elements in the system but would also form the units from which many of the representatives to the Regional Boards would be selected. The nature of the relationship between the CHC's and the health facilities and staff in each community would be very different from that which had existed prior to transfer and give the CHC's a greater influence and say. However, there was not a very strong network of CHC's before the transfer. In fact, many that had been formed under federal jurisdiction had become inactive.

This was the result of a combination of little attention being paid to them by the federal government and their being purely advisory or being confined largely to matters of environmental health. Therefore the GNWT Department of Health mounted a campaign prior to the full transfer to reactivate or reestablish CHC's where necessary. A series of workshops was held for the CHC's that did exist and efforts were made to establish new ones where they did not.[24]

One of the aspects of the devolution process that should be briefly noted was that once underway it involved remarkably little input from politicians at either the federal or the territorial level. At the federal level, Mr. Epp, the Minister of National Health and Welfare, was supportive and this support was clearly important, especially for the freedom of action it accorded the Director of the

MSB, Dr. Nicholson. At the territorial level few of either the territorially elected federal MP's or the members of the territorial legislature had much to say about the health transfer per se and certainly had little input to either the process or the details of the content of the process. Most of the public statements in the course of the health devolution process were made either by the leaders of Native organizations or by senior bureaucrats, with only a few coming from the two Ministers involved and very few from politicians generally. However, the politicians were largely sympathetic to health care devolution.

Although the views and actions of most politicians were not critical to the health care transfer, the importance of other personalities to the process should not be underestimated. In fact, the officials within both the GNWT Department of Health, the MSB, and other affected agencies such as the Devolution Office worked well together. In addition, despite many political and other differences among the members of the Steering Committees they by-and-large managed to put aside most of their differences in their efforts to reach the general outcome that they all wanted to see achieved.

While not without difficulties, as the next section will detail, the health care devolution process worked relatively well. In part this was because of the lessons learned in the earlier abortive Yukon health transfer. The key lesson being that it was absolutely vital to retain the support of aboriginal organizations. To do this they had to be assured that the devolution process was a participatory one and one that would, therefore, likely result in the creation of a new health care system that would treat all territorial residents fairly. Another lesson learned from the Yukon experience was that the devolution of health should be accomplished by a process that was slow and staged.

5 The Content of Health Care Devolution

The content of the health care devolution involves those topics that were discussed and resolved by the three sets of Working Committees, namely Finance and Administration, Personnel, and Operations and the three Steering Committees. The topics dealt with by each will be analyzed in turn.

The three Steering Committees established to discuss the detailed content of devolution were the Arctic, Inuit and Western Steering Committees. The Regional Director of the MSB and the Deputy Minister of Health of the GNWT were on all the Steering Committees. An official of the GNWT Devolution Office, Mr. Home, acted as the Secretary to all of the Committees. Each of the Steering Committees was otherwise representative of the major groups within each of the three regions. To take the Inuit Health Transfer Steering Committee as an example it included representatives of the Inuvialuit Social Development Fund, the Dene/Metis Mackenzie Delta Regional Development Council, the Beaufort Delta Conference Group, the Shihta Regional Council, the Inuit Hospital Advisory Board and the Town of Inuvik.

The Steering Committees were responsible for guiding and negotiating the preparation of all the appropriate documentation, coordinating the efforts of the Working Committees that reported to them and making the final decisions on issues that arose.[25] The work of these Steering Committees was obviously vital. It is fortunate that the prior Baffin transfers had set the pattern for discussions because there was the possibility of a variation in approaches that might have made the production of a single transfer document difficult. In the final result a single transfer document was drawn up. The discussions of the Steering Committees concentrated upon the broader issues, as would be expected. Prime among these were the issues of the degree of autonomy and the degree of authority that the Regional Health Boards would have. To focus these discussions the GNWT Department of Health developed a model Regional Health Board framework based upon the Baffin example.

The three Finance Committees had to identify all of the financial resources that should be transferred and assess their adequacy. In addition, they had to identify all of the properties affected, inspect them and value them.[26] In terms of the finances, everyone was reasonably confident that they could obtain an accurate estimate of the sums involved. The method by which this was obtained was by analyzing a five-year financial history of the finances of a particular region provided by the federal government. This document was used as a base line and it was assumed that staff costs were the authorized person years whether or not particular positions were actually filled and expenditures made. To this base a wide variety of adjustments were then made for all the likely reasonable cost variations. For example, it was clear that the Regional Board structure would entail additional expenditures and thus estimates were made to cover them.

Although the sums involved were large (the full transfer added $58.6 million or 7% to the total GNWT budget for 1988-89) everyone was confident that their estimates would turn out to produce adequate finances. This was largely because the Baffin Regional Hospital transfer ($3.1 million to the 1985/86 GNWT budget) had been accurate.[27] In addition, a special audit of the transfer of the nursing stations in the Baffin region (which added $3.8 million to the 1987/88 GNWT budget) indicated that the estimates made prior to that transfer had also been accurate. It should be noted that of the $58.6 million involved in the full transfer, $49.9 million was added to the expenditure base of the GNWT used for the calculation of formula funding from the federal government. The remaining sum was a payment to the GNWT for the administration of Indian and Inuit health care and is negotiable annually.

Discussions in the Working Committees on facilities were lengthy and complicated. For each building the cost of construction at the time of construction was obtained and the cost of any renovations added to produce the current cost of the building. Every building was then inspected by a team comprised of members from both the GNWT and federal Departments of Public Works to obtain an estimate of the number of useful years of life left, using the assumption that every building only had a life span of 25 years. The useful life left for each building was then averaged by region. The cost of replacing all the buildings at the end of their useful life was then made. This was then divided by the years remaining to get a yearly amount required and this was then transferred.[28] It should be noted that the property on which each building stood was also transferred to the GNWT. Any buildings that were in the process of renovation or construction at the moment of transfer would remain the property of the federal government until the work was completed and then additional calculations would be made and the buildings and property transferred. In addition to the building and land upon which they stood, all of the public property listed in the Health Public Property Register had to be taken into account. This included vehicles, equipment, food, linen, drugs and supplies on hand at the time of transfer.

The three Personnel Working Committees had to re-classify all the federal jobs to the GNWT system, counsel all affected employees and liaise with the unions involved.[29] This proved to be the most contentious and problematic area in the lead up to transfer despite the fact that both the federal government and the GNWT went to considerable lengths to assure employees that they would be treated fairly. Both said that one of their major concerns was employee well-being. All those who did not want to be transferred from the federal public service to that of the GNWT were to be given every opportunity for re-employment with the federal civil service. All those who did want to be transferred were assured by the GNWT that every precaution would be taken in relation to such matters as levels of responsibility and pay in the process of job re-classification. It should be noted that the task of re-classifying all the jobs to the GNWT's personnel system was a lengthy and complicated process. In addition, the federal government and the GNWT agreed that all those transferred had the opportunity to return to the federal public service with priority status for reemployment if they did not want to remain with the

GNWT. Clearly this was offered as an inducement to federal employees to make the switch.

. At the time of transfer most of the federal employees did change employers, including 85% of the nursing staff which was the single largest group. This was a pleasingly high percentage as far as the GNWT was concerned, especially in view of the fuss created by nurses just prior to the transfer. The idea of changing employers quite naturally created a lot of uncertainty despite the assurances provided by both governments.[30] The problems involved tended to become focused on the issue of union membership. Many nurses said that they would not sign on with the GNWT if they had to drop membership in the Professional Institute of the Public Service (PIPS) and become members of the Union of Northern Workers (UNW). In fact, a group of nurses even took the matter to court but their arguments were rejected by Justicc M. M. de Weert.[31] However, despite these concerns, most of the nursing staff did change employers as previously indicated. It should be noted that just prior to the date of transfer the federal government had difficulty replacing those who left because of the impending changes, although some say that the federal government didn't try very hard to replace them knowing that transfer was in the offing and the hiring problem would soon become one for the GNWT.

It is likely that most of the nursing staff eventually made the change because despite all the problems and uncertainties employment with the federal government was becoming less attractive and employment with the GNWT more attractive. The MSB was undergoing rapid change and with the Northwest Territories transfer, a possible Yukon transfer as well as the possible transfers south of 60° to Native self government the MSB was obviously likely to pass out of existence almost entirely at some point in the future. Thus there was as much, if not more, uncertainty with employment with the MSB as with the GNW Department of Health. At the same time the career path possibilities were getting better with the GNWT as it expanded in size. Moreover, it was also becoming a more sophisticated and responsible employer as the various transfers proceeded.

The difficulties with the nurses looked as if it would be the only major problem area in personnel terms until just a few months prior to the April 1st, 1988 full transfer. However, in February of 1988, the GNWT announced a Transfer Policy that caused a great deal of upset.[32] The newly announced policy called for those people who worked in the field of personnel, public works and the like within the federal health care system to be transferred not to the GNWT Department of Health but to the appropriate line department, such as Personnel or Public Works. The members of the Regional Boards and the major Native organizations saw this as a move deliberately undertaken to reduce the significance of Native participation and reduce the span of control of the Regional Health Boards. Some of the Native organizations said the policy indicated bad faith on the part of the GNWT, especially since the policy was not going to be applied ex post facto to the Baffin Region.[33] The GNWT said the policy was not intended to reduce the influence of the Regional Health Board and was, in fact, intended to help them since they would not have the capability of dealing with a wide range of personnel when only very small numbers would be involved in each category. However, officials of the GNWT did agree that the timing of the announcement, though they said it was accidental, was not the most appropriate.

The three Operational Working Committees had to identify the level of health services to be transferred, define the residual responsibilities of the MSB and identify the monitoring data for non-insured health benefits.[34] This was not a particularly easy set of tasks. The two levels of government possessed different types of programs prior to the transfer. The federal government's services such as community health programs in relation to nutrition, careers, environmental health, dental health and communicable disease control had to be blended at an appropriate level with the GNWT's medical and hospital insurance programs and programs in the area of pharmacare, family life education, health information and promotion, and physician recruitment. This adjustment was made with little rancor although some personnel were not happy that some of their programs were "messed with."

It was not particularly difficult to identify the residual responsibilities of the MSB but it was not very easy to decide exactly how to organize, deliver and pay for them. The residual responsibilities were largely those related to non-insured health services which are drugs prescribed by a licensed physician, prescribed appliances, optholmic services, dental treatment, transportation and alcohol treatment. However, they also included health services to federal employees, civil aviation medicine and health services under the Quarantine and Immigration Act. It was decided that non-insured health services could not be transferred to the GNWT but could be administered by them under the terms of a Contribution Agreement.[35] This agreement stipulated that the staff, offices and services would be provided by the GNWT with the federal government paying for them. In other words, the GNWT would become the administrative agent for the federal government. As such, it would have no role in determining the nature and level of services to be provided, this would be decided by the federal government in consultation with Native organizations. The consultative arrangement was specified in the Contribution Agreement and consisted in a committee in each of the region broadly representative of the Native groups but also including a representative of the GNWT Department of Health and chaired by a federal official. It should be noted that the sums involved in the area of non-insured health services were sizeable, they were $22.3 million in 1989/90.

6 The Policy Impact of Health Care Devolution

The policy impact of the health transfer can very broadly be divided into two areas. The first is its impact upon health policy outputs and health status, that is its impact upon the health system and health. The second is its impact upon the two governments involved, namely the GNWT and the federal government and especially upon the two line departments offered, namely the GNWT Department of Health and the Department of National Health and Welfare or, more specifically it's Medical Services Branch. While it is somewhat early to be able to assess some of the policy impacts it can be observed whether or not the new arrangement is likely to have an effect.

The transfer has created a more unified system and one that should result in a greater focus of attention on problems specific to the NWT. While the federal government still retains real authority in non-insured services the GNWT does administer them and have some say in what they will be. This means that the focus of the GNWT Department of Health will be upon a broad range of health problems specific to the NWT. Under the previous federal system the MSB had to deliver services to both of the territories and south of 60° in most of the provinces. Clearly then the MSB's main focus was not just the NWT. The new devolved health care structures incorporate a Territorial Health Board that has the role of ensuring that public participation in both policy and management continues to have a territorial-wide focus, that is, it is charged with maintaining reasonable equatability as between regions in terms of facilities, services and standards.[36] This is done both for its own sake but also to stop each of the Regional Boards competing with each other over staff and other matters.

This greater NWT focus within a more unified system is to some degree reflected in the stated intention of the Minister of Health and the Department of Health to provide more health services and have more health facilities in the GNWT.[37] This is coming to fruition as there is a significant upgrading of the Stanton Yellowknife Hospital being undertaken and the construction of a boarding home for Inuit in Yellowknife. Clearly the intention is to replace the multiple north to south referral routes that existed before transfer to a referral route that will see most patients going to the Stanton Yellowknife facility. It is likely, therefore, that in time other facilities changes will occur such as the replacement of the use of the Churchill Health Centre in Manitoba with a small hospital in the Keewatin region of the NWT.

The transfer has created the possibility of greater local influence over, and control of, health care services. Implicit within this is also a greater degree of influence or control by Natives and Native organizations, which is why the Native organizations were in favour of health care devolution in the first place. The transfer has set the basis for this because of the regionalized nature of the system to which health care has been devolved. There are five Regional Health Boards in the NWT, the Keewatin, Kitikmeot, Mackenzie, Inuit and the Baffin. Each Board is broadly representative of the groups within each region and each of the Boards has major responsibilities in the planning, management and delivery of health care services, both medical and dental, and the operation of hospitals and nursing stations within their regions. Thus the Regional Boards are important administrative units. The GNWT has stated it is in favour of strong local control via these bodies because this is likely to make health services more responsive to both local and inter-ethnic needs and, thereby, improve the general level of satisfaction with them.

The Regional Boards are very representative of their regions. For example, the Keewatin Regional Health Board is comprised of one member from each of the eight communities in the region as well as a representative each for the Keewatin Inuit Association, the Keewatin Regional Council, the Churchill Health Centre Board, the Department of Health and Welfare (ex officio and non-voting), and the Northern Medical Unit of the University of Manitoba (ex officio and non-voting). The members are appointed by the Minister of Health from nominations made by municipal or band councils and the nominees have generally been members or chairpersons of Community Health Committees (CHC's).[38] Initially the chairmen were the GNWT Regional Directors (who no longer have line authority) but lay chairpersons have now been appointed following the Baffin model.

However, representatives of membership does not guarantee the desired outcome although it is a precondition. The local representatives also have to be individuals who are willing to work and gain a certain degree of expertise in relation to the health care system. Even if a willingness to work is present many Board members may have difficulty with actually performing the work as there is a situation of overload on capable local representatives. The general trend to regionalization and local control has placed a considerable burden on many people, especially the most active and able. Indeed, in our example of the Keewatin this was precisely why a number of the CHC's had become largely defunct prior to transfer. Admittedly the GNWT has recognized the problem and has tried to do something about it. They tried to revitalize the CHC's before the transfer with reasonable success and they did establish a training program for CHC members in co-operation with Arctic College. In addition, the Department of Health has prepared a trustee manual to help with the training of members of the Regional Health Boards.

The Regional Boards also do clearly have significant authority on paper. They will operate as autonomous managers of health program delivery as described in a master agreement between the GNWT and each of the Boards. They will each negotiate separate support service contracts with the GNWT service departments for the provision of direct and indirect services.[39] Each of the Boards has appointed a Chief Executive Officer (called an Executive Director in those regions without a hospital). While this is laudable, the fact remains that it is an inexpert lay group that will be attempting to control experts and, indeed, experts of another race. It is quite possible that the Chief Executive Officers may be able to dominate the Regional Boards because of their expertise. It is also possible that the physicians, or possibly another expert professional group such as the nurses, will come to dominate both the Regional Boards and the CEO's. Another possibility is that the Department of Health in Yellowknife might also impose its own administrative expertise eventually either via the CEO's or via the use of an extensive and uniform regulatory system imposed by the Territorial Health Board.

While local or regional control, if effective, should ensure that there is a much greater degree of Native influence and control all of the potential problems just cited could detract from such influence. Moreover, there will be a continual problem if influence or control is exercised by one racial group over those of another. While the structure being put in place is in theory, and hopefully in practice, a better one than what was there before, it is still inherently unsatisfactory. A satisfactory situation will only result when the services are provided by and administered by people of much the same racial and other background as those who are the clients of the system. Prior to transfer the efforts to train Native health care professionals were woefully inadequate both in absolute terms and in comparative terms with nations such as the USA. However, there are hopeful signs in the post transfer situation. The GNWT Minister of Health, Nellie Cournoyea, has stated "we expect to make inroads into the area of attracting Native people into health careers."[40] In the long run the NWT will only have a truly responsive health care system when that system is reasonably representative in terms of its composition of the population it serves.

The health transfer had a major impact on both the MSB and the GNWT Department of Health. For the MSB and, therefore, the Department of National Health and Welfare, the transfer meant a significant downscaling of staff and operations. It was clearly the predecessor of future transfers to the Yukon and to self-government units south of 60°. While the transfer meant that the DNHW could relatively easily achieve its downsizing targets the future prospects for the MSB led to morale and employment problems. It was clear that employment prospects with the MSB were becoming both uncertain and truncated, thus it became more difficult to attract people and more particularly good people. To some degree the sense of mission was adversely affected. In the early years especially, the MSB attracted some very highly motivated and able people because of its sense of mission. With the onset of the era of transfer the mission had not gone but was now linked to an obvious process of self-destruction of the unit in a relatively short period of time. As in any field it is especially difficult to find people who are dedicated to work themselves out of a job.

The impact on the GNWT was, of course, almost the reverse of that for the MSB. The transfer meant expansion, an enhanced career path for employees and a chance for some to try and put new ideas or approaches into effect. The GNWT Department of Health was restructured as 500 people were added to its staff.[41] A three column structure (Programs and Standards, Hospital Operations and Health Insurance Administration) headed up by chiefs[42] was replaced by a two column structure (Community Health and Standards and Institutional Health) headed up by Assistant Deputy Ministers.[43] It was argued that this structure would be better able to cope with a regionalized structure and the new responsibilities as well as the added staff.

Another significant impact of the transfer may well be in the nature of health policy itself. The concept of a more unified system for the entire NWT plus greater local control via the method of regionalization has always been linked with a desire to effect some program reorientation. Many of those involved in the health policy matters believe that the existing curatively biased, doctor dominated, hospital based, highly technological form of health care delivery has come close to reaching the limits of its effectiveness and also is not very likely to be able to successfully combat the new pattern of sickness and death in the north. The argument is that emphasis has to be shifted from curing infectious diseases to tackling chronic illness and a variety of essentially social pathologies and that this shift will require a more preventive set of measures and closer links with other social services. Such a shift is often advocated for Canadian society in general but it has greater applicability in the north given comparative morbidity and mortality statistics.

There are some efforts being made to effect a change in orientation in the post-transfer period. The nursing stations have been renamed "Community Health Centres" which, while it may not be of much practical significance, is of some symbolic importance. Here it should be noted, however, that the change of name was accompanied by the requirement that nursing staff would henceforth live in the community and buy food there like everyone else, rather than live in the nursing station and have their supplies provided separately. In addition, visiting specialists and the like will now stay in the community not at the nursing stations. Also the GNWT has stated its intention of placing a greater emphasis on health promotion and health education than was the case under the MSB. A new health education program is being developed and efforts are being made to increase the number of certain types of health care workers such as Community Health Representatives. While these are relatively small beginnings the stated intention is to build upon them and gradually effect a significant reorientation via the mechanism of enhanced local input in a regionalized system.

However, there are forces which are likely to impede progress toward such a shift in orientation. These forces are much the same as those likely to impede progress towards a greater degree of local control. It is quite likely that there will be professional resistance to a significant reorientation. As in the south it implies a change in the pecking order or power structure among the health professionals and the currently dominant professional, the physicians, are bound to be resistant. Many residents of the NWT have long been conditioned, as we all have, to think that the only true form of health care is that provided by doctors in hospitals. Consequently, there is a tendency to think that if such services are not readily available one is being short-changed. Thus even many tiny communities in the NWT feel they are being hard done by or discriminated against if they don't have a resident physician. It will take a lot of effort in the north as in the south, to reorient peoples attitudes and expectations. In addition, the GNWT Department of Health and the Regional Boards have taken over the facilities and programs developed under the older way of thinking and they represent sunk costs making it expensive and difficult to change them or add to them.

7 Conclusions

The health care devolution process in the NWT has set the stage for a potentially valuable reorientation of the health care delivery system and it has indicated that even in a policy field with a great many potential difficulties, reasonably efficient transfer can be effected. As such, it sets the stage for the future transfer of health services in the Yukon and may even provide useful lessons for how to deal with health care transfers south of 60°.

The health transfer in the NWT has set the stage for positive developments in health care. A more integrated system with a high degree of local input and input by Native peoples has resulted from the transfer. This, in and of itself, is a positive outcome but one which, as has been observed, is fraught with difficulties that could lead in time to the erosion of public or consumer input and its replacement by the dominance of "experts" or professionals of one kind or another.

The health transfer has also resulted in a system which may be able to reorient itself to better tackle the current pattern of health care problems in the North. However, that reorientation is also fraught with difficulties. Despite decades of fine phrases generally in Canada about the need to reorient the health care system very little has actually changed, as indicated by the fact that no greater a percentage is spent on broadly preventive approaches than was the case several decades ago. As has been observed even greater local or Native control is no guarantee that the needed reorientation will occur as the association of "health" with "curative" rather than "preventive" health services is widespread at all levels and among all groups in society.

In purely procedural terms the transfer worked remarkably smoothly given the potential pitfalls. The explanation for this in part resides in the fact that all the interested groups involved were convinced that a devolved health care system was likely to further their interests and, in so doing, improve health services and health status for all residents of the Northwest Territories . The slow, staged and experimental or fluid process managed to retain the support of most of the major policy participants largely by giving them a considerable say in both the process and the outcome and to observe in the first stages that what was intended did, indeed, result.

Notes

1   K. Coates, *Canadia's Colonies,* Toronto: James Lorimer, 1985.

2   See Geoffrey R. Weller, "Self-Government for Canada's Inuit: The Nunavut Proposal," *The American Review of Canadian Studies*, 18:3 (Autumn 1988), 341-358 and Gurston Dacks, "The Case Against Dividing the Northwest Territories," *Canadian Public Policy*, 10:11, 202-223.

3   See Geoffrey R. Weller, "The Delivery of Health Care Services in the Canadian North,"

Journal of Canadian Studies, 16:2 (Summer 1981) 69-80.

4   See John O'Neil, "The Politics of Health in the Fourth World: A Northern Canadian Example," *Human Organization,* 45:3 (Summer 1986), 119-128.

5   See Geoffrey R. Weller, "The Delivery of Health Care Services in the Canadian North," *Journal of Canadian Studies,* 16:2 (Summer 1981), 69-80.

6   Canada, *Establishment of Northern Health Services,* Memorandum to Cabinet by Paul Martin. Ottawa: Department of National Health and Welfare, October 12th, 1954.

7   This structure is described in A.P. Ruderman and Geoffrey R. Weller, *Report of a Study of Inuit Health and Health Services in the Keewatin Zone of the Northwest Territories 1980,* Ottawa: Department of National Health and Welfare, 1980.

8   See R. Quinn Duffy, *The Road to Nunavut,* Kingston and Montreal: McGill-Queen's University Press, 1988, Chapter 2 "Looking After Health" pp. 51-94.

9   See P. Ruderman and G. Weller, *op. cit.,* p.30.

10 See *Healthbeat,* 9:2 (Summer 1987), 2.

11 See Janet Moodie Michael, *From Sissons to Meyer: The Administrative Development of the Yukon Government, 1948-1979.* Whitehorse: Yukon Education, Libraries and Archives Branch, June 1987, p. 29.

12 Canada, Task Force on Program Review, *Improved Program Delivery: Health and Sports,* Ottawa: Supply and Services Canada, 1986.

13 See John O'Neil, *op.cit.*

14 This tendency is discussed in A. P. Ruderman and Geoffrey R. Weller, "Health Services for the Keewatin Inuit in a Period of Transition," *Inuit Studies,* 5:1 (Spring 1981), 49-62.

15 See Government of the Northwest Territories, *Annual Report 1985.*

16 Government of the Northwest Territories, Dene Nation and Metis Association of the Northwest Territories, *Memorandum of Understanding on Devolution of Power and Authority to GNWT from Canada with the Involvement of the Dene and Metis,* Yellowknife, 24th April 1986.

17 Janet Moodie Michael, *op.cit.* p. 29.

18 Ibid, p. 28.

19 Ibid, p. 99.

20 Interview with Mr Horne, Manager, Devolution Office, GNWT, 13th February 1989.

21 Government of the Northwest Territories, *Planning for Devolution: Principles, Process and Guidelines,* Yellowknife: Devolution Office, 1987.

22 Lynn Elkin Hall and Associates, *A Recommended Outline of the Devolution Process Based on the Baffin Health Phase II and Forestry Transfers.* Yellowknife: Lynn Elkin Hall and Associates, December, 1986, p. 10.

23 Government of Canada, The Commisioner of the Northwest Territories, and the Dene Nation, *Participation Agreement on the Devolution of Health Services within the*

Dene/Metis Settlement Area in the Northwest Territories, 13th February, 1987.

24 Interview with J. McGraw, 14th February 1989.

25 Government of the Northwest Territories, *Steering Committees.Transfer of the N.W.T. Region, Terms of Reference.* Yellowknife: GNWT, 14th January 1987.

26 Government of the Northwest Territories, *Administrative and Finance Sub-Committee, Transfer of N.W.T. Region, Terms of Reference,* Yellowknife: GNWT, 14th January 1987.

27 Government of the Northwest Territories, *Audit Report, Baffin Regional Health Board, Transfer of Health Care Responsibilities,* File 91-04-31-800, no date.

28 Interview with Mr Horne, Manager, Devolution Office, GNWT, 13th February 1989.

29 Government of the Northwest Territories, *Personnel Sub-Committee, Transfer of N.W.T. Region, Terms of Reference,* Yellowknife: GNWT, 14th January 1987.

30 See Hon. Jake Epp, *Notes for an Address at a Ceremony Transferring Responsibility for Health Care to the Government of the Northwest Territories,* Yellowknife, August 25th 1988, p. 5.

31 See *News North,* 25th April 1988, "Most Nurses Accept Job Offers."

32 Government of the Northwest Territories, *GNWT Transfer Policy,* Yellowknife: GNWT, 24th February 1988.

33 See, for example, Inuvialuit Regional Corporation, *Press Release on Transfer Policy,* Inuvik: Inuvialuit Regional Corporation, 30th March 1988.

34 Government of the Northwest Territories, *Operations Sub-Committee, Transfer of N.W.T. Region, Terms of Reference,* Yellowknife: GNWT, 14th January 1987.

35 Government of Canada and Government of the Northwest Territories, *Contribution Agreement,* Tabled Document No. 127-88(1), 7th April 1988.

36 See Government of the Northwest Territories, *Institutional Structures, GNWT Health System,* Yellowknife: GNWT, 6th July 1987, pp. 9-10.

37 The Hon. N. Cornoyea, *Address at the Health Transfer Ceremony,* Yellowknife, 25th August 1988, p. 4.

38 See J. Epp, *op. cit.* p. 6.

39 See Government of the Northwest Territories, *Institutional Structures, GNWT Health System,* Yellowknife: GNWT, 6th July 1987, pp. 7-8.

40 N. Cournoyea, *op. cit.* p. 4.

41 See Hon Jake Epp, *op.cit.,* p. 5.

42 See Government of the Northwest Territories, *Main Estimates, 1989/90,* Yellowknife: GNWT, 1989, p. 14-04.

43 Ibid, p. 15-02.

Part Three

Current Problems Related to the Northern Fourth World: Canada and the Nordic Countries

Current Problems Related to the Northern Fourth World: An Attempt at Comparative Understanding

Tom G. Svensson

Introduction

The *Northern Fourth World* includes all indigenous ethnic minority groups living in the Arctic and Sub-Arctic regions. For comparative purposes we tend to leave the native peoples of northern Siberia aside, concentrating instead on northern Fennoscandia, as well as Greenland, Canada and Alaska. Indigenous people in the latter areas are all part of nation-states characterized by western democratic traditions which makes systematic comparison feasible. There are, moreover, reasons for incorporating the Ainu in Hokkaido, northern Japan, in this delimitation, and, if the process of large scale political change continues in the USSR, we will no longer need this kind of separation of native peoples based on diverse political systems.

Having said this, it is obvious that a comparison between, e.g., native peoples in Canada and the nordic countries, referring to life conditions in modern times, could be a starting point in furthering our understanding and insight about the Northern Fourth World in general. This brief presentation, which should be viewed as a tentative commentary, intends to draw attention to a kind of research which is both interdisciplinary in approach and inter-cultural in empirical content and theoretic focusing.

A Note for Comparison

There are three independent variables which appear to be specially significant: one deals with *ecology*, another with *politics*, and a third with *legal conditions*. All three variables relate to the North-South axis, where the North in most instances is considered the home land for native peoples representing the *original* parties in ecological terms, the weak, more or less *powerless*, parties politically speaking, and, from a legal point of view, parties having their basic *rights* still *unresolved*. As I hope to demonstrate, the situation is as valid for the Nordic countries as for Canada.

Referring to *ecology* we can identify two contrasting factors, both leading to conflict having a detrimental effect on the life conditions of indigenous minorities. First, the development of non-renewable resources by the industrial society stands in glaring contrast to the traditional mode of extraction of renewable resources characteristic of native cultures. The second factor has to do with differences in land use patterns; the larger society uses the land far more intensively than native people traditionally do; most of the time the land use pattern of the latter is very extensive, demanding huge areas of land. Frequently, due to these differences in resource extraction, indigenous minorities lose ground; their ecological basis for cultural sustenance is gradually circumscribed, an irreversible process of change.

The above discussion views the ecological variable from one perspective only. In order to complete the picture, however, the creation of a great number of new opportunities for wage labor should be accounted for as well. In certain areas such opportunities are quite necessary if native peoples are to be able to remain in sufficient number on their home land and carry on their particular way of life. Because of the marked increase in production costs, far more cash than before is required to maintain an optimal adaptation based principally on a subsistence economy. This problem is in no way different for people who are occupied in hunting and trapping than for those with a pastoralist means of livelihood. This is the price all have to pay if they wish to continue being part of a culturally distinct way of life. On the other hand, the continued development of non-renewable resources, on which most wage labor opportunities are based, will render traditionally defined resource extraction more difficult, as well as more expensive. In other words, this shift of opportunity situation for native peoples must be connected to a penetrating cost and benefit analysis. Socio-cultural change, not only redirection of economic circumstances, must be subject to such a close calculation.

Turning to *politics*, what focal aspects concern us the most? One issue is central and in many ways superordinate to others; that is the one referring to *distribution of relative power*. It goes without saying that most power and influence over the Northern Fourth World is assembled and consolidated in the South of each nation-state. This state of affairs has become more or less a tradition which indigenous minorities have long had to cope with; it constitutes an essential part of their history. This means that decisions regarding many vital native concerns are taken by non-natives and very far from core regions of native habitation.

The distribution of power is, moreover, utterly imbalanced in the sense that indigenous ethnic minorities have no means of influencing life conditions of the majority society, whereas the latter is in possession of a huge structural apparatus through which decision making, both indirectly and directly, has a constant impact on native interests and circumstances. Despite their demands, the devolution of power, in terms of general decentralization, has so far not reached the aboriginal peoples of the North. Presently the Sami in both Norway and Sweden claim *veto power* concerning cases of exploitation caused by the industrial society, exploitations which may undermine their very cultural existence in particularly vulnerable areas. The Sami have so far been denied the right to veto, which means that the devolution of power is still more symbolic than real. The Sami Rights Committees, which currently are preparing new legislation regarding fundamental Sami rights in both Norway and Sweden, have demonstrated discrepant opinions in this respect; they are willing to allow Sami self-determination, viewed as a basic human right and founded on recognized aboriginal status, but in concrete matters, or in practical politics, the Sami are disallowed the right to veto concerning far-reaching ecological changes in their home land. This aspect of devolution of authority has been explored more thoroughly by Gurston Dacks relating to changing conditions in NWT and Yukon. (Dacks, 1990; see also Dacks' chapter included in this volume.)

From the problem of distribution of power follows *degree of self-determination*, i.e. the right for native people to decide as much as possible about their own affairs. Indigenous ethnic minorities have long been engaged in a process, without exception initiated by themselves, which aims at an increased degree of self-government crucial for their cultural survival, and, at the same time, the decrease of southern influence and involvement. This transfer of relative power, even though the process in most instances has been extremely slow, constitutes one of the most important aspects of socio-cultural change northern aboriginal peoples have experienced during the last 40-50 years. As this process of transformation has taken place at unequal rate, from culture to culture, I am more concerned about accurately defining the degree of self-determination than maintaining a simplified either/or position. Because absolute self-government still is very far from being realized in such a way as to fully satisfy the needs and aspirations of native people, the degree of self-determination must be determined empirically in each case. John Anderson has recently made an overview of the important question of self-government and native peoples in Canada and how it stands at present. (Anderson, 1991).

Bureaucracy is closely related to the above mentioned political aspects. The Sami, as well as most other northern indigenous peoples, have long been subject to extensive bureaucratization. To begin with, indigenous minorities become encapsulated as social units to be administered under terms and style determined entirely by the dominant society. Efficient bureaucracy in this sense affirms and reinforces the uneven distribution of power to the disadvantage of native peoples. In order to cope with the situation in an appropriate way, native people are both forced and inspired to adopt bureaucratic life styles and forms of social organization foreign to them. New expertise which mainly derives from the larger society and its educational opportunities is required. This expertise in various fields, such as economics, law, social work, education, agronomy, etc., must be attained at the same time as original cultural competence is maintained. *Dual cultural competence* is vital for indigenous people if they are to handle their administrative matters vis-a-vis the larger society and to shape their own bureaucracy in a culturally appropriate manner. This factor of competence building to meet new demands probably differs a great deal from culture to culture; however, it is a matter of increasing importance, especially in later years. Referring to the Inuit/Inupiat conditions in Alaska and NWT respectively, Knelson Daley in this volume argues firmly for the adaptive strategy of bi-culturalism covering the same phenomenon. (Knelson Daley, 1991; see also Svensson, 1988:81-82.) In a recent article for a special volume on education and cultural differences I have explored the problem of native competence building more fully. (Svensson, n.d.)

Aboriginal people, then, have to adopt their own bureaucratic style without losing their cultural uniqueness. While maintaining a clear cultural identity, they must simultanously aim to reduce as much as possible the negative effects of the encompassing bureaucratic apparatus of the larger society. It is most crucial to come to terms with this complex matter of bureaucratic duality in order to realize the ultimate goal of cultural survival despite constant pressure from the outside. The Sami, as well as many indigenous peoples in Canada I know of, are at present trying to remedy this socio-cultural dilemma. This is a road of no return, because without bureaucracy in both forms cultural sustenance becomes an impossibility in the complex modern world.

What is extremely important for native peoples, however, is the capacity to check and constrain the bureaucracy of the larger society which influences their internal affairs, thus avoiding the impact of tutelage from which most of these people have suffered for too long already. Consequently, the aspects of politics discussed are closely interdependent, and they all point toward cultural survival as the overall problem indigenous minorities persistently are facing and trying to cope with.

The third variable refers to *law*. Certain legal aspects can be isolated as particularly salient for indigenous minorities in their realization of cultural viability and continuity. The predominant factor in this respect is *aboriginal rights*, i.e. comprehensive rights based on distinct status, a kind of right which is reserved exclusively for people who claim to be, and are acknowledged as, aboriginal. Aboriginal rights are a set of two-dimensional rights; they comprise both *political rights* in terms of right to self-determination, and *legal rights*, mainly referring to the material basis of a culture, i.e. right to land and water. (Cf. Asch, 1984.) In itself, the factor of land is crucial for practically all indigenous ethnic minorities; it represents the core issue of cultural survival. All cultures, small and large, are anchored in a territorial base to which they belong; land, then, has definite meaning both in a real, materialistic sense and symbolically. This is the reason why native claims to land and water constitute the number one issue for so many indigenous people in the Fourth World at present. (Cf. Billy Diamond's key note address for this conference: Diamond, 1991.)

The question of *land rights* has to be determined in both legal and political terms; without clarification of these rights the indigenous minority will not acquire real *negotiation power*. Rights can never be obtained unless a party with opposing interests is confronted with the issue. The ongoing struggle for improved land rights, therefore, reflects a stage of profound confrontation between the majority society and various indigenous minorities encapsulated therein. And, the outcome of these efforts will to a large extent determine the capability indigenous minorities will have to sustain viable and distinct cultural units in the future.

A few years ago in a total confrontation between the Swedish Crown and the Sami in the entire South Sami region concerning ownership rights to what is named the taxed mountains, the Sami lost the dispute in specific matters but gained some important ground on principles.

The decision by the Supreme Court stated that the Sami are entitled to exclusive and firm usufructuary rights to land and water; these rights are considered to be equally strong as private ownership rights in regard to rights to compensation for losses caused by external encroachments, or in regard to protection of their land base. Moreover, these usufructuary rights are based on *immemorial usage* and *custom* and should in no way be perceived as privileged rights handed down by the state. Statements of this kind expressed by leading representatives of the legal system of the nation-state are extremely significant; it is the first time in Sami history that the Supreme Court makes a decision which both clarifies and gives ample specification to existing rights ascribed to the Sami as an indigenous minority. (HD, 1981.)

Because of such precise specification, the former ambiguity as to contents and quality of Sami rights has been eliminated, a change which will be most advantageous to the Sami in future cases of conflict of interests.

Rights to land is also a *human rights* issue, in the sense that belonging to a culture and taking part in its cultivation and continuity is a fundamental human right. Human rights, then, especially that part which is collectively enjoyed and exercised, are legal properties derived from international law having great implications for native people in their attempts to strengthen their position in terms of cultural and political autonomy.

And now I come to my final point in my discussion of legal perspectives, that is the one referring to *legal pluralism*, which is more instrumental and strategic in nature. Lasting gains can never be attained unless the argumentation and plea for improved conditions, which in most instances are highly justified, are shaped in a legal pluralistic framework. What we usually observe is a confrontation between two cultures, or rather between certain actors whose behavior and articulation, as well as identity, are reflected by clear difference in cultural background, and, furthermore, a conflict between two legal conceptions. In order to legitimize a claim, or even to open for an actual trial, a relevant section of *national law*, such as, for example, *the law of landed property*, must be fused with significant aspects of *natural law*. The latter consists of customary law paired with international law, in particular legal constituents embedded in human rights which have a definite bearing on cultural concerns.

The legal foundation of land rights for indigenous people, e.g., refer to: 1) *international law*, serving as an instrument for protection of the material basis of cultural maintenance; and 2) *customary law*, from which land rights claims can be defined as legitimate. In other words, *cultural distinctiveness* justifies legal claims of a special order, which otherwise are very difficult, or next to impossible, to make. Legitimate claims must be expressed in legal terms; references to *customary law* blended with significant sections of *international law* represent the juridical argumentation which can adequately translate legitimacy based on culture-political conditions into legally valid terms. In court, then, all substantial pleas and arguments must relate to core features of national law. On the other hand, referring exclusively to, e.g., the law of landed property, would make native claims very poor and most unrealistic; the establishment of a level of legitimacy, therefore, is rather compelling. Indigenous peoples are engaged in a process of adapting to the modern world and its new circumstances and I would go as far as to maintain that the strategy to acquire improved rights based on legal pluralism in a very broad sense is about to become part of *native culture*.

Summing up

What I have done in this brief account is to try to elucidate certain interconnected factors which are pertinent in Northern Fourth World situations. By means of breaking up each primary variable--*ecology, politics,* and *law*--into relevant elements, or essential building blocks, I hope to have demonstrated how these variables are interrelated. The superordinate objective, *cultural survival* under premises defined by the native people themselves, depends to a great extent on how well a given indigenous minority is able to adapt to pressing life conditions and environmental circumstances generated by its peculiar minority situation. Consequently, the interrelationship between the three primary variables derives its *meaning* from specific cases of native readaptation and management, where empirical variation as to form and contents can be determined. The tentative schema for systematic comparison in the Northern Fourth World just outlined should be viewed with this perspective in mind, i.e. it is a broad theoretical schema which aims to increase our understanding of a comparable but widely dispersed cultural reality.

Strengthening of aboriginal rights, viewed as highly comprehensive rights, is crucial for the realization of the ultimate goal of *cultural survival.* And the latter end can never be attained unless indigenous people in their continuous adaptation to the interrelationship between themselves and the majority, i.e. the nation-state, are able to shape and influence the interconnection between the three independent variables. Despite empirical variations in regard to vulnerability in ecological terms, command of natural as well as social resources, and choice of strategy, e.g. emphasizing one factor over others, the schema reflects generalities without which no systematic comparison is feasible. It is important to note that the adaptive process is never ending. The argument can be summarized in the following diagram.

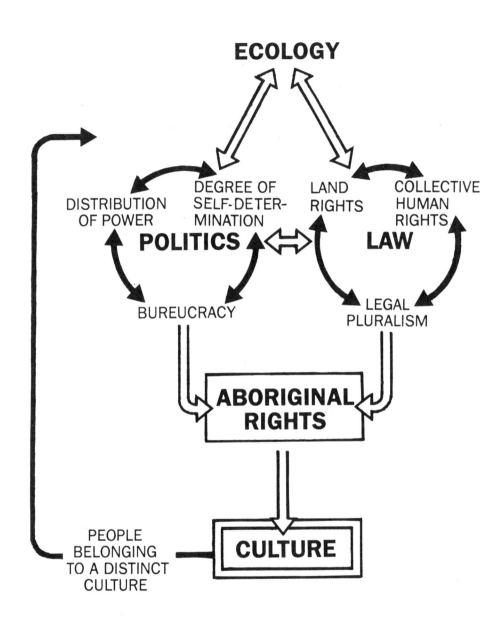

ECOLOGY

DEGREE OF
SELF-DETER-
MINATION

DISTRIBUTION
OF POWER

LAND
RIGHTS

COLLECTIVE
HUMAN
RIGHTS

POLITICS

LAW

BUREUCRACY

LEGAL
PLURALISM

ABORIGINAL
RIGHTS

PEOPLE
BELONGING
TO A DISTINCT
CULTURE

CULTURE

Tentative Scheme for Systematic Comparison of Adaptive Processes
in the Northern Fourth World

References

Andersson, J., 1991. "Self-Government and Canada's Aboriginal Peoples," NACS Text Series, Vol. 6.

Asch, M., 1984. *Home and Native Land* : *Aboriginal Rights and the Canadian Constitution.* Methuen, Toronto.

Dacks, G., ed. 1990. *Devolution and Constitutional Development in the Canadian North,* Carleton University Press, Ottawa.

Dacks, G., ed. 1991. "The Devolution of Authority from the Government of Canada to the Governments of Canada' s Northern Territories: Issues of Self-Determination," NACS Text Series, Vol. 6.

Diamond, B., 1991. "The Development of the North: Confrontation and Conflict," NACS Text Series, Vol. 6.

Högsta Domstolen, HD, 1981. *Dom Nr DT 2 Skattefjällsmålet*, Stockholm. The Court Decision is reproduced in B. Jahreskog, ed., *The Sami National Minority in Sweden.* Humanities Press, N . J .

Knelson Daley Pearson, N., 1991. "The Impact of the Development of Non-Renewable Resources in the Canadian and American Arctic on Inuvialuit and Inupiat Women," NACS Text Series, Vol. 6.

Svensson, T., 1988. "Patterns of Transformations and Local Self-Determination: Ethnopower and the Larger Society in the North: The Sami Case," in G. Dacks and K. Coates, eds., *Northern Communities: The Prospects for Empowerment*, Boreal Institute Occ. Publ. Nr. 25, University of Alberta, Edmonton.

Svensson, T., n.d., 1988. "Education and the Struggle for Adequate Cultural Competence in the Modern World: The Sami Case," in D. Poonwassie and D. Ray, eds., " Tomorrow can be Better: Education and Cultural Differences" (in press).

Self-Government and Canada's Aboriginal Peoples

John Anderson

Introduction

Aboriginal self-government has become one of the major issues for first nations in Canada. It has also become a key element in the continuing debate on constitutional change in Canada. This paper attempts to give an overview of this crucial topic and to explain the relevance of self-government to the wider constitutional crisis after the failure of the Meech Lake accord.

At the end of July 1990, a rally was organized in Oka, Quebec, by the Assembly of First Nations to support the demands of the Mohawk people of Kanesatake for recognition of their nearly three centruries old claim to land at Oka, Quebec. At the rally, there were representatives from many of the first nations of Canada. One of the chiefs present was Max Gros-Louis of the Huron nation, historically an enemey of the Mohawks, but here to show solidarity with the demands of a fellow first nation. When I witnessed him interviewed by a television crew from France, Chief Gros-Louis was asked why the native people had still kept up their demands for land claims and a distinct status in Canada? Why had they not integrated with the rest of Canadian people? Gros-Louis replied that the question should rather be framed why had the Europeans not integrated with the indigenous peoples when they came here? "When I go to your country, France, and I have been there over twenty times, I speak French, and adopt your customs and laws." One could not ask for a better statement of why self-government is such a necessity for the first nations of Canada.

Most of mainstream Canadian political science, economics and history has exluded or marginalized the study of Canada's first nations. Most general works, with a few important exceptions, either leave out completely the role of the first or indigenous nations, or reduce their place in Canada's history to their involvement in a series of early wars and to their role in the so-called Riel Rebellions. Very little has been written in an integrated way of the role of native political systems in pre-European Canada or the continued history of

229

those societies after the European colonization. And what little has been written is generally from the last ten years and is often viewed as a separate field which is not integrated into Canadian social sciences. In the past, only a few historians such as H.C. Pentland, have told the true story of white enslavement of aboriginal people in New France, or like anthropologist Diamond Jenness even written about the diversity and depth of the culture of Canada's first peoples.

The perspective has been, in general, that of, as Abele and Stasilius have pointed out, presenting Canada as a white settler colony where the first nations only rarely intervene in the study of Canadian politics, history and society. Canada, from this perspective, is seen as essentially different from South Africa or Mexico because aboriginal people in Canada are now only a minority! In a recent article, in *The Toronto Star* ("Indians Reject View of History," Aug. 4, 1990), two prominent Indian intellectuals were asked to list the historic dates they thought as of most significance for aboriginal peoples. Their choices which included the Royal Proclamation of 1763 also included the arrival of corn and beans in the eighth century. Both events, I am sure, would be unknown to almost all of Canada's white population. For example, in the eighties, one of the principal textbooks in Canadian political science used for many introductory courses at the university level contained only four pages where aboriginal people were even mentioned; and most of this was to relate the economic situation of aboriginal people.

But recent struggles of aboriginal peoples and the more widespread broadcasting of the truth about the situation of Canada's aboriginal peoples has forced, and is forcing, a drastic revision of our previous views of many aspects of how Canadians of European origin view the past and the future.

To situate the present state of steps towards self-government for Canada's first nations requires, first of all, putting into perspective some of the important changes which are taking place as far as the political and economic situation of Canada is concerned.

First of all, in political terms, there has been the whole Meech Lake process, and its final failure in June 1990. The aboriginal opposition to Meech Lake, and the process which has brought it about, as has been said many times, was not a rejection of Quebec but rather a rejection of yet another constitutional accord which failed to recognize and entrench aboriginal self-government. Aboriginal people wondered aloud how Quebec could be recognized as a distinct society, and one of the two founding peoples, when they were excluded from any special status.

The failure of Meech has meant that, as far as Quebec is concerned, the already growing movement for a new relationship with the rest of Canada has been accelerated. The goals of this movement range from a version of sovereignty association (or in other words some much looser form of federation) to outright independence. The provincial government is proceeding to establish an anlarged parliamentary committee which will conduct hearings throughout the province, elaborate a new constitutional proposal and present it to the government by March 1991. In the West, the governments of the four western provinces have recently met in Lloydminster, Saskatchewan and have elaborated a series of proposals including collection of their own income tax, and other forms of increased autonomy from Ottawa.

Secondly, there has been the ability to judge some of the first real effects of the free trade agreement signed in January 1989 between Canada and the United States. The net result of this agreement so far has been the loss of some 105,000 manufacturing jobs mostly in Ontario and Quebec in 1989 alone (*Pro Canada Dossier*, June 18, 1990 p. 4) and a sure trend towards greater integration of the two economies. The free trade agreement has accelerated the trend towards a post-fordist economy based on smaller automated manufacturing units, service industries and greater flexibility.

Thirdly, there has been the move towards yet another free trade deal between United States and Mexico. This is a deal which, if it is consummated, will have a profound impact on Canadian economics. The United States is clearly moving towards some kind of North American (and perhaps even eventually the Americas') free trade zone as a counterweight to the 1992 end of tariffs in EEC (the Common Market).

Going into the nineties, the Canadian federation is then faced with seemingly contradictory trends. On the one hand, there is the centripetal tendency for greater regional autonomy and even independence for some parts of the federation. Only Ontario and some of the Atlantic provinces seem somewhat content with the constitutional status quo. But, even in the latter, the first talk for many years of economic, and/or political, union of the Atlantic provinces and even of possible political union with the United States, if Canada breaks up, has been heard. A recent poll in *The Globe and Mail* noted that 20% of people in Quebec and 15% in the rest of the country were favourable to Canada joining the United States if Quebec left. (July 9, 1990.) In the same poll, some 76% of Quebecers thought independence was likely or very likely and 46% of those in the rest of Canada agreed.

On the other hand, there is the centrifugal trend which sees Canada becoming part of a larger economic zone. As we all know now, with the Common Market economic union is the mother of political union, and it is only a matter of time, if the FTA remains as it is, when the nascent political structures which now are supposed to regulate trade disputes and which were created as a result of the FTA are enlarged.

And then there is the position of many, particularly in the Liberal Party, as represented by its old leader Trudeau and by the new leader Jean Chretien, who would like to see a return to a stronger federal government and stop the drain of power from the centre and particularly to Quebec. In the debate over Meech Lake Accord, Clyde Wells, the Premier of Newfoundland, probably best articulated this view of a strong central government treating all provinces equally.

On the left, particularly in the union movement and in such movements as Pro-Canada, yet another vision has begun to be elaborated by such spokepersons as Mel Watkins and Daniel Drache, who disliked Meech, in part, because they would like to see a more unified and centralized English Canada, but one which is willing to deal on an equal basis with a more autonomous or even independent Quebec. In other words, no more powers for the majority English language provinces, but a new relationship with Quebec.

A History of Betrayal

Any attempt for Canadians of European descent to understand the issue of aboriginal self-government must begin clearly with a re-definition of the historic relationship between Europeans and indigenous peoples. We must dispense with a series of myths that overlay our understanding.

Myth one: Canada's relationship with first nations was fundamentally different from the American approach.

While Canada perhaps did not send in the cavalry as frequently in the nineteenth century as the United States, military force was the final weapon in the occupation of the Canadian West as the outcome of the Northwest Rebellion of 1885 indicates. But more importantly, because Europeans in Canada are one of the oldest white settlements in North America we must remember that the use of force was not simply a nineteenth century phenomenon but that it began at a much earlier date. Witness the extermination of the Beothuk people in Newfoundland by the early nineteenth century or the French wars against the Iroquois in the 17th century.

But one must link the similarity of the relationship, between aboriginal peoples and white settlers in Canada and the United States, fundamentally to the denial of aboriginal rights including the right to self-government and the imposition of a colonial ruling apparatus. Strangely enough, the American government has for many years now recognized, at least in words, the right of self-government and has had, in many cases, a better recent record of recognizing aboriginal sovereignty.

Myth two: At the time of the arrival of the Europeans, the aboriginal people were primitive people, who had no government or state institutions and no understanding of democracy.

First of all, it is important to note that the colonial powers of Britain and France which stripped away the aboriginal right to self-government and seized aboriginal lands, were not democracies as we understand the term today. There was no universal suffrage in either country until after the First World War as women were excluded from the vote. Late seventeenth century France was an absolute monarchy, and Britain a monarchy with a very limited franchise for certain property-owning male citizens. The system of government of most aboriginal peoples was based on some form of consultation and usually some form of system of checks and balances. One of the most elaborate systems of aboriginal governments was the Iroquois or Haudenosaunee Confederacy which involved a formalized constitution, an important role for women and a federal system which the American Congress has recently (November 1988) acknowledged serveds as a model for American federalism. With the horrible total of deaths in wars waged by Europeans in this century as well as the European/North American advanced destruction of the environment, our claim to having a superior society of government institutions appears quite vacuous. (Purich 1986, Mitchell in Richardson 1989.)

Myth three: Indigenous peoples are relatively small in numbers and could not possible govern themselves.

After doing all in its power to reduce aboriginal numbers through genocide, slavery, famine and disease, white society turned to assimilation, cultural genocide, territorial deprivation and discrimination in the provision of virtually every main service of a civilized society, from health care to housing and education. Aboriginal language speakers have been reduced to only about 150,000. Life expectancy remains eight years less than the Canadian average. But Canada's indigenous peoples have refused to disappear.

Today there are some 444,000 status Indians and some 33,000 Inuit. (*Globe and Mail*, June 14, 1990.) This figure must be supplemented by the some 750,000 to over a million Metis and non-status Indians. (Purich 1986, Frideres 1988.) The situation of aboriginal peoples is, in many ways, similar to that of many small nations inside the Soviet Union who are demanding self-rule. The post-war independence movement has demonstrated that size in terms of population is no criterion for state status. Greenland which is home to Inuit peoples is already self-governing and is moving towards independence.

Self-Government: A Brief History

The political division of North America between the United States and Canada, and of Canada into different provinces and territories, is a purely white invention which has divided many indigenous peoples. Aboriginal peoples have always referred to the Royal Proclamation of 1763 as the basis for any discussion of first nation rights. This proclamation of the British crown in the pre-American revolution period notes that "the several Nations or Tribes of Indians with whom We are connected, and who live under our protection, should not be molested or disturbed in the Possession of such parts of our Dominion and Territories as, not having been ceded to or purchased by Us, are reserved to them or any of them as their hunting grounds." (Smith 1975.)

The Royal Proclamation is important in that it recognizes the right of native people to their land and deals with aboriginal peoples on a nation to nation basis. Land had to be purchased or ceded by aboriginal people in signed treaties in order to be claimed as no longer owned by them.

After that time, and, particularly after Confederation and the imposition of the Indian Act of 1876, the federal government ceased to deal with the indigenous as equal nations. Treaties that were signed were often not lived up to; large parts of Canada including Newfoundland, the Maritimes, most, if not all, of Quebec, Sothern Ontario, British Columbia, the Yukon and much of the far north were never covered by any treaties at all. (Frideres 1988.)

The British North America Act of 1867 accorded the specific responsibility for Indians to the federal level of government under Section 91 (24). The federal government later unilaterally developed this power in the Indian Act of 1876, amended in 1951 and 1985. The aim of the Indian Act was to maintain a colonial rule, reduce native people to marginal status and then to assimilate them. The Act was administered successively by the Department of the Interior until 1880; later after 1936 by the Department of Mines and Resources; in 1949 by the Department of Citizenship and finally by the Department of Indian Affairs and Northern Development. While showing the low importance attached to native affairs, this colonial administrative regime also demonstrated that in the eyes of white governments, native people were an obstacle in the way of the development of mines, natural resources and the North. The Federal government gave itself the power to define who was an aboriginal person, and what services, and the quality of services, to be offered to aboriginal people as second class citizens, who were restricted in their rights to vote and in many other ways.

By the late 1940s, the federal government after a Joint Committee of the Senate and House of Commons Report, began transferring powers for administering certain programmes to the provincial governments. (Boldt, Long and Litte Bear 1988.) In 1969, the Trudeau government White Paper (put out by Jean Chretien, the then minister) promoted the elimination of all constitutional and legal distinctions between Indian people and other Canadians. It was this report which galvanized the modern Indian movement into action. The massive Indian rejection of this clear attempt to force the assimilation inssue and the 1969 Nishga land claim case led to a breakthrough in terms of the 1973 recognition by the federal government of the existence of non-treaty Indian land claims and the principle of aboriginal title to land.

But since in inception, the process has been bogged down in federal bureaucracy in a deliberate attempt to slow down the process. Even *The Globe and Mail* recognizes that it has "limped along since its creation in 1973. It has stumbled into 1990 with some successes, a massive backlog and widespread unhappiness with its slow pace and inflexible rules." (*Globe and Mail*, Aug. 6 1990.) Only four comprehensive settlements have been reached since its inception: James Bay 1975, Northeastern Quebec 1978, Inuvialuit 1984 and Nunavut 1989. One expert recently estimated that as the federal government only handles six land claims at any one time and there are hundreds pending, it would not be until some two hundred years before all the cases would be dealt with in court!

While this breakthrough over land claims appeared more promising at the time than it later turned out, the next period, from 1981 to 1987, involved the attempt to have aboriginal rights entrenched in the new Constitution. The issues of land and self-government are obviously linked together in a symbiotic relationship. Bowing to provincial pressure, the federal government dropped all mention of native rights from the proposed constitution of 1982 and only later included them as a result of aboriginal protest. Even then, the clause was so worded to include the term "existing" to attempt to water down the effect of section 35(1) which states that the "existing aboriginal and treaty rights of the aboriginal peoples of Canada are recognized and affirmed."

This half-hearted endorsement of aboriginal rights was to be coupled with a series of constitutional (federal-provincial) conferences to settle the issue of aboriginal rights. These conferences were important because, for the first time, the provinces were specifically included and given a role in determining aboriginal rights. Secondly, aboriginal groups were included as participants but in typical fashion without a vote. The major theme of the conferences turned around the issue of entrenching aboriginal self-government in the constitution.

The project was in many ways doomed from the start, as any amendments required seven provinces, representing 50% of the population. As Quebec refused to participate (due to its own exclusion from the 1982 accord) and as British Columbia, Alberta, Newfoundland and Saskatchewan opposed the final federal proposal, it was impossible to see a coalition of forces passing the proposal. Thirdly, aboriginal leaders did not agree with the federal proposal which saw self-government as being derogated from federal and provincial powers. Aboriginal organizations viewed self-government as being part of the right of self-determination of aboriginal peoples. (Long, Boldt and Bear 1988.)

The Penner Report of 1983, which was the result of a special all-party committee on Indian Affairs, gave a developed meaning to the issue of self-government. The Penner Report recommended that self-government be immediately entrenched in the constitution; that Indian governments be recognized as First nations forming a distinct order of government; that Indian nations have the right to determine their own membership and have full legislative powers; that a Ministry of State for Indian First Nations, linked to the Privy Council Office be established to co-ordinate federal relationships with Indians; that the Department of Indian Affairs and Northern Development be phased out within five years; that a special tribunal be established to settle disputes between First Nations and the federal government; it also recommended that First Nations be financed through direct grants and that a new land policy be based on the non-extinguishment of native rights. Each band would be free to choose whether to form its own government or join with other bands. (Cassidy and Bish 1989, Menno, Boldt and Little Bear 1988 and Frideres 1988.)

The recommendations of the Penner Report were considered too radical by Liberal and Conservative governments and were never implemented. Today, the idea of the DIAND seems to be to try to devolve power and responsibility to the provinces for Indian Affairs and to experiment with models of self-government along the Sechelt lines. But much more radical steps are necessary. Even *The Globe and Mail* calls, in typical Canadian fashion, for a Royal Commission (as if we did not already know the situation) and demands some kind of quick and comprehensive land settlement policy.

After the failure in 1987 of the consitutional talks the aboriginal movement moved into a phase which emphasized direct action and use of legal channels to affirm aboriginal claims. Aboriginal people saw these as the only channels left after the betryal of their hopes during the six year period of constitutional activity. This latest phase has resulted in hundreds of actions across the country including road blockages, hunt or fish-ins, hunger strikes and many other forms including the use of legal parliamentary moves to block the Meech Lake Accord. Aboriginal peoples were particularly incensed that the Meech Lake Accord could be reached in 1987 so relatively easily between the federal government and the ten provinces when it concerned a distinct self-governing society for Quebec, whereas no such agreement was possible for aboriginal peoples.

Models of Self-Government

While, after the break down of the 1987 meeting, the road to entrenchment of self-government seemed blocked, aboriginal peoples have had to content themselves with such models of self-government which have been allowed to evolve so far by Ottawa and the provinces.

The main two existing models of aboriginal self-government in Canada are the James Bay Settlement and the Sechelt band Agreement in British Columbia. Meanwhile, the settlement of the Nunavut territorial land claims in the Eastern Arctic may indicate that in the future, a territorial status, and then a provincial status, for this region might become a reality, if the provinces do not maintain a veto over the creation of new provinces. It seems all right to have a majority white province with a very small population (Prince Edward Island) but the creation of Northern provinces with aboriginal majority or near majorities seems a more difficult proposition. Let us look briefly at the two current forms of recognized self government.

The James Bay Settlement was signed ino law in 1975 and the Northeastern Agreement was signed in 1978. These agreements with the Quebec provincial government were later followed by legislation at the provincial level and the Cree-Naskapi Act of 1984 at the federal level. The 1975 and 1978 agrrements offered Indian peoples guaranteed rights to land and monies in return for extinguishment of their rights over vast tracts of landt to be used for hydro-electric development. Through these agreements, a large measure of self-governments was won. However, many of the services, such as health and education, which are administered by the Crees through their own institutions, are funded, and are part of, the provincial government network of services. In this sense, the self-government of the Crees has been limited by continued ultimate provincial jurisdiction. Funding for the various programmes is shared between provincial and federal levels of government.

The Sechelt Indian Band Self-Government Act came into effect in October 1986. The Sechelt Act along with a parallel provincial accord gives the Sechelt delegated federal and provincial authority for self-government. The Sechelt government has a wide range of economic and political powers including the right to enter into contracts and to borrow or invest money. Undoubtedly the Sechelt legislation is a step forward over the previous situation. However, some provisions of the Indian Act still apply and all power is delegated by federal and provincial governments. The land question or rather the land claims of the Sechelt are still pending and have detached from this model of self-government. (Cassidy and Bish 1989.)

The problem with both of these agreements, and the reason why the Assembly of First Nations has been so critical of these policies, is that neither one stems from the innate right of aboriginal people to self-government. Both are a result of delegation of powers from the federal government and the provinces; powers which can always be taken away at will or modified when the white governments decide that they want the aboriginal land or new powers over resources, or various government sectors from education to health care and justice.

The lack of entrenched powers for these native governments is one problem. Another question which faces all land settlements and all Indian governments is the issue of extinguishment of rights. Here is certainly a double standard. While federal and provincial governments certainly seem to have the "right" to re-open any treaty or negotiated settlement, native people cannot as governments try to put the case for the extinguishment of rights once a treaty has been signed or a settlement made. But Quebec's aboriginal people did not have to wait very long before the Quebec provincial government put out its plans in 1990 for a massive new project which will flood huge new areas of northern Quebec.

The idea of aboriginal government as some form of glorified city administration still seems to be the mainstream form for federal and provincial governments. As Mark Krasnick, executive director of the Ontario government's aboriginal affairs directorate, says, this government will take the form of "super municipal" governments, excercising some provincial, federal and municipal powers. (*Globe and Mail*, Jan. 3 1990.) Even the most advanced version of this policy in Quebec, to quote the words of John Ciaccia, the Quebec minister of Indian Affairs, calls the future status of aboriginal peoples as "a nation within a state." Ciaccia affirmed this status when talking of the future self-government for the Mohawks of Kahnawake. (*Globe and Mail*, Jan. 6, 1989.) By outlining this new status which is to include native administration of justice, Ciaccia was following the ideas of successive Quebec governments since the resolution of the Quebec National Assembly of March 1983. In that resolution the Quebec government recognized the existence of ten aboriginal nations in Quebec." (Resolution in Boldt, Long and Little Bear.) Krasnick called this limit attached to self-government "a line beyound which they [federal and provincial governments] will not go." (*Globe and Mail*, Jan. 3, 1990.)

But aboriginal peoples have gone far beyond this limited idea of provincial and federal governments setting the limits of self-government.

The head of the Assembly of First Nations, Georges Erasmus, has called for the federal and provincial governments to accept "aboriginal governments as similar in status to the provinces." (Erasmus in Richardson 1989.) Erasmus has advocated direct funding by the federal government to aboriginal governments. (Richardson 1989.) As Winston Maclean, a co-ordinator for the Saskatchewan Federation of Indian Nations, has noted: "We see ourselves as nations with different systems of original communities equal to the Canadian government." (*Macleans*, July 23, 1990.)

Some aboriginal nations reject any special political links with Canada. The Mohawks of Akwesasne, whose community straddles the frontier between New York State, Ontario and Quebec, see themselves as governing themselves outside of any frontiers imposed by white governments. After all, Mohawks were here before the frontiers were imposed. As Mohawk activist and scholar Kahn-Tineta Horn recently wrote, "It may be unrealistic to expect the border to disappear but why can't Akwesasne be considered a single sovereign entity as it once was?" (*Globe and Mail*, May 3, 1990.) Mike Mitchell, the Grand Chief of the Mohawk Council of Akwesasne, has noted that Mohawks have never considered themselves part of Canada, "Only one Akwesasne person has ever voted in a Canadian election, and that was in the 1950s. Our people felt betrayed and incensed by his action, and his house burned down." (Mitchell in Richardson 1990.)

Indigenous peoples have the right to self-determination in exactly the same way as the Quebec people have the right to choose their own destiny. Some aboriginal peoples may want provincial status, some a more limited form of powers and some complete independence. It is their right to choose the form that best suits their needs.

First Nations after Meech

The summer of 1990 will be remembered in Canada and in the world as the summer of direct action by indigenous people in Canada in defense of their rights. It will also be remembered as the summer which showed that the Canadian state apparatus still retains the power to use massive force or firepower against aboriginal people rather than negotiate, as was the case at Oka, Quebec that summer when som 250 Quebec provincial police attacked Mohawk barricades.

Aboriginal peoples are unlikely to sit back and wait for self-government to be granted by different levels of government. While aboriginal peoples have come a long way in having their demands about self-government accepted from the days when native negotiators (according to Michael McGoldrick, an adviser to Inuit organizations) were called "lunatics" and "unreasonable" in the late seventies for bringing up the issue, much remains to be won. (*Globe and Mail*, Jan. 3, 1990.) Both provincial and federal governments are worried still about the implications of self-government and the cost ot settling land claims, a cost which has escalated (according to federal estimates) to some 4.6 billion dollars. (*Macleans*, July 1990.) But cost is not the only concern of white-majority governments in Canada. Behind the much stated fear of the Balkanization of Canada or the creation of an apartheid system is undoubtedly an element of racism. For white Canadians, the granting of self-government for aboriginal people could, in the final analysis, mean that the majority of Canada's surface could be ruled by aboriginal governments. Canada's white population has tended to cluster in the south by the American border and aboriginal people still form the majority in much of Canada's north; not simply the northern territories but rather the north of Quebec, Labrador and all provinces to the West.

The post-Meech era may be the best chance for aboriginal people to have their demands heard in the re-formulation of the Canadian federation. Canada is unlikely to stumble along without important constitutional renewal. There can surely not be another constitutional proposal which excludes aboriginal people. Even a sovereign Quebec would have to renegotiate the position of native people. As Cree Grand Chief Matthew Coon Come recently noted when talking about the future Crees in an independent Quebec, "We don't want to be baggage that is tranferred from the federal government to Quebec." If Quebec is to move towards sovereignty or independence, aboriginal people feel they have the right "to decide to stay with Canada and keep the land with us." (*Toronto Star*, July 21, 1990.) This may not be the choice in the end but it does mean that no majority white government in Canada can refuse to negotiate with aboriginal peoples.

What Solutions?

Canada is rapidly moving to what can be called a postfordist economy. A

240

post-fordist type economy, which is decentralized and relies on more service industries and on smaller units of production, may offer aboriginal peoples renewed possibilities of economic development. No longer does a successful economy of the future necessarily have to be based on a huge labour supply or massive resources. But success in a post-fordist world would mean important investments in education and training as well as targeting specific areas of economic development. However, the potential is there for relatively small (population-wise) aboriginal self-governments to be very viable economic propositions.

Secondly, the breakdown of economic frontiers (and eventually political ones) such as has occurred in the EEC and is occurring in Europe causes a dramatic decline of many old-style fordist economies with unemployment and closing down of whole regions industrially. It means particularly for Canada, locked in a very unequal partnership with the American giant, a loss of sovereignty and the closing down of many branch plant industries. Paradoxically, and this is not an argument in favour of free trade but only a possible appreciation of the situation, it may give smaller economic units a chance to function while acquiring increased political sovereignty, particularly if they are economically independent and culturally distinct.

This is the idea which motivates the renewed drive for autonomy and/or independence in many regions of Western Europe (such as the Catalonian and Basque regions of Spain and Scotland in the United Kingdom). Many in Quebec welcomed free trade in the same manner because it broke the economic dominance of English Canada. The difference between the FTA and the EEC is that of course the EEC joins together a number of relatively equal states and many smaller ones, whereas the FTA takes two states who are equal only in geographic size.

But taking advantage of changes brought about by FTA is not, in my opinion, the best way for aboriginal peoples in the Canadian state to proceed. This way may hold the seeming potential of more political independence but will bring with it the potential for renewed economic subjugation to an even more powerful state. And unlike the EEC where for instance EEC social legislation is more progressive than for example British laws in the same areas, politically the FTA is most likely to lead to a harmonization of laws with American practice on a whole range of issues from unemployment insurance regulation to state or community ownership. To aboriginal communities with terrible social problems and lack of private economic resources, the free enterprise model state is unlikely to hold much of a solution.

At the present time a much better way would be the restructuring into some

241

form of an independent Canadian federation which would guarantee the rights of sovereignty and self-determination to Quebec and to aboriginal peoples. In the future, other arrangements between aboriginal peoples of the northern regions outside of Canada could also be a possibility.

Whatever the future holds for relations between English-Canada and Quebec, we must be ready to deal with the First Nations on a nation to nation, or equal to equal, basis. This way of dealing with indigenous people will mean the recognition of self-determination for Canada's aboriginal peoples, which means their right to decide on whatever form of government and whatever link, if any, they wish to have with the non-aboriginal population, no matter what the consequences for English or French Canada might be. It means that aboriginal people may decide to set up independent states or negotiate a new form of federalism. It is only through this kind of open and transparent politics that both indigenous and non-indigenous Canadians can hope to create a true bond of friendship based on equality and self-determination.

The Canada of the future may and hopefully will be radically different from Canada as we know it. It is heartening (though very late) that the Canadian government was finally able to compensate Japanese Canadians for their totally unjust imprisonment and loss of personal property and livelihood during World War Two. But aboriginal peoples in Canada have demanded compensation for injustices committed over nearly four centuries and have an equal right to redress of their demands of which self-government is only the most crucial.

Bibliography

Boldt, Menno; Long, Anthony; and Little Bear, Leroy (Editors): *The Quest for Justice - Aboriginal Peoples and Aboriginal Rights* (Toronto: University of Toronto Press, 1985) (especially Boldt and Long, "Native Indian Self-Government: Instrument of Autonomy or Assimilation?").

Cassidy, Frank and Bish, Robert: *Indian Government: Its Meaning in Practice* (Halifax: Institute for Research on Public Policy, 1989).

Cassidy, Frank and Dale, Norman: *After Native Claims?* (Halifax: Institute for Research on Public Policy, 1988).

Clement, Wallace and Williams, Glen (Editors): *The New Canadian Political Economy* (Montreal: McGill-Queens University Press, 1989) (especially Frances Abele and Daiva Stasiulis, "Canada as a 'White Settler Colony': What about Natives and Immigrants?").

Franks, C. E. S.: *Public Administration Questions Relating to Aboriginal Self-Government* (Kingston: Institute of Intergovernmental Relations, 1987).

Frideres, James, S.: *Native Peoples in Canada - Contemporary Conflicts* (Scarborough: Prentice Hall Canada Inc., 1988).

Gagnon, Alain and Bickerton, James (Editors): *Canadian Politics: An Introduction to the Discipline* (Peterborough: Broadview Press, 1990).

Hawkes, David and Peters, Evelyn: *Implementing Aboriginal Self-Government: Problems and Prospects* (Kingston: Institute of Intergovernmental Relations, 1986).

Hawkes, David: *Aboriginal Self-Government: What Does it Mean?* (Kingston: Institute of Intergovernmental Relations, 1985).

----The Search for Accomodation (Kingston: Institute of Intergovernmental Relations, 1987).

----*Aboriginal Peoples and Government Responsibility* (Ottawa: Carleton University Press, 1989).

Gary Paget, "Federal/Provincial Responsibility and the Sechelt," and Evelyn Peters, "Federal and Provincial Responsibilities for the Cree, Naskapi and Inuit Under the James Bay and Northern Quebec and Northeastern Quebec Agreements."

Purich, Donald: *Our Land - Native Rights in Canada* (Toronto: James Lorimer & Company, 1986).

Richardson, Boyce (Editor): *Drumbeat - Anger and Renewal in Indian Country* (Toronto: Summerhill Press, The Assembly of first Nations, 1989) (especially Georges Erasmus, "Introduction: Twenty Years of Disappointed Hopes," and "Epilogue: The Solution We Favour For Change," and Grand Chief Michael Mitchell, "Akwesasne: An Unbroken Assertion of Sovereignty").

Schwartz, Bryan: *First Principles, Second Rights: Aboriginal Peoples' Constitutional Reform and Canadian Statecraft* (Montreal: The Institute for Research on Public Policy, 1986).

Smith, Derek (Editor): *Canadian Indians and the Law: Selected Documents, 1663-1972* (Ottawa: Mc Clelland and Stewart, 1975).

Articles

Dutton, Don: "Indian act changes causing tribal rifts, native inquiry told," *The Toronto Star*, January 9, 1990, p. A9.

Fulton, E. Kaye: "Looking for dignity: Oka's Mohawks are not alone," *Maclean's*, July 23, 1990, 22-23.

Henton, Darcy: "Indians stake their claim to Quebec," *The Toronto Star*, July 21, 1990, pp. D 1-4.

Horn, Kahn-Tineta: "The Akwesasne war: why can't the Mohawks settle it themselves?" *The Globe and Mail*, May 3, 1990, p. A7.

Howes, John: "Western union," *Maclean's*, August 6, 1990, A17.

Jenish, D'arcy: "Power to burn," *Maclean's*, May 21, 1990.

"Judge rules Micmac treaty no longer valid," *The Globe and Mail*, January 6, 1990, p. A11.

Mackie, Richard: "Rules issued for talks on native self-government," *The Globe and Mail*, December 15, 1989, p. A13.

McInnes, Craig: "Agreement reached on Inuit land claim," *The Globe and Mail*, December 9, 1989, p. A5.

----"The lot of native peoples," *The Globe and Mail*, June 14, 1990, p. A18.

Picard, Andre: "Quebec Mohawks to be 'nation within a state,'" *TheGlobe and Mail*, January 6, 1990, p. A9.

Platiel, Rudy: "Wider self-rule for natives foreseen in '90s," *The Globe and Mail*, January 3, 1990, p. A3.

Priegert, Portia: "Indians across the country step up protests in quest for power," *The Globe and Mail,* July 17, 1989, p. A11.

Smith, Donald B: "Canada's third solitude," *The Globe and Mail*, July 17, 1989, p. A11.

----"To address native land claims," *The Globe and Mail*, August 6, 1990, p. A10.

Watkins, Mel: "Once more unto the Meech - A Final Assault on the Accord," *This Magazine*, 23:8 (April-May 1990).

The Devolution of Authority from the Government of Canada to the Governments of Canada's Northern Territories: Issues of Self-Determination

Gurston Dacks

Introduction

In Canada's North, constitutional and political development are engaged in an intricate dance, each guiding the pace and direction of the other in ways which are complex and fluid. In part, these complexities reflect the fact that the constitutional development suite involves the intricate orchestration of a variety of simultaneous motifs in the North. These include the pursuit of regional government, territorial division and changes to the form of public government in the Northwest Territories, and, in both territories, aboriginal claims, aboriginal self-government and the approach to provincial status. The dance is also complicated because northern politics brings together different traditions of political practice and widely divergent goals; the partners in the dance do not always understand each other or want to move in the same direction. At the same time, increasingly, they do share common purposes. They recognize a need to seek common goals and thus must choreograph their movements as an interplay between competition and co-operation.

The subject of this paper is how devolution influence the dynamics of the dance. Devolution will be the focus because it has been one of the most prominent themes of northern policy since the Progressive Conservative Party gained office in Ottawa in 1984. While now overtaken by progress on aboriginal claims, it appeared in the 1980s to be accomplishing more tangible results than any of the other policies, hence provided a context in which the other processes unfolded, a great opportunity for some northern policy actors and a serious threat for others.

Constitutional and Political Development

Constitutional development is a process of increasing jurisdictional span,

245

autonomy and structural refinement of public government. Political development is the ability of the members of a society to make binding, legitimate decisions concerning their affairs. Critical to the attainment of a high level of political development is a consensus on the boundaries of the polity and on the nature of the politically relevant entities in society whose interests must be represented in the institutions of government if it is to be legitimate. In the larger Canadian context, a consensus exists that the individual is the primary political entity. The principles of universal suffrage and relatively uniform constituence sizes, at least within each province, aim at the representation of individual interests. At the same time, Canadian practice recognizes the relevance of ethnicity and regionalism through the federal system and provincial representation in the Senate and the cabinet. However, even the pan-Canadian system is challenged by debates about the representational needs and the basic rights of particular groups in Canada's social structure. Most dramatically, the debate about the now-lapsed Meech Lake Accord centred on the question of how to reflect the special circumstances of Quebec in Confederation. Calls for a triple-E Senate from western and Atlantic Canada suggest that national institutions do not adequately reflect the special needs of Canada's hinterland. The constitutional status of Canada's aboriginal peoples remains a sadly unresolved question.

In these and similar issues constitutional and political development are linked; even legally powerful and elaborate institutions need to rest on an adequate political foundation in order to function effectively and to be accepted as legitimate. Processes must be in place which enable significant groups in society to communicate their desires to government. These groups must feel confident that the social consensus on basic issues will assure their concerns a fair hearing. Until these groups feel this confidence, entrenching institutions will be a risky enterprise. They may function, reach decisions promptly and administer policy efficiently. However, they may not act responsively or gain the trust of important groups in society. Constitutional development which is not accompanied by appropriate political development may become a trap for these groups, as present federal government structures appear to some hinterland, aboriginal and other Canadians to be.

The Role of Collectivivity in the Canadian North

In Canada's North, this interaction between political and constitutional development turns on the significance of social collectivity in its society and politics. As the literature on consociationalism demonstrates, the political role of social collectivities challenges a great many countries. In Canada, for example, politics is struggling with the questions of how to fit Quebec into Confederation and how to balance collevtice rights--such as "distinct society" in the terminology of the Meech Lake Accord--and individual freedoms. The northern analogue to these questions is how to accommodate aboriginal peoples within the political and governmental frameworks of the North. While this issue also appears in southern Canada, it exerts less pressure on southern governments for several reasons. Aboriginal people constitute only a small fraction of the southern population, very much more in the North. These numbers give aboriginal northerners substantial strength at the ballot box and also mean that they have the potential to create relatively powerful forms of self-government in the future, should they wish to do so. Moreover, the institutions of the territories, and particularly the NWT, are not yet fully formed, hence the aboriginal people have an opportunity to share in the shaping of them which the established forms of government in the provinces deny to their aboriginal peoples.

Accommodating aboriginal peoples means accomodating aboriginal collectivities. While generalizations always admit of exceptions, aboriginal people traditionally see themselves as social collectivities--in effect as distinct societies. Their relationship to their aboriginal roots remains rich and vital; it is usually a fundamental source of their identity, more so than ethnic background tends to be for many other Canadians. The security and future of their aboriginal group are basic elements of their political agenda. This traditional valuing of the collectivity has been reinforced by two modern-day political processes. The first of these is the land claims process. This process caused aboriginal people to develop strong representative organizations which serve as voices for their aboriginal collectivities. The claims themselves are collective claims whose settlements will convey collective rights and benefits. For the foreseeable future, the pursuit of these rights and the management of settlement benefits will engage aboriginal peoples in collective activities. These will encourage them to conceive of their interests as collective and their relationships with non-aboriginal people and institutions as at least in part collective in character. The second, and related, process has been the attempt to constitutionalize the meaning of aboriginal rights through the first minister's process. This process sensitized them to the issue of their collective self-determination. Its failure to date has reinforced the determination of northern aboriginal people to seek regional constitutions which avoid the national failure of aboriginal peoples to achieve a satisfactory collective relationship with the Canadian state.

In contrast, non-aboriginal northerners tend to hold the individualistic values of North America liberal-democracy. Tending not to see themselves a part of a social collectivity, a sub-group in northern society, they feel no need for the institutions of public government in Yellowknife and Whitehorse to reflect any ethnic collecitivity of which they might be a part. They recognize aboriginal rights but feel that they should be expressed through the settlement of claims and possibly aboriginal self-government. In this way, they view as, at best, unnecessary and burdensome and, at worst, a violation of the principle of equality public government structures which aboriginal leaders see as logical extensions of their aboriginal rights, essential to securing the benefits of their claims settlements and acknowledging their distinctness as societies within northern society.

The constitutional uniqueness--and complexity--of the North flows from the immediacy of the question of how to express the interests and protect the rights of aboriginal collectivities within northern public governments which must conform to the individualist bias of the *Charter of Rights and Freedoms.* If not for this issue, the direction of constitutional development in the North, responsible government through the Westminster model reflecting non-aboriginal political culture, would be completely predictable. Indeed, it is almost guaranteed to come to pass in the Yukon, and may also do so in the N.W.T. Whether it will depends on the answers to several questions. First, how much cross-pressure do aboriginal people feel between their collective interests and their self-interest as individuals? Second, how important are factors--including the responsiveness of the present Government of the Northwest Territories (GNWT)--which undercut the mobilization of effective pressure for constitutional innovation to reflect the aboriginal collectivites in northern society? Third, what is the likelihood that other forms of government will develop to express collective interests in the North, thus reducing or eliminating the need to modify the Westminster model to provide for this representation within the public government?

The experience of the devolution process provides a number of insights into these questions. However, before devolution can be considered, some context and important contrasts between the two territories must be indentified.

The Yukon

Responsible government is already institutionalized in the Yukon. Canada's three national parties contest elections and participate in the legislative assembly in ways which mirror behaviour in the legislatures of southern Canada.

Because aboriginal people account for about one quarter of the territorial population, they have no prospect of using the ballot box to pursue a restructuring of the institutions of public government in the territory. Moreover, because they live in a widely dispersed pattern in the Yukon, it would not be possible to identify a portion of the territory which could be allotted to them as their own--an application of the logic of federalism to their need for collective representation and self-determination.

In any case, they have not sought to change the nature of the Government of the Yukon (YTG) for at least three reasons, in addition to the minimal likelihood of success. First, the Yukon Indians tend to view their fourteen communities as their prime political units. Indeed, the agreement in principle for the settlement of their aboriginal claim anticipates the creation of fourteen locally-based aboriginal self-governments, with no reference to any territory-wide institution.[1] The local focus of Yukon Indian political culture disinclines them to seek territory-wide constitutional change. Second, the presence of disciplined political parties provides a link between government and the aboriginal people and enables the latter to exercise a degree of accountability over the former, enhancing governmental responsiveness. Third, the present New Democratic government of the Yukon, in power since 1984, has taken as its first constitutional priority the settlement of the aboriginal claim of the Council for Yukon Indians. This had led it to give a lower priority to devolution. As a result, devolution has not proven to be a source of changes which complicates claims negotiations or threatens understandings once they have been negotiated.

All of these factors underpin a clear social expectation that the form of government of the Yukon has already been decided. Collective interests are not given institutional expression in this structrue, but this has not led to aboriginal calls for a new form of public government. Rather there is a clear consensus that these interests will have to be expressed through other institutions, if they are to receive institutional expression at all.

The Northwest Territories

The NWT presents a very different picture. Its form of government is significantly less institutionalized than is the Government of the Yukon. While it largely resembles the Yukon Government in having a cabinet composed entirely of elected members of the assembly and responsible to the Assembly, it cannot be said to be fully a system of responsible government.[2] The reason for this is the absence of party affiliation in what is termed a "consensus" form of government. This absence impedes the operation of cabinet solidarity and denies the accountability which party politics gives to the parliamentary system as one of its greatest strengths. This feature displeases many, primarily non-aboriginal northerners, who value the accountability which responsible government entails. However, aboriginal people in particular resist the development of party politics because they feel that it would entrench a system which would subordinate the expression of their collective interests to the dictates of party discipline. However, in taking this position, they deny themselves the instrument of party discipline and accountability which has proven effective in improving relations between Indians and government in the Yukon.

Demographics make this resistance by the aboriginal people of the NWT more than plausible. According to the 1986 census, they account for about fifty percent of the territorial population. This does not guarantee them domination of territorial politics through the ballot box. However, it makes them a very significant force, particularly in the future in view of their high birth rate and the possible adoption of a two year residence requirement for voting, a requirement which would disenfranchise quite a few non-Natives but, of course, no aboriginal people. In addition, the Inuit of the NWT account for over eighty percent of the population north of the treeline. This and their conviction that the GNWT does not and cannot govern them responsively[3] has led them to promote a federal solution to their representation needs. Division of the NWT into a western territory and an eastern territory to be called Nunavut would give them a jurisdiction which they could be assured would support their collective interests yet do so through the same type of institutions of government which are found elsewhere in Canada.[4] Nunavut has not come into existence because it has proven impossible to resolve the issue of where to draw the boundary.[5] However, this state of affairs should not be taken as evidence that the Inuit believe that the present Government of the Northwest Territories satisfactorily protects and promotes their collective interests. To the contrary, the Tungavik Federation of Nunavut (TFN), the body which represents the Inuit of the NWT, emphasizes that division of the territories complements their claims settlement in a way which is not only essential, but inevitable.[6] The Inuit Agreement-In-Principle reaffirms the commitment of the territorial and federal governments to support division in principle and promises that a process for creating Nunavut will be initiated promptly after the signing of the final claim settlement.[7]

Similarly, while the Dene and Metis of the western NWT continue to take part in the Government of the NWT, their pursuit of aboriginal self-government strongly suggests that they find its present format not fully satisfactory as a vehicle for expressing their collective needs. For example, in 1988, the Dene and Metis argued that,

> . . .for aboriginal peoples, the existing GNWT is still an interim government, because it has yet to represent them directly or directly incorporate their values or priorities. . . Aboriginal self-government has not been achieved in the Northwest Territories by the participation of aboriginal people in the public government.[8]

The Dene and Metis achieved a comprehensive land claim agreement in 1990. However, because of the constraints of the federal government's aboriginal claims policy, this not-yet-ratified agreement will not afford the Dene and Metis the full range of protection of their rights and interests which many, particularly Dene, feel they must have to secure their culture and lifestyle in the future. They therefore feel compelled either to change the structure of the GNWT to make it more responsive or escape its jurisdiction to some degree through the mechanism of aboriginal self-government.

It would appear that the Government of the NWT is less institutionalized and accepted than governments elsewhere in Canada. In particular, the criticisms it encounters from aboriginal organizations suggests that they may be closer to aboriginal people than it is. What is probably closest to the truth is that the government and the aboriginal groups are locked in a struggle for the support of aboriginal northerners.

For its part, the Government of the Northwest Territories argues that "...many of the goals of a aboriginal self-government are already in place or potentially in place within the present (GNWT) system."[9] It often points to the aboriginal majority among the members of the Legislative Assembly and the ample representation of aboriginal peoples in the cabinet to legitimize itself in reply to criticisms that it is a "white government."

However, the GNWT cannot be an institutional voice for the collective interests of the aboriginal peoples in the way that their own groups can. The GNWT is not structured directly to represent the collective interests of the aboriginal groups of the territories as contrasted with the interests of aboriginal persons as individuals. It must govern in the interest of all northerners, not just aboriginal people. This responsibility, the outlook of the primarily non-aboriginal bureaucracy and the need in some cases to conform to southern models to gain the cooperation of Ottawa[10] can lead ministers, even ministers who are themselves aboriginal, away from the agendas of the aboriginal groups. The absence of party politics prevents aboriginal people from electing a government committed to their collective goals and holding it accountable for its fidelity to those goals once in office. In the more remote constituencies, a good many voters are much more concerned with local issues than with territorial matters. This feature of the N.W.T.'s political culture may combine with the absence of party politics to make the success of ministers and ordinary members as advocates of local interests a more important determinant of their electoral fate than is their promotion of aboriginal constitutional interests. All of these structural factors can work together to lead the GNWT to develop policies inconsistent with aboriginal goals, and to pursue its institutional interest vigorously at the expense of the interests of the aboriginal groups when and to the extent that they have come into conflict.

At the same time, the Government does represent aboriginal people as individuals and serve their individual interests quite effectively. In addition to supplying the services which the provinces deliver, such as health care, education and social assistance, it provides housing and electricity. It is the biggest employer in the territories, employing many aboriginal people.

Moreover, the Government can appeal to the aboriginal interests of aboriginal voters. As noted above, it can claim legitimacy on the basis of number of aboriginal people in the assembly and the executive. As would be expected of such a group of politicians serving such a large aboriginal constituency, the Government of the Northwest Territories does often respond to a significant degree to the collective needs of the aboriginal peoples of the territories. For example, it has supported the settlement of aboriginal claims and the positions which the aboriginal groups advocated during the 1983-1987 national constitutional process which attempted to define the concept of aboriginal rights.[11] It also helped fund the court challenge to uranium development which the Inuit community of Baker Lake launched on the basis of aboriginal rights.[12]

In addition, the Government of the Northwest Territories has cooperated with attempts to restructure it to achieve collective representation within it. It participated in the Constitutional Alliance of the Northwest Territories from its inception in 1982 until 1990, when it ceased to exist. This advisory body, composed of MLAs and representatives of aboriginal groups responsible, was responsible for preparing a plan for dividing the territories, including recommending a form of government for the western NWT which, in the words of Bob MacQuarrie, then an MLA and member of the Alliance, would establish "an appropiate balance between individual and collective rights."[13] In 1990, it committed itself in both the Dene/Metis and TFN claims settlements to pursue processes of constitutional development which, if they reach fruition, could diminish its power significantly.[14]

The responsiveness of the GNWT to the principle of aboriginal collectivity can be debated. What is less debatable is that the aboriginal groups have failed to press effectively for changes in the structures of government which would institutionalize the representation of their collective interests. They have presented some rather extensive proposals, such as the Dene/Metis statement, *Public Government for the People of the North* [15] and the Nunavut proposal of the Inuit. However, these have not accomplished any change to date in the operation of the government. As will be argued below, devolution makes such change less likely in the future.

The aboriginal groups have failed in pursuing their constitutional agenda for a range of reasons. The first is that the support they enjoy from their people is less than absolute. For one thing, aboriginal people may experience a degree of cross-pressure over the pursuit of their collective interests. Instances can arise in which aboriginal people must weigh their interests as members of ethnic collectivities against their interests as wage earners or residents of particular regions. For example, their collective interests have led the Dene Nation and the Metis Association to seek a delay in the construction of a natural gas pipeline in the Mackenzie Valley until their aboriginal claim is settled.[16] However, the desire of individual Dene and Metis to work on the construction phase of the pipeline leads many of them to support the stance of the territorial government in favour of construction. In addition, the government can appeal quite persuasively for aboriginal support on the representational and policy grounds suggested above. Finally, there is no aboriginal tradition of pursuing politics over as large an area as each of the aboriginal groups covers. Aboriginal people feel a strong indentification with their extended family and their linguistic group, but their loyalty to the umbrella organizations which brings these groups together at the territorial level is a relatively recent phenomenon. This means that the leaders of the aboriginal organizations cannot count on unequivocal support and may have to face difficult internal politics as they attempt to manage the relations among the diverse components of their organizations. Thus, for example, the leaders of the Dene Nation found in 1987 that they could not ratify the agreement on a boundary for dividing the NWT which they had negotiated because of pressure from a small minority of Dene people.

This case illustrates a second general problem--that aboriginal political culture, while admirably suited to meeting the needs for which it traditionally evolved, imposes some severe liabilities on aboriginal leaders attempting to work effectively in non-aboriginal political settings. Because of the dispersion of authority in aboriginal communities, it is more difficult for leaders of the aboriginal groups to commit themselves than it is for the government to do so. In addition, aboriginal political culture calls for extensive consultation between leaders and their people. For example, before approving their claims agreement in principle, the Dene and Metis held Assemblies attended by large numbers of their people lasting five days. The need for this type of consultation forces aboriginal leaders to work in a different time frame than politicians working in a non-aboriginal setting who can make executive decisions with quite limited consultation, if they wish. Moreover, aboriginal leaders find that they must manage the gap between aboriginal and non-aboriginal political culture. They must operate in two different modes, dealing with elders and communities on one hand and the policy processes of public government on the other. They respect the former, but must deal with the overwhelming power of the latter. This is not only extremely stressful for them, but also limits their ability to steer a proposition all the way through governmental policy processes. When the needs they may encounter to deal with issues internal to the aboriginal community distract them from their policy goals or force a revision of plans, relations with government suffer.

A third set of problems of a more practical nature has kept the issue of representing collectivities from coming to a head. One problem is that aboriginal groups' resources are usually quite modest, yet they are called upon to respond to a variety of external developments ranging from devolution itself to pipeline proposals to issues of northern sovereignty and strategic policy, not to mention doing what is necessary to maintain the flow of federal government money to fund their activities. Even more labour-intensive is their preoccupation with negotiating the settlement of their all-important aboriginal claims. Faced with challenges such as these, the aboriginal groups simply lack the personnel they need to devote to issues of governmental structure. This is particularly the case because no occasion, such as a decision to proceed with dividing the territories, has presented itself to make this issue immediate and pressing.

A fourth problem is that the various aboriginal groups have pursued different strategies of constitutional development. The Inuit have pursued Nunavut and ignored discussions about reforming the structure of the government of the NWT, because it will not govern them after division. Through much of the 1980s, the Dene and Metis focussed on reforming the public government; more recently they have begun to explore options for separate institutions of self-government. For their part, the Inuvialuit, the Inuit people of the western Arctic, have sought a strong regional government as a vehicle for their self-detemination. The pursuit of these different goals has divided the strength of the aboriginal people of the territory and prevented their representatives in the Assembly from forming a voting bloc, although the members from the eastern Arctic have sometimes voted as a group.

These various infirmities on the part of the aboriginal groups of the territories pose a basic problem of political development. The determination with which they have pursued their aboriginal claims demonstrates indisputably that the aboriginal people feel a strong collective identity and share important collective interests. However, they have to date proven unable to bring sufficient pressure to bear on the political system to ensure that the public government of the territories is structured in a fashion which would facilitate the expression of this identity and these interests. The result is a continuation of incoherence in territorial politics, a continuing absence of consensus on the political role of social collectivities and how to represent the aboriginal collectivities in public government. The resulting inability to achieve a broadly based approach to planning constitutional change has allowed other forces, such as devolution, to determine the direction of constitutional change. This is a basic feature of the dance as it is done in the NWT:constitutional development proceeds, but political development not only does not lead it, but fails to keep pace with it.

In this uncertain climate, and driven by the universal desire of governments to be as fully empowered as possible to serve their people, the government of the Northwest Territories has sought to increase its strength. Devolution has been one of the basic elements of its strategy. Indeed, the high priority it has attached to devolution stands in contrast to the subordination of devolution to claims in the priorities of the Government of the Yukon.

Devolution

The devolution of authority over provincial-type jurisdictions from the federal government to the governments of the two territories was a priority of the first two Conservative Ministers of Indian Affairs and Northern Development, David Crombie and Bill McKight. From 1984 to 1988, management of forests, forest fire suppression and electrical generation were transferred to both terrritorial governments. The Government of the NWT also assumed jurisdiction over hospitals and health services, a responsibility whose transfer the Yukon and federal governments began to negotiate in the Spring of 1989. The completion of these devolutions will bring the span of authority of the territorial governments very close to that of the provinces. They and not the federal government will provide their people with the vast bulk of services which Canadians South of 60° receive from their provincial governments.The major powers the territories will lack are few, but very important: oil, gas and minerals, land management and ownership and the prosecution of criminal court cases. The pace at which the territories acquire these powers and the conditions which are attached to their transer bear important implications for the overall processes of constitutional and political development in the North.

Some of these processes touch directly on the issue of how representation of northern aboriginal collective interests can be accomplished. These include the claims themselves, possible forms of aboriginal self-government and the structures of the public government--the YTG and the GNWT. Other changes would indirectly represent aboriginal interests by creating or strengthening institutions whose constituencies would be predominantly aboriginal. These include division of the Northwest Territories and the pressure for powerful regional governments, which is strongest in the regions of the territories where the Inuit comprise the bulk of the population. A final constitutional process which devolution affects, but which only very indirectly relates to the issue of collective representation is the attainment of, or at least the approach to, provincial status by the territories. The rest of this paper will examine the linkages between devolution and these processes in both the Yukon and the Northwest Territories.

Devolution and the Form of Public Government

Devolution will add to the powers of the government of the Yukon, but it will not alter the government's basic structure or its approach to representation. In the Yukon, the process of molding the institutions of public government is largely complete; a parliamentary system of responsible government based on party competition has operated there for more than a decade. No one expects it to change in the foreseeable future, nor is any sentiment being expressed that it do so. Indeed, the only remaining step for it to take is for its basis to be changed from minsterial directive, which can be unilaterally altered or withdrawn by Ottawa (a highly unlikely prospect) to constitutional entrenchment. While devolution may raise a variety of questions in the Yukon, its impact on the underlying structure of its government is not one of these questions.

In contrast, devolution does affect constitutional development in the Northwest Territories by adding to the credibility of the present direction of evolution. Each additional power which the government receives symbolizes

256

the acquiescence of the federal government to the development in the NWT of the institutions of representation and responsible government found everywhere else in Canada among the federal and provincial governments. This symbolism build the confidence of northerners who support this evolution and who see it as natural and preordained. It is not that devolution has shaped the government of the Northwest Territories. Rather, each instance of devolution represents the closing off of an opportunity to force a joining of the issue about the shape of government, leading, perhaps, to an altered direction of constitutional development.

In a practical sense, devolution is institution-building. Devolution gives the government more money, more person years and more services to provide. In this way, it enables the government to expand its clientele, whether they be employees who depend on the GNWT for their jobs or citizens who receive GNWT-provided services. As the government becomes larger and more powerful, the contrast grows between it and the smallness and the inability of the aboriginal groups to deliver equivalent benefits. As time passes, it becomes less and less credible that aboriginal institutions might be developed which would be as effective as is the government of the NWT. It becomes harder for the aboriginal groups to scrutinize the activities of the government to ensure that the interests of their people are being served. Their opposition to devolution in the absence of accommodation of their collective interests in public government institutions becomes less and less credible each time it is ignored. Increasingly, the aboriginal groups look less like governments in wating or the voices of sovereign peoples and more and more like mere interest groups.

The Northwest Territories has been interesting for politicial scientists because it has been the only jurisdiction in Canada which has held out some promise of deviating from the model of public government found elsewhere. The operation of the Assembly in a non-partisan, "consensus-government" fashion and the consideration of a form of consociational government for the western NWT after division[17] have suggested that room exists for some form of institutional innovation which would lead to the more effective representation of aboriginal collective concerns than the parliamentary system has tended to provide throughout Canadian history. Devolution has reduced the odds of this type of development by enabling the government of the Northwest Territories, in instances which will be discussed below, to seek and to acquire powers without having to confront the issue of how it represents the collective interests within it society.

Devolution and Aboriginal Claims

The purpose of the aboriginal claims in the North is to protect the material basis of the traditional economies of the aboriginal peoples and in this way to ensure their economic wellbeing and the sense of identity and spirituality which is based on their relationship to the land and water. In the words of Michael Whittington, " . . .the land (and one might add for the Inuit, 'the arctic waters') holds a central place in the social, economic and spiritual lives of the native peoples, and as such it is the disposition of that land that is the dominant concern of the Dene, Metis and Inuit alike."[18] In particular, the aboriginal people are concerned that government may approve large-scale non-renewable resource development projects such as pipelines or uranium mines, which may make it impossible or at least much more difficult for them to hunt, fish and trap. The settlements of aboriginal claims have given or will give the aboriginal peoples substantial control over the land. The settlements confirm aboriginal ownership of large areas of land. On some of this land, the aboriginal people own the subsurface as well as the surface rights. This enables them to prevent non-renewable resource development by the simple expedient of not developing their property. In the other portions of aboriginal lands, where companies do hold subsurface rights, the aboriginal groups will be able to negotiate fair compensation for granting the companies access to their lands.[19] However, they have not been in a position to control the pace at which government makes exploration and development rights available to developers nor such policies as royalty rates, incentive grants, tax arrangements and worker and environmental safety requirements, which will determine the impact of non-renewable resource exploitation on their use of the land.

The devolution process will interact with the claims settlements to answer the absolutely fundamental question of the extent to which the aboriginal peoples will be able to escape their historic inability to protect the lands and waters on which they depend. The federal government is currently negotiating with the GNWT, and will soon begin to negotiate with the YTG, "Northern Energy Accords" which will devolve jurisdiction over oil and gas exploration and production. If these negotiations are successful, the Accords will empower the territorial governments to develop and implement northern energy management regimes. It remains to be seen how emphatically the transfer will instruct them to treat aboriginal interests as a principle consideration in their policy making.[20] Equally unclear is how effectively the settlements have safeguarded aboriginal interests. The settlements will create planning, land and water use and impact assessemnt bodies. While these will be public government bodies, they will be compelled to treat aboriginal needs very seriously because of the numbers of aboriginal people who will sit on them and because they own their existence to claims settlements, not to the devolution process. It would appear therefore that, while devolution dominated claims in the late 1980s, the claims process gained the upper hand at the start of the 1990s. This judgement may prove premature in that, in the final analysis, government ministers can reject what will be recommendations--not binding decisions--of these bodies. Ministers will be discouraged from doing so by having to state their reasons publicly, but, whenever push comes to shove, they will have the authority to proceed on their own judgement, not that of the boards. Furthermore, they may be able to point to the technical resources of their public services to legitimize their decisions as better supported than the views of boards which may not rest on a comparable base. In the end, the vision which will dominate the northern land and seascapes of the future will reflect two factors. The first is the degree to which the territorial governments and the resource planning and management boards share common values and cooperate. The second, to the extent that they work at cross purposes, is the balance of technical resources and political legitimacy between them.

A final note must be added to complete the story of the relationship between devolution and claims. While in the 1980's they appeared to be parallel and at times competing processes, the approaching settlement of the claims at the start of the 1990s has caused them to converge. In one sense, the settlement of claims has enabled at least the GNWT to assert more aggressively the need to devolve jurisdiction over land and water to it. The argument is not merely that this transfer is now timely in that it has been consistent with the ongoing federal devolution policy, but has been held up pending the settlement of the claims. Rather than merely seeing claims in this way as a roadblock now removed, the GNWT is hoping to harness the momentum of the land claims process to pull the devolution cart. It argues:

> The result of the past approach (of separate processes for claims and for political and constitutional development) has been a largely ad hoc and poorly coordinated approach to political and constitutional development. While this has worked in a fashion in the past, it will not any longer because land claims implementation and devolution have merged into a single process. Land claims have also added the requirement of a higher level of discipline, because claims agreements have set deadlines for the implementation of claims institutions, particularly public institutions which regulate the use of land and water...it does not make any sense to contemplate the implementation of public institutions created by land claims other than pursuant to territorial legislation. It would be inconsistent with

federal and territorial policy and objectives. It would also be unworkable, certainly confusing and inefficient, if reneawble and nonrenewable resource use continues to be regulated by a mixture of territorial and federal legislation.[21]

From this perspective, devolution and the settlement of claims are linked. The latter provides an occasion for the former--for creation of a comprehensive territorial government regime for managing all the resources of the North, a development which would bring the span of powers of the territorial government very close to that of the provinces.

The issue of the relationship between claims--based resource management structures and those which devolution may provide arises in both territories. An energy accord may itself not stir great interest in the Yukon because relatively few areas of the Yukon offer much promise of oil and gas deposits. As a result, relatively few areas of the territory are likely to be disturbed by energy exploration. However, to the extent that an energy accord will accelerate and provide precedents for the transfer of jurisdiction over mining, which does effect the Yukon very significantly, the linkage between the devolution of land and resources management and ultimately ownership, and aboriginal claims will be an important issue in both territories. In the negotiations, the Yukon can expected to advance the argument of the GNWT that resources can only be managed coherently if there is a single hand at the helm--the hand of the territorial government.

Aboriginal Self-Government

In the Yukon, devolution has not significantly influenced the Council for Yukon Indians' (CYI) pursuit of aboriginal self-government. As has been noted, the Government of the Yukon has tried to avoid pushing the devolution process in a way which would complicate or pressure the negotiation of the claim. This has enabled the CYI to devote relatively little attention to devolution while developing the *Framework Agreement* for its claim, including the approach to self-government which it contains. This approach reflects the consensus that the Government of the Yukon has achieved its final form. It also reflects Yukon Indian political culture, which, as in the N.W.T., holds the local community to be the prime focus of political allegiance. As already noted, the lack of emphasis in the Yukon Indian *Framework Agreement* on a territory-wide Indian self-government makes a power struggle between it and the Yukon government quite unlikely, although conflict may arise over the transfer of powers to the community-based Indian nations. In theory, the issue of how governments--the aboriginal self-governments and the Yukon government--will share power over land use, when this power is devolved in the future does relate self-government and devolution in the Yukon. However, this issue is largely resolved by the rather modest provisions of the *Framework Agreement*. For all of these reasons, while devolution is important to Yukon Indians, they have not felt that it has frustrated their pursuit of their claim; devolution has not motivated them to seek self-government.

The Northwest Territories presents a very contrasting picture. While many territorial residents would welcome the completion of the present evolution toward parliamentary government, this pattern is far from universally accepted. This is the case precisely because this model does not provide for the representation of aboriginal collectivities as collectivities.

Moreover, the aboriginal groups feel that past actions by the GNWT relating to devolution have undercut their interests and pre-empted opportunities for the development of aboriginal self-government. For example, the aboriginal groups supported the devolution of jurisdiction over health care out of a belief that the GNWT would decentralize the administration of this activity by empowering strong regional health boards. The aboriginal groups feel that their expectations were not realized and that the GNWT has denied them the power over their health care which they believed devolution would provide them.[22] The experience of the aboriginal groups regarding the signing of the enabling agreement for the Oil and Gas Accord in 1988 reinforced their belief that, when faced with a conflict between their interests and its own institutional growth, GNWT would invariably opt for the latter.[23]

This feeling has caused them to fear that future devolution will continue to pre-empt aboriginal self-government. In some instances, as in the case of the Inuit position regarding health care and the Dene and Metis interest in forest management and fire suppression, aboriginal groups support devolution as a way of gaining much needed improvements in the quality of service. In other instances, such as the involvement of the Inuit in the Northern Accord process, they sense that they cannot stop devolution from occurring. Whatever the considerations which involve them in the devolution process, they are very concerned that they have as full an influence over its course as possible and that, in particular, future devolution does not limit the scope of aboriginal self-goverment which they may seek to put in place or the rights which they have negotiated as part of their claims settlements.

In this way, devolution has two impacts on aboriginal self-government in the N.W.T. First, the approach of the territorial government has added to the aboriginal groups' feeling that it is more interested in state-building than it is in respecting their interests. This suggests that the territorial government has little real interest in institutionalizing within its own structure the expression of the collective interests. This conclusion only adds to the argument for pursuing aboriginal self-government. Second, devolution can frustrate the development of aboriginal self-government if powers are devolved to the territorial government before the aboriginal governments have been established to receive them. The assumption is that once the territorial government assumes formerly federal powers, it will not be possible to cause it to share these powers.

If the territorial government and the aboriginal groups do not find more mutually satisfactory accommodations on devolution, the aboriginal groups can be expected to pursue strong forms of self-government. In the case of the Inuit, this will mean an intensified pursuit of division of the territories. Should it become evident that this option is unattainable, the Inuit will probably fall back to a position of seeking the strongest possible forms of regional government. Several alternative futures could flow out of this situation. The first is that aboriginal self-governments in the West and strong regional governments in the East take shape and co-exist relatively successfully with the GNWT. Such a co-existence is unlikely, however, if the genesis of these governments involves tension between the territorial government and the aboriginal groups and if their jurisdictions overlap concerning such crucial issues as oil and gas management. A second, and more likely, scenario would involve the development of significant aboriginal and regional governments in the West and the East, respectively, and the development of conflict over policy and competition over resources between the territorial and the other governments. The hostility and waste of resources which would accompany this outcome would likely lead to calls for constitutional revision. In this way, if the government of the Northwest Territories does not change in the near future to represent aboriginal collectivities within its structures, it may find itself revisiting this issue ten years from now. However, by then its structure may have become entrenched and the unique constitutional opportunity which the N.W.T. presents may have been irretrievably lost.

This could also be the consequence of the third scenario, which is that strong aboriginal and regional governments do not come into existence. This scenario would lead the aboriginal groups back to the pursuit of restructuring the territorial government to embody aboriginal self-government, or at least directly represent their collective interests. Should they fail, the result will not be intergovernmental conflict as in the previous scenario. Rather, the government will continue to include aboriginal collective interests among a number of factors--regional concerns, interest group desires, its own institutional needs; electoral prospects of its members--which shape its decisions. These decisions will likely serve aboriginal people better than have the similarly derived policies of the provincial governments because the proportion of aboriginal people in the N.W.T. is greater than in the provinces. However, it will not give the weight to the collective interests of these aboriginal people which they need if their claims settlements, their land base and their culture and identity are to be secure.

The last two scenarios would produce the situation anticipated at the start of this paper, a situation in which constitutional development is well advanced, but political development is blocked. The absence of a consensus on the appropriate basis of representation in the territorial government can only leave a part of the population alienated from the government, frustrated by its policies and difficult for the government to appeal to support its intitiatives. This situation, characteristic of many third-world nations, tends to reduce the responsiveness and the effectiveness of government. Particularly in a region experiencing the effects of rapid social change and economic challenges such as high unemployment and a dependence of natural resource production the pace of which is determined largely by factors which are global, hence out of its control, government needs to be as strong and well supported as it possibly can be. In other words, the issue of collective representation must be satisfactorily resolved if the GNWT is to be best able to provide its people with the effective government they need.

This is the context in the Northwest Territories in which devolution brings together the issues of the form of public government, land claims and aboriginal self-government. Indeed, devolution and claims represent two competing processes. Each has the ability to shape governmental institutions, devolution by denying powers to aboriginal self-government and claims by denying them to public governments. These two processes also shape the motivations and tactical considerations of the government and the aboriginal leaders. Devolution without recognition of aboriginal collectivities reduces the pressure the government feels to involve aboriginal groups significantly in future devolutions or to make significant concessions to their concerns. On the other hand, it reinforces the determination of the aboriginal leadership to resist future devolution and to seek to go it alone through the development of aboriginal self-governments or division or, failing that, regional governments. The measure of the outcome of this struggle between devolution and claims will be the importance accorded to collective representation within the totality of government institutionas in the territory.

Devolution and the Attainment of Provincial Status

The territories face significant opposition in their pursuit of provincial status.[24] Much of this concern focuses on how their transformation into provinces would affect the operation of federal-provincial financial arrangements and of the constitutional amending formula. This suggests that other aspects of provincial status which would not affect the general pattern of federal-provincial relations may be attainable by the territories in the near future.[25] These aspects could include fuller participation at first ministers conferences, the establishment of crowns in right of the territories and entrenchment of territorial institutions, so that they could not be altered without the consent of the assembly of the territory affected.

However, status in Canadian Constitution and in intergovernmental relations is only one of two basics sets of provincial attributes. The second is the range of powers, of jurisdiction, which they exercise. As with the linkages between devolution and other forms of constitutional development, the two territories differ regarding the approach they have taken in relating devolution to their strategies for promoting the attainment of provincial status. The Yukon strategy has been to emphasize the status of provinces.[26] The GNWT has focused its efforts on broadening the range of its powers.

By way of example, the government of the Yukon attacked the Meech Lake Accord most vigorously. It condemned the provisions of the Accord which require unanimous federal and provincial approval for the creation of new provinces and which deny the government leaders of the territories a guaranteed role at future constitutional discussions. It even went so far as to launch an unsuccessful challenge to the constitutionality of the provisions of the Meech Lake Accord which affect the status of the territorial governments. For its part, the GNWT condemned the Accord and lobbied actively against it. However, it avoided the stridency of the Yukon government. It recognized that the pursuit of provincial status would bring it immediately in conflict with the provinces on issues about which they felt strongly, such as the constitutional amending formula. It also recognized that it could not compete with the provincial governments on these issues, particularly in view of the insistence of all of the parties at the time that Meech Lake could not be renegotiated. In any case, provincial status would represent the fullest expression of constitutional development. While the territories can continue, although at a significant cost, to develop institutionally in the absence of consensus on division, the form of public government and the role of aboriginal self-government, to grant provincial status would create a degree of constitutional development unacceptably ahead of the territorial level of political development. For this reason, and because it was blocked in seeking enhanced status, the GNWT emphasized gaining enhanced powers through devolution.

In this way, devolution has not been a signficant part of the strategy by which the Yukon government has sought provincial status. In contrast, devolution has been the centerpiece of the GNWT's strategy. With the devolution of jurisdiction over health care completed, the GNWT now is responsible for all the major social development functions which the provincial governments carry out. Should it prove possible to negotiate a Northern Accord and thereafter the transfer of the jurisdiction over land and water which will enable it to legislate into existence the management regimes anticipated by the claims settlements, the territorial government will exercise a great deal of control over policy making in the the realm of economic development. These functions involve large financial and personnel resources and the development of very substantial technical competence in the public service of the territorial government. Even if provincial status remains in the distant future, the GNWT will be able to deliver to the people of the territory almost the full range of services which the provincial governments deliver. When the provincial status does become attainable, this institutionalization of the territorial state which devolution has promoted will make it easier for the GNWT to credibly press its case to the other governments of Canada.

However, to the extent that this institutionalization does not rest on a societal consensus, then the other governments may resist provincial status for the NWT. At the head of the dissenters will be the federal government which will fear that the rights of aboriginal people, for whom it has a special constitutional responsibility, may be inadequately served by a government which is enstranged from them. It will fear that some territorial government action may compel it to violate the norms of intergovernmental equality which have led it to deny itself the use of the disallowance power for the last half century. Any resort to this power, however, justified, would undoubtedly create a crisis in federal-provincial relations. While the likelihood of such a scenario is remote, Ottawa may feel that the prudent course in the absence of a degree of political development high enough to ensure the GNWT's sensitivity to aboriginal collective needs is to avoid taking the risk att al. In such a situation, provincial status would become impossible.

Conclusion

Devolution is linked to both political and constitutional development in

Canada's northern territories, and these two processes are themselves linked in ways which devolution significantly affects. While national factors such as equalization and the arithmetic of constitutional amendment will affect the growth of status of the territories, regional factors will also prove influential. The more each of the territories is able to demonstrate a societal consensus supporting or at least accepting the institutions it has developed, the more likely Ottawa and the provinces will be to accord it more status. Assuming that the aboriginal groups' collective consciousness and desire for collective representation do not dissipate in the face of assimilating forces, the obstacles they face in bringing their political agenda to bear on the debate about public government in the N.W.T. represent a problem of political development which may impair its constitutional development.

The more power is devolved to the territories, the more technically competent and similar to the existing provinces they are likely to appear to be, developments which ought to weaken the rationale for discriminating constitutionally against them. If power is devolved and status accorded northern governments which are taking shape in ways which enjoy the support of the major social groupings, then this process of empowerment can promote the development of the social consensus required for successful government. Here again, the ability of aboriginal groups to bring their potential political weight to bear on these issues and the responsiveness of government, particularly in the NWT, will be the deciding factors in striking the balance between collective and individual representation.

Until recently in the N.W.T., both of these factors contributed to a balance which tended to favour the latter over the former. This outcome encouraged aboriginal groups to seek separate vehicles--divison, claims and self-government--rather than public means of representing their collective interests. The recent settlement of aboriginal claims has empowered the aboriginal peoples of the territories, assuming the ratification of the Dene/Metis agreement, and has redressed the balance to a degree. It remains to be seen what status this development will encourage the territorial government to accord its aboriginal peoples. It could continue to respond to them as interest groups, albeit very powerful ones and risk the continuation of incoherence, of diverging values, loyalties and agendas. Alternatively, it could acknowledge that the devolution and claims processes have now converged; in recognizing its aboriginal peoples as "distinct societies" within it, it could lay the groundwork for resolving the difficult issues of political development and building the foundation of legitimacy on which further constitutional development should rest.

The author wishes to thank the Donner Canadian Foundation, the Social Sciences and Humanities Research Council of Canada and the Department of Advanced Education of the Government of Alberta for their financial support of the research on which this paper is based.

Notes

1   Executive Council Office, Government of Yukon, *Yukon Indian Land Claim Framework Agreement* (Whitehorse: Government of Yukon, 1989), Sub-Agreement 20.

2   Graham Englington, "Matters of Confidence in the Legislative Assembly of the Northwest Territories" in Special Committee on Rules, Procedures and Privileges, Tenth Legislative Assembly of the Nortwest Territories, *Third Report* (Yellowknife: 1986).

3   See, for example, Canadian Arctic Resources Committee, *Aboriginal Self-Government and Constitutional Reform* (Ottawa: CARC, 1988), p. 68.

4   Nunavut Constitutional Forum, *Building Nunavut* (Yellowknife: Nunavut Constitutional Forum, 1985).

5   Peter Jull, "Nunavut" in Rebecca Aird, ed., *Running the North: The Getting and Spending of Public Finances by Canada's Northern Governments* (Ottawa: Canadian Arctic Resources Committee, 1988). See also John Merritt, *et. al.*, *Nunavut: Political Choices and Manifest Destiny* (Ottawa: Canadian Arctic Resources Committee, 1989), Chapter 2.

6   Paul Quessa, President,, Tungavik Federation of Nunavut, "Notes for an Address on the Signing of the Nunavut Agreement-In-Principle Between the Inuit of the Nunavut Settlement Area and Her Majesty in Right of Canada," Igloolik, April 30, 1990, p. 14.

7   Indian and Northern Affairs Canada, *Tungavik Federation of Nunavut Land Claim Agreemnt-In-Principle* (Ottawa: 1990), Article 4.

8   Dene Nation and Metis Association of the Northwest Territories, *Devolution of Powers to the Government of the Northwest Territories: Provincehood and Aboriginal Self-Government*, Eleventh Legislative Assembly of the Northwest Territories, Tabled document No. 51-88 (2), tabled November 2, 1988, pp. 1 and 3.

9   Government of the Northwest Territories, "Opening Address of Commissioner John H. Parker to the Fourth Session of the Eleventh Assembly, February 8, 1989," p. 3.

10   Gurston Dacks, "The Quest for Northern Oil and Gas Accords," in Gurston Dacks, ed., *Devolution and Constitutional Development in the Canadian North* (Ottawa: Carleton University Press, 1990).

11   Government of the Northwest Territories, *First Ministers' Conference on Aboriginal Rights and the Constitution* (Yellowknife: GNWT, 1983) and *Directions for the 1990s*

12   This case is discussed in Robert Page, *Northern Development: The Canadian Dilemma* (Toronto: McClelland and Stewart, 1986), pp. 247-50.

13   Bob MacQuarrie, "Address to Standing Committee on Indian Affairs by the Western Constitutional Forum, March 21," 1984, reprinted in Western Constitutional Forum, *Partners for the future* (Yellowknife: WCF, 1985), p. 11.

14   Dene/Metis Negotiations Secretariat, *Comprehensive Land Claim Agreement between Canada and the Dene Nation and the Metis Association of the Northwest Territories* (mimeo, April 9, 1990), Section 7, and Indian and Northern Affairs Canada, *Tungavik Federation of Nunavut Land Claim Agreement-In-Principle* (mimeo, 1990), Article 4.

15   Yellowknife: Dene Nation and Metis Association of the NWT, 1981.

16   *The Globe and Mail*, Wednesday, March 15, 1989, p. B4.

17   Western Constitutional Forum and Nunavut Constitutional Forum, "Iqaluit Agreement" (Ottawa: Canadian Arctic Resources Committee, 1988), Part II.

18   Michael S. Whittington, "Political and Constituional Development in the N.W.T. and Yukon: The Issues and Interests" in Michael Whittington, coordinator, *The North* (Vol. 72 of the research studies of the Royal Commission on the Economic Union and Development Prospects for Canada, Toronto: University of Toronto Press, 1985), p. 81.

19   See for example Dene/Metis Negotiating Secretariat, *op. cit.*, Section 30, and Department of Indian Affairs and Northern Development, *Western Arctic Claim: The Inuvialuit Final Agreement* (Ottawa: DIAND, 1984), pp. 15-16.

20   This question is examined in detail in Gurston Dacks, "The Quest for Northern Oil and Gas Accords."

21   Letter from Bob Overvold, Principal Secretary, Office of the Government Leader, GNWT to Rick Van Loon, Senior ADM, Department of Indian and Northern Affairs, Government of Canada., April 12, 1990.

22   *Ibid.*, p. 5.

23   See Dacks, "The Quest for Northern Oil and Gas Accords."

24   See, for example, Gordon Robertson, *Northern Provinces: A Mistaken Goal*, (Montreal: Institute for Research on Public Policy, 1985).

25   Gurston Dacks, "The View from Meech Lake: The Constitutional Future of the Governments of the Yukon and Northwest Territories" in Rebecca Aird, ed., *Running the North: The Getting and Spending of Public Finances by Canada's Northern Governments* (Ottawa: Canadian Arctic Resources Committee, 1988).

26   Executive Council Office, Government of Yukon, *Green Paper on Constitutional Development* (Whitehorse: Government of Yukon, 1990), p.10.

The Impact of the Development of Non-Renewable Resources in the Canadian and American Arctic on Inuvialuit and Inupiat Women

Nelda Knelson Daley Pearson

From interviews in 1987 in both Canada (funded by a grant from the Canadian Government) and Alaska it is clear that Inuvialuit and Inupiat women, both sub-groups of the Inuit, have had very different opportunity structures. Although the development of the North Slope Borough (NSB) in Alaska has been heavily criticized and has been rejected as a model by the Inuvialuit of Canada it has provided Inupiat women in Alaska with a chance to acquire significant economic power and political autonomy. In Canada the struggle to create a self-government through the Nunavut proposal and the lack of economic development and diversification have hindered similar opportunities for the Inuvialuit women. Although select women among both the Inupiat and the Inuvialuit by force of their own character have gained some power and voice in the community, the opportunities created by development in the NSB have benefited Inupiat women in more systematic and formal ways.

Unfortunately this development and its benefit to women can only be sustained through the development of non-renewable resources. Most of the opportunities generated for women are in the government funded support system for this development. The questions of who will gain and who will pay and what will happen when resources run out is a serious issue. The NSB must now face the fact that Prudhoe Bay is past the fifty percent mark and capital improvement has dwindled to a standstill. Whether continued development can be sustained is the key issue and will impact heavily on opportunities for Native women in both Canada and Alaska.

This is an ethical issue of potential long run losses versus short term gains which can not be addressed by nonindigenous peoples, neither those who wish to preserve nor those who wish to develop these areas. The degree of social change can only be resolved by the Inupiat and the Inuvialuit themselves.

The differential development of the NSB of Alaska and the Mackenzie Delta/Beaufort Sea Region of the NWT in Canada has led to very different

269

forms of political and social organization. These differences in organization have impacted heavily on the roles of women in the two communities. In the NSB the impact of petroleum exploration and development at Prudhoe Bay and the subsequent capital improvement projects generated by petroleum revenue have made the Inupiat a relatively wealthy people. This wealth has been administered through the development of Native corporations and selfgovernment by the Inupiat within the broader government of Alaska. Although this approach has been heavily criticized and the borough's leaders are under investigation for their mishandling of funds, it has meant that the Inupiat have been forced to become bi-cultural, to acquire the skills necessary to deal with the "white man's" social institutions while maintaining significant, not just symbolic, dimensions of their own culture. These social institutions such as the school board, health clinic, crisis center and borough commission, although foreign to Inupiat culture, have been more or less successfully incorporated into Inupiat culture and now present an opportunity structure for young Inupiats who wish to remain in the borough but have been educated at university. This has been especially beneficial to Inupiat women who have been somewhat more eager than their men to move into these opportunity structures. Inupiat women, for example, fill clerical, administrative, and staff positions at the NSB School District. These positions provide women with an opportunity to use knowledge they have gained through formal education, develop new skills and knowledge, and to acquire power within the community. Although the corporate system and oil development has been and can be criticized on several levels, it is clear that it has provided Inupiat women with an avenue to develop a larger role in their community.

The Inuvialuit of the Mackenzie Delta/Beaufort Sea, on the other hand, have not undergone the kind of economic, social and political dislocation created by the petroleum development of Alaska, and the Inuvialuit, except for those transplanted from Aklavik to Inuvik, lead a life that has been considered much closer to authentic Inuit culture. Although there have been various assessments of the Inuit women's power position in general (Friedl, 1975; Briggs, 1974), it is clear that their power is not equal to that of the men which is an exception to most contemporary hunting and gathering societies (Martin and Voorhies, 1975). Without the development of interface institutions between the Inuvialuit and dominant culture and the subsequent bi-culturalism, Inuvialuit women have only the opportunities for power traditionally open to the women of a minority group within the culture of the dominant group, to be guardians of the traditional values (Lewis, et al., 1978) or to become low income workers in the dominant culture, often providing illegal sales and services such as bar girls and hookers (Interviews, 1987).

This comparison of the Inupiat and the Inuvialuit will address two key issues. The first is the unique benefits received by Inupiat women from the introduction of a wage economy into a hunting and gathering society. Their economic, social, and political position does not conform to the position of other women in development models for the third and fourth world. The second issue addressed is whether or not the development that brought about their unique benefits is sustainable in a society which can maintain a wage economy only as long as non-renewable resources hold out. Examination of the data and arguments pro and con lead us to conclude that the question ultimately is an ethical one best decided by the Native peoples themselves.

Theoretical Background

Traditional approaches to economic development and employment of underdeveloped regions in North America have stressed the acquisition of the knowledge and life style of the dominant culture. This approach has assumed that minorities are disadvantaged due to "inadequate socialization," i.e. they have not only not acquired the requisite formal education and certification but they have not acquired the beliefs, values, norms, and attitudes of the dominant culture. Lewis (1966) points to a culture of poverty common to minorities. This culture has a set of values which are dysfunctional in the broader dominant culture and were believed to be the "problem," the reason why minorities were not succeeding in the "better" developed dominant culture. Lewis' theory is merely a formalization of a conventional wisdom that underlies the missionary movements throughout North America among Hispanics, North American Indians or the Inuit. In all cases eradication of indigenous culture was the goal. Frequently, this was done in the name of God as the missionaries brought religion to the heathen or in the name of law and order as in the case of the RCMP or the empire as in the case of the Hudson Bay Company. This attitude was incorporated into less overtly biased efforts once the missionaries were replaced by government agencies and their agents. Nonetheless, indigenous people were seen as backward, inferior, heathen, etc. and efforts to eradicate native culture and deny autonomy were formally perpetuated through government policies (Whittington, 1985).

The assumption behind the "inadequate socialization" approach was that if "inferior" groups were "resocialized" i.e. acquired both the formal knowledge and life style of the dominant culture they too could join the mainstream of success and achievment. As implemented in third world nations this approach

271

has meant that as more "advantaged" members of the Native population become educated and outmigrate to neighboring urban areas they leave behind a native region depleted and underdeveloped. Once "the chosen" have been absorbed by the dominant culture, the development tends to come to a standstill. Subsequent education creates overeducation for the unskilled jobs available. Since Native and non-Native upper class educated individuals have saturated the market and control the college education level jobs, education of the less advantaged does not increase their opportunities.

As several authors (Boserup, 1970; Blumberg, 1978; Burke, 1978; Etienne, 1980; Kelly, 1981) point out men are more likely to benefit from this development/re-education approach because resocialization tends to be based upon a western European androcentric view of men and women. Native men are trained and educated when defined as "bright" by western standards to do low level functionary jobs. Native women are usually defined in traditional homemaker terms and directed toward education specific to their role as mother/homemaker. In third world countries this has tended to "mainstream" men into the wage economy while women have been left with subsistence horticultural and domestic chores. Or, for example, if women do move into the wage economy it tends to be at the very bottom of the secondary labor market. At some point the balance between college level jobs available and level of education shifts so that the educated outnumber the appropiate jobs available. At this point life stagnates for the indigenous peoples because no new opportunities have evolved and this stagnation impacts heavily on women in the secondary labor market. This outcome has been documented in such diverse areas as Appalachia (Daley, 1986) and Kenya (Thomas, 1985) and has been recognized as a serious concern by planners in the Canadian north (Whittington, 1985; Dacks, 1985).

Although dependence on a single industry economy creates economic dependence on a boom and bust cycle, if the economic benefits of that industry can be redirected to create social institutions which will foster a degree of diversification and economic opportunity for indigenous people within the native region, then there is potential for the development of some degree of self determination and economic/political autonomy. A possible strategy for native peoples would be to become bi-cultural, i.e. be able to speak "the language" of the dominant culture while maintaining a commitment to and credibility with their own peoples (Lewis et al., 1978). In the past re-education theory has encouraged the indigenous peoples who mastered the life style of the dominant culture to accept that culture as superior, co-opting them (Fanon, 1967; Memmi, 1965). The bi-cultural person, however, can deal effectively with the dominant culture while not "buying into" this definition of his own inferiority and/or developing the life style of the dominant class. Initially, it is this bi-culturalism that appears to be the bridge between northern reality and southern education, development and economic opportunity. In the interviews conducted in both Alaska and Canada it was clear that those most effective in leading their people, dealing with the dominant culture and in maintaining Native cultures were bi-cultural.

Initially bi-culturalism appears to be "the answer" for indigenous women's need to empower themselves and break the tendency for men to benefit from the introduction of a wage economy at a cost to women. The Inupiat women of the NSB appear to be an excellent case study of this "break" with the documented impact of development on women. However, a second issue which mediates against this bi-culturalism is the impossibility of industrializing the north and developing economic diversification along southern lines. Northern development depends on the extraction of a non-renewable resource. When that resource is exhausted what happens to the social structures that have been created during the boom cycle of extraction and to those women who have become bi-cultural in order to fill positions in these structures? Because northern development can not encourage economic diversification and the development of an indigenous middle/professional class, once the boom is over economic decline is nearly a certainty.

As Berger has pointed out most theories of development misunderstand the nature of the north. Southern development followed what has been seen as a natural development process of "clearing the forest, the rise of agriculture, establishment of manufacturing, the proliferation of cities as centers of commerce" (Berger, 1985:34). It is clear that the millions of acres of frozen tundra are not amenable to this type of development. There really exists only two possibilities, exploitation of non-renewable resources, especially gas and oil, which requires huge capital investments and "southern" technical know-how or management of renewable resources, primarily wild game management, which requires "northern" field knowledge. The uniqueness of northern development calls into question the effectiveness of using formal education and the encouragement of bi-culturalism as a policy, as we shall see below.

The Beaufort Sea Regions of Alaska and the Northwest Territories

The Beaufort Sea regions of both Alaska and the NWT are unique in Inuit culture in that they have known oil/gas reserves and therefore both the Inupiat and the Inuvialuit have had some reservations as to their participation in the Native land claims settlements in both Alaska and Canada. The North Slope Borough of Alaska which exists within the native corporation of the Arctic Slope Regional Corporation resisted the corporate arrangements of the Alaskan Native Claims Settlement Act (ANCSA) (Berger, 1985) due to its mineral wealth that was already under developemnt at the time of settlement. In the settlement native corporations that make profits must share up to seventy percent of those profits with other native corporations that are not showing a profit. It is clear that the ASRC saw its own petroleum revenues being dispersed to other less advantaged regions.

Similarly in the effort to settle native land claims in the Mackenzie Delta/Beaufort Sea Region of the NWT, the Unuvialuit are aware of the importance of the gas/oil reserves although Norman Wells is not currently producing at the rate of Prudhoe Bay. In their negotiation with Native peoples and the federal and territorial governments to create Deneneh and Nunavut, the Inuvialuit have developed a negotiation organization, Committee for Original People's Entitlement (COPE) separate from the Inuit Tapirisat of Canada (ITC), the Dene or the Metis. They wish to create their own municipality, Western Arctic Regional Municipality (WARM) which will have a good deal of autonomy. Although culturally the Inuvialuit are more similar to the Inuit of the eastern Arctic than to the Dene, they fear exploitation as a "wealthy" minority whether they are part of Deneneh or Nunavut.

Both the Inupiat and the Inuvialuit have some commonalities due to their exploitable non-renewable gas/oil reserves. Although both groups have a common concern with all other Native peoples in the north, namely a wish to preserve traditional subsistence economies, a wish for some degree of autonomy and self-determination, and a wish for the delivery of services to Inuit by Inuit, they also recognize not only the potential benefits of their wealth but the possible costs of that wealth as well as potential conflicts with other Native peoples. The benefits include "southern style" economic development which could lead to an easier more comfortable life. Costs include increased dependence on revenues from non-renewable resources which will eventually run out and a concurrent deterioration of indigenous subsistence skills and activities. Conflict with other Native groups who wish the land preserved for only subsistence activities are inevitable and can currently be seen with pressure toward further exploration in Alaska as Prudhoe Bay passes its fifty percent depletion point (Udall, 1987; Berger, 1985).

On the other hand the specifics of development differ between the NSB and The Mackenzie Delta. To date Native land claims in Canada have not been settled and the negotiated settlement involves not only the land claims themselves but the creation of a Native homeland and a potential new province as well as the Constitutional status of Native Peoples, a low federal priority now that Meech Lake has failed. In Alaska ANSC settled Native land claims within the existing structures of both a state and federal government. It appears that the opportunities for negotation were more limited for the Inupiat than the Inuvialuit and that the Native corporation concept was presented to the Inupiat and other Alaskan Natives without their full understanding. These corporations have used a "cart before the horse" approach to economic development which has led to a good deal of waste. Most Inupiats feel that non-natives have benefited more from ANCSA than have Natives.

> The Native corporations were created by a reversal of the usual process whereby some individuals notice an economic opportunity, then organize to exploit it by forming a corporation and looking for capital. The Native corporations were not formed to meet a particular need in an established market. ANCSA required Natives to organize corporations, provided them with capital, then urged them to find or create economic opportunities. They had to formulate their business purposes after the fact (Berger, 1985:28).

For most Native corporations more money is spent implementing ANCSA and on maintaining the corporate structure than on economic development. The most rapid expansion has been in the area of government services fueled by revenue of the oil boom and it has been the expansion of these services that have most directly benefited the Inupiat of Barrow, as we shall see below.

A major concern of the Canadian government in developing the oil and gas reserves of the Mackenzie Delta/Beaufort Sea Region has been to combine such development with an equitable sustainable life style for all Native peoples. Both the Berger Commission Report and the MacDonald Commission struggled with the question of how to develop non-renewable resources without creating the inevitable dependence of the Inuvialuit people as well as other Natives on the boom/bust cycles seen in other areas of the north. The concern is to create a society which respected indigenous culture, and which would attempt to avoid the mistakes of the Native Corporations which had been used in Alaska unsuccessfully and with slightly more success in the James Bay Inuit/Cree settlement. These concerns came out of a national vision of Canada as a *northern* nation with a special mission toward the north (Page, 1986).

Out of the conference on Northern Development commissioned by the Royal Commission on the Economic Union and Development Prospects for Canada there evolved the following set of concerns. First, a concern arose for developing an economy based on non-renewable resources with government, service, and support spin-offs while maintaining a traditional subsistence economy. Secondly, a concern arose that education for Native people be directed toward both encouraging them to enter the wage economy while enhancing yield in the traditional subsistence economy. Finally, a concern developed that some form of self-government emerge for Native peoples.

All these concerns arose within the problem of how such a society can be maintained. As pointed out by Stabler (1985) dependence on jobs generated by the non-renewable resource sector could not meet the demand for jobs needed to have all Natives fully employed, nor could these support, service, and government jobs be generated fast enough to take up the slack. Such jobs are dependent on the revenues generated by non-renewable resources and are dependent on their fluctuations due to market demands and availabilities of resources.

A realistic fear of those dealing with northern development is: what happens when the resources are depleted. Canada has looked to Alaska and seen the incipient decline in wages from capital improvements and the drop in income as oil reserves as well as market demands decline. Their concern is that if a support, service, and government system is put in place at high initial cost and continued high maintenance costs, what will happen when the non-renewable resources are depleted. In Prudhoe Bay over fifty percent of the oil reserves have been pumped out in less than ten years and additional exploration must be initiated to maintain current lifestyles or the NSB will have to revert to a subsistence hunting and gathering economy. Canadians, both Native and non-Native have noted the overdependence of the Inupiat on this single industry economy, its inevitable decline, and the social dislocation that has occurred with both the increase and decrease in revenues.

The Inupiat

The Inupiat are among the wealthiest of the Inuit, benefiting both from the petroleum revenue from Prudhoe Bay and from increased economic opportunity due to the spinoff from Prudhoe Bay in the form of capital improvements. For example, the high school at Barrow was completed in 1983 at a cost of 75 million dollars. This meant that capital improvements generated high paying jobs for the Inupiat which required very little training, i.e. unskilled day labor. Most of these jobs went to men. With these jobs came many of the serious social dislocations experienced by remote areas when there is a relatively quick influx of money but not real economic development, diversification, or empowerment. Family violence increased as did alcoholism and drug abuse, sexual assault and suicide (Worl and Smythe, 1986).

Meanwhile women had moved into the rapidly expanding need for trained clerical workers, administrators, and staff personnel as well as organizing to cope with the social dislocations created by capital improvement income. Although most Native women (an estimated 75-80 percent) have no special skills, those women who do have training have good paying white collar jobs that are not dependent on labor demand fluctuations and give them power in the broader community. As of 1985 sixty percent of all Inupiat women in Barrow were fully employed year round (Worl and Smythe, 1986). The demand for trained Inupiat women is extremely high. For example there are currently no native teachers in the schools not because none have been trained and certified but because they can receive higher pay as administrators in the NSB government agencies. It is projected by both whites and Natives (Interviews 1987) that as more and more Inupiat receive college educations (currently between 25 and 50 percent of each high school graduating class go on to college) they will fill the professional positions now held by whites. Since most of these jobs are traditionally female occupations such as teacher, counselor, social worker, nurse, etc., there will be a continued demand for Inupiat women in the labor force, and in particular college educated Inupiat women.

Two pulls have encouraged Inupiat women to adapt to the white culture, expanding opportunities for education and the availability of jobs for women that encourage education. There is also a "push." Women still participate in traditional subsistence economic activities but these can be more easily combined with work outside the home than can men's traditional activities. For example sewing skins can be done in the evenings while whale hunting, a male acitivity, is a continuous activity, and interferes with ongoing wage labor (Worl and Smythe, 1986; Kruse, 1986). However, women have decreased their subsistence activities, especially the more demanding preparation of skins, which has led to a shortage of good sewers for umiats (Klienfeld, 1981; Kruse, 1986). Traditional activities that were continuous for women such as tending oil lamps have been abandoned and replaced by electricity and natural gas.

These conveniences require cash. Women can enter the wage economy to help pay for these conveniences while maintaining some traditional activities. Women have a greater opportunity, then, to acquire expertise in the dominant culture and can more easily combine work outside the home with traditional Inupiat women's acitivities. Women have more chances than do the men to become bi-cultural. They also have more reasons to become bi-cultural.

B., a female Inupiat and an administrator in the NSB, stated that "Inupiat men equate education and office work with the white world while their identity is in the outdoors and physical strength. . .hunting and the land." She pointed out that men more than women in the NSB had turned to substance abuse because "men's pride as head of household was threatened." C., a native woman who works as a counselor at Arctic Women in Crisis confirmed this view. She pointed out that as capital improvement jobs declined, which they have been doing with a drop in hourly wage from $25.00/hour to $11.00/hour, women who work in offices become the providers while the men's role through subsistence acitivity as head of household becomes symbolic. Although whaling and hunting continues, greater and greater dependence on "storebought" white man's food has become the norm. Women not only are gaining power within the community, they are also gaining power within their families.

The issue of food is very real and at the core of the bi-cultural difference between men and women. As women replace men as head of households and wage earners, the role of men as hunters becomes more marginal and there is less inducement for them to become bi-cultural. I. states there is great tension in her own family. Her brothers are "great hunters" and see her office work as a "sell out." Despite this personal pain I. sees bi-culturalism (and she uses this word) as the only alternative for the Inupiat. She wants to see the schools teach native children how to use the corporations and to be able to handle their shares intelligently. But at the same time, she wants native language and culture taught in the schools. When I pointed out that only white women went to skin sewing classes, I. retorted indignantly that the women learned these things at home and didn't need the white man's classes for this. This opinion is not supported by Klienfeld's (1981) findings that only ten women in Barrow were expert skin sewers.

A major concern of the schoool board is to encourage bi-culturalism in order to keep NSB children in college. Fairbanks is the nearest university and students experience severe culture shock. They haven't seen trees, parking meters, mountains or flush toilets. They have never walked on grass. The school board has mounted multiple efforts to encourage more contact with the "outside" to deal with this. Sports teams are flown all over Alaska to keep students in touch with the experience of other Alaskan students. A support system has been developed to keep Barrow and other NSB students in college, including a newsletter.

I. sees education as both organizing point for native autonomy and empowerment as well as the vehicle for bi-culturalism. She stated that it was distress over how the Bureau of Indian Affairs handled Native schooling that brought about the organization of the NSB as a political entity. I. stated that parents felt a "lack of control" and that the BIA sent children away to boarding schools and were "breaking up families." The school made "you feel bad about yourself." The Inupiat formed their own school board and "made many mistakes" but now they make policy and are not "just rubber stamps" for the white administrators. Several Native women admit that there have been many mistakes. They said: "We made many mistakes. We got bad advice. We didn't know how to spend money. A lot of money was wasted."

This is directly linked by them to lack of bi-culturalism on the part of the Inupiat and their lack of understanding of "white ways." N. a bush pilot pointed out that a main source of knowledge about white ways is TV. "If the only wealthy man you ever saw was J.R. Ewing on *Dallas,* you'd act like J.R. or try to." Despite this, all the women interviewed believed Native children educated at "outside" universities would return to Barrow and take over more and more of the jobs currently filled by whites in the schools, the professions, and as scientists. Several whites echoed this. Most whites saw their days at Barrow as numbered and had already made plans to retire in the lower forty-eight. Current data is insufficient to determine whether this trend will occur.

Although women currently have been able to benefit from combined increased educational and economic opportunities in ways that men have not, they project a future in which their men will also accept bi-culturalism. Within their memory they see a shift from the hard life before the coming of petroleum development to the greater comfort of heated homes, TV., guns, and snowmobiles. There followed a period of serious social dislocation and abuse. This developed a sense of loss of the past and a yearning for that past. Now, the women feel that they can have the best of both worlds if bi-culturalism can be developed through the schools. Whatever the future, the role of the women at Barrow has been such that they have been empowered and are seeing themselves as the leaders who will transform Inupiat society.

The Inupiat women's increased power through economic development is an exception to the role women usually play in economic development. As several writers on women and economic development (Boserup, 1970; Blumberg, 1978; Burke, 1978; Etienne, 1980; Kelly, 1981; Rubbo, 1975) have pointed out men are usually the first to benefit from contact of an idigenous population with a developed culture. Women generally lag behind, "stuck" in "backward" ways. In the case of the NSB, the organization of the borough around education and the development of the crisis center to deal with social dislocation created an opportunity structure for native women that encouraged them to gain education and take on stable white collar employment. This they believe they have been able to successfully combine with their traditional native activities. A pattern that more nearly fits the model developed by Kelly (1981) can be seen when we turn to the Inuvialuit.

The Inuvialuit

Compared to Alaska Canada has moved more slowly to develop the types of administrative positions developed in the NSB of Alaska.

> However, it soon became clear that most residents of the N.W.T. and Yukon had strong views about the nature and pace of development, and more significantly northern leaders began to ask questions about the social and environmental costs of development (would have to pay?) and about the economic benefits (who would reap them?). Basically, what northerners, both native and non-native and in both the N.W.T. and Yukon want is greater control over their destinies. They want a say in determining the pace of development and the form that development takes; they want assurances that development will proceed in a manner that does not destroy the existing social fabric or the natural environment; and they want a piece of the action--a fair share of the economic rents and job opportunities that will flow from the resource development projects (Whittington, 1985:79).

Inuvialuit women have less access to developing bi-culturalism and empowerment in either the white or Native society since development of a support system of government agencies has been slower than in Alaska. It was for this reason in part that interviews among Inuvialuit women were more difficult and less productive than among the Inupiat. From a limited number of informants, mostly male, it was clear that the NWT's attempts at "indigenization" of public service had appealed more to males than to females. The most common public sector job is that of wildlife officer, a low education male occupation. Secondly, field experience with low levels of managerial professional training was a prime criterion for promotion to senior positions. (However, these positions are currently being replaced by southern trained professionals who tend to be non-Native.) This trend conforms more closely to the model developed by Kelly (1981) in third world nations in which men are the sex most likely to be absorbed into the wage economy and trained for work in that economy. Outside of Inuvik the adoption of white technology has been limited and highly selective. High powered rifles are common and highly desired while snow machines are seen as more trouble than they are worth (Interviews, 1987). The men do not speak eagerly of their women entering the labor force and currently no Natives, let alone Native women occupy positions in the hospitals, schools, or other public human service delivery areas.

Currently, the best hope for the development of opportunity structures for women that would parallel those found in the NSB would be the establishment of the Western Arctic Regional Municipality (WARM) which would enjoy a degree of autonomy in control of such matters as education, policing, health servcices and renewable resource management. This would hopefully allow for a form of bi-culturalism in which Native values and mores could be incorporated into white economic, political, and social structures. If this is the case then many of these jobs that are traditionally female such as clerical, social service, nursing, teaching, will create the push-pulls toward education, employment in the wage economy, and empowerment for Inuvialuit women that it has for Inupiat women. Several authors see government expansion as the only real source of development in the north (Whittington, 1985, Stabler, 1985, Weller, 1987).

Summary and Conclusion

The socio-political and economic shifts of the NSB of Alaska are an accomplished fact. The benefits and costs have been well documented (Worl and Smythe, 1986; Worl, Worl and Lonner, 1981; Smythe and Worl, 1985). It is clear that Inupiat women have greatly enhanced their position in Inupiat society as it is currently shaped by petroleum revenues. The question remains as to what will happen to these women when and if revenues decline. Currently, most job expansion in Alaska has been in the increase of government spending and not in development of resources. As resources dwindle, retrenchment must occur (Berger, 1985). This is clearly a major concern for the development of the Mackenzie Delta. As Whittington so eightly points out employment in the wage economy clearly disrupts the indigenous culture of the Inuit. It disrupts consensual decision making that places the good of the group over the interests of the individual. Wages create inequalities and thus undermine traditional patterns of authority in the community which are based on ability in the subsistence economy. It tends to mean geographic mobility to urban areas where jobs are available, and if failure occurs it tends to mean dependence on a welfare economy. Finally, it means alienation of native peoples from the land.

> The wage economy implies individualism, competition and inegalitarianism, while native culture espouses collectivism, consensus and egalitarianism. Similarly, where the native social structures see authority in terms of a functional division of labour based on

ability, the wage economy implies that power and status are determined by income.

Finally, and possibly most significantly, the wage economy also leads to the alienation of native people from the land. . .If this central fact of their lives is removed and replaced with either a wage or welfare economy, the most significant determinant of their culture will disappear and with it ultimately the culture itself. (Whittington, 1985:69.)

If economic development can continue to sustain the types of opportunities available for Inupiat women we will see a unique example of how women rather than men benefit from a wage economy. But as Whittington points out, these benefits are likely to create a society in which true Inuit culture slowly fades away. Bi-culturalism for one generation may in fact deteriorate into dominant culture in subsequent generations (Worl and Smythe, 1986). As Stabler (1986) points out the number of jobs that the NWT would need to generate in order to bring the Inuit population up to full employment are not cost effective and could not be sustained by the development of non-renewable resources. But, of course, these resources will be developed. The question posed by Whittington of who will pay and who will benefit are the key issues. The data from the Inupiat of the NSB suggest that, in the short run, development will benefit women most, but not without social costs and not without serious dislocation in the future.

This study has addressed two issues. The first was the unique benefits by Inupiat women from the introduction of a wage economy into a hunting and gathering society. Their experience is truly unusual and presents us with counter data to the standard development model. The second issue addressed was whether or not this kind of development is sustainable in a society which can maintain a wage economy only as long as non-renewable resources hold out. Opinion in Alaska is that eventually the outlying Inuit villages will move to major urban areas. If this is the case then Inupiat women may find themselves in the same position as their sisters in third world nations, competing for low income unskilled jobs no matter what their previous level of training and employment has been.

The implications for Inuvialuit women are unclear. If they resist movement into the wage economy they will remain in a weak position when development inevitably comes. On the other hand their entrance into the wage economy is nearly guaranteed to create tremendous personal and social dislocation. The final decision is an ethical one best made by indigenous peoples themselves and summarized by Berger.

Enclaves of indigenous peoples who live within a nation's boundaries cannot fit neatly into a standard pattern for decolonization. In the past, from the point of view of the international community, indigenous peoples were seen as requring legal protection from economic exploitation, racial discrimination, and the denial of human rights. Today, with the support of international law, they are asserting rights to land and to their own institutions (Berger, 1985:178).

In the final analysis white efforts to romanticize Native culture as superior or something to be preserved is not the issue. The issue is whether Native peoples prefer present gains with possible long run losses or whether they prefer to maintain their subsistence economy.

Bibliography

Berger, Thomas R, 1985. *Village Journey*. Hill and Wang.

Blumberg, Rae Lasser, 1978. *Stratification: Socioeconomic and Sexual Inequality*. William C. Brown.

Boserup, Ester, 1970. *Women's Role in Economic Development*. Allen and Unwin.

Briggs, Jean L., 1974. "Eskimo Women: Makers of Men," in Carolyn J. Matthiasson (ed.), *Many Sisters: Women in Cross Cultural Perspective*. The Free Press.

Burke, Mary P., 1978. "Women: The Missing Piece in the Development Puzzle," *Agenda* 1(3):1-5.

Dacks, Gurston, 1985. Comments from a seminar on the North as quoted in Michael S. Whittington (ed.), *The North*. The University of Toronto Press, p. 23.

Daley, Nelda K., 1985. "The Familiar Outsider as Community Developer." Paper presented at *Appalachia: The Land and the Economy*. The University of Kentucky, Lexington.

Etienne, Mona, 1980. "Women and Colonization," in Mona Etienne and Eleanor Leacock (ed.), *Women and Colonization*. Praeger.

Fanon, Franz, 1967. *The Wretched of the Earth*. Monthly Review Press.

Friedl, Ernestine, 1975. *Women and Men*. Holt, Rinehart and Winston.

Kelly, Maria Patricia Fernadez, 1981. "The Sexual Division of Labor and Women's Status," *Current Anthropology* 22(4): 414-419.

Klienfeld, Judith, 1981. "Different Paths of Inupiat Men and Women in the Wage Economy," *Alaska Review of Social and Economic Conditions*. Anchorage: University of Alaska.

Kruse, John A., 1986. "Subsistence and the North Slope Inupiat: The Effects of Energy Development," in Steve J. Langdon (ed.), *Contemporary Alaskan Native Economies*. University Press of America.

Lewis, Oscar, "The Culture of Poverty," *Scientific American* 215:19-25.

Lewis, Helen, et al., 1978. *Colonialism in North America: The Appalachian Case*. The

Appalachian Consortium Press.

Martin, M. Kay and Barbara Voorhies, 1975. *Female of the Species.* Columbia University Press.

Memmi, 1965. *Colonizer and Colonized.* Grossman.

Page, Robert 1986. *Northern Development.* McClelland and Stewart.

Rubbo, Ann, 1975. "The Spread of Capitalism in Rural Columbia: Effects on Poor Women Rayna Retier (ed.), *Toward an Anthropology of Women.* Monthly Reviw Press.

Smythe, Charles W. and Rosita Worl, 1985. *Monitoring Methodology and Analysis of North Slope Institutional Response and Change.* U.S. Department of the Interior, Technical Report 117.

Stabler, Jack C., 1985. "Development Planning North of 60: Requirements and Prospects," in Michael S. Whittington *The North.* University of Toronto Press.

Thomas, Barbara P. 1985. *Politics, Participation, and Poverty: Development Through Self Help in Kenya.* Westview Press.

Udall, James R., 1987. "Polar Opposites," *Sierra*, October.

Weller, Geoffrey R., 1987. "Self-Government for Canada's Inuit: The Nunavut Proposal." Paper presented at Western Social Science Association, El Paso, Texas, April.

Whittington, Michael, 1985. "Political and Constitutional Development in the N.W.T. and Yukon: The Issues and Interests," in Michael S. Whittington (ed.), *The North.* University of Toronto Press.

Worl, Rosita and Charles W. Smythe, 1986. *Barrow: A Decade of Modernization.* U.S. Department of the Interior, Technical Report 125.

Worl, Robert, Rosita Worl, and Thomas Lonner, 1981. *Alaska OCS Socioeconomic Studies Program: Beaufort Sea: Sociocultural Update.* Bureau of Land Management Report 64.

Part Four

Comparative Approaches to International Arctic Cooperation: The Experiences of Canada and Norway

FRAM

International Scientific Cooperation in the Norwegian Arctic

Odd Rogne

Although Canada and Norway both are Arctic rim countries and to some extent have similar needs in the Arctic, they show differences as to international Arctic cooperation. The main reason is the difference in the national control of their Arctic area. While the Canadian Arctic is a physical part of Canada's mainland and follows national regulations, the Norwegian high Arctic--the archipelago of Svalbard--is governed under a special treaty. The Spitsbergen Treaty gave Norway the sovereignty of the area, but with certain rights to citizens from countries having signed the Treaty. As a consequence Svalbard has for decades been an area of multinational activities both in industry and in science.

Why Polar Research?

If we want to understand international arctic science cooperation, we have to go behind the scene and ask: Why are we doing polar research? What are the motives?

These motives can be divided into six groups:[1]

1 Administrative Needs

The administrative responsibility for an area implies a need for data such as maps, survey of resources, environmental data etc. A major part of the institutional Arctic research has taken care of these needs.

By nature this research is of less interest to international cooperation. However, a cooperation between Arctic rim nation scientists would be logical in some methodological issues such as environmental assessment studies, but till now only some exchange of information has occurred. There seems to be a need for an organized contact forum.[2]

2 Basic Research

Many problems in basic research are studied with advantage in the polar regions. Some examples: In upper atmosphere physics, "the polar clift" has made the polar regions attractive to these sciences. The biologists can take advantage of the simple ecosystems and the adaption to an extreme environment. The Quaternary geologists are able to study active glacial processes such as sedimentation from glaciers, and the glaciologists are naturally in their right environment. Similar opportunities are found in the marine sciences.

Most of the international cooperation in polar research has up till now been done in basic research--often on a bilateral project basis, although some multinational projects have been organized. There are some differences between the sciences depending on the field's need for large-scale cooperation, tradition for international cooperation, etc.

3 Environment

Also the environment issue has been focused upon in the polar regions. It is studied both as a regional problem (with investigation of, for instance, pesticides and heavy metal in the food chain) and as a worldwide problem (with monitoring of such global enivironmental issues as the ozon depletion and climate change).

Environmental monitoring and research is likely to become a major field of scientific activity in both polar regions and a field where international cooperation is fundamental, as data are needed for the whole region. The pollution of the Arctic has been a key issue in the recent discussions between the Arctic nations ("the Finnish Initiative"), and a need for both monitoring and research has already been expressed.

4 Industrial/Economic Motives

The quest for new resources has been the driving force for industrial activities in the polar regions, as also was the case for major efforts in the earlier exploration of these regions. Mapping of resources and related research are often financed by industry, supplementing the nation's own surveying.

Environmental regulations have in the last decade created a need for data on environmental implications of industrial activity. The industry has been compelled to produce documentation of these effects (environmental assessment studies), which in sum has produced new knowledge on the Arctic environment. However, so far international or multinational cooperation in this field has been the exception rather than the rule.

The polar areas present challenges to the engineering industries to come up with new technical developments, for instance equipment that can function in a cold climate. Also within such sectors of activity as transport, housing and tourism do the areas present special needs to be meet.

So far this field has few examples of international cooperation Competition is more typical than cooperation.

5 Political Motives

Polar research has served as a means to mark national presence in regions where sovereignty questions are not solved. Today Antarctica would be the best example. Earlier this has also been the case in the Arctic, and "incidents" in the Arctic may still occasionally lead to politically motivated Arctic research.

6 Military/Strategic Motives

Military/strategic motives have been an important driving force for some of the Arctic research. Oceanographic data, including sea ice, is useful knowledge for oceangoing vessels of any type. Military agencies have been a source of financing also for open university research in the Arctic.

Although the military tension may decline as a result of improved relations between east and west, the need for improved data still exists, so the research may well continue at the present level.

Melting of the Ice Curtain

Except for a few cooperative projects among scientists from western Arctic countries, the majority of cooperative projects in the Norwegian Arctic have a represented a north-south cooperation.

Until recently there has been an "ice curtain" in Arctic research between east and west. However, in 1984 USSR signaled a change in their policy offering bilateral cooperation. As for Norway, the Soviets had suggested bilateral cooperation some 20 years earlier. However, it then turned out that the cooperation was limited to Norwegian territory--a possibility of less interest to us.

The new policy aimed at a balanced cooperation covering both countries' Arctic areas. The Norwegian-Soviet discussions started just after the conclusion of the general agreement on scientific cooperation in the Arctic between Canada and USSR. However, it was quite clear that the USSR's change of policy only referred to the Arctic rim countries and only to bilateral agreement.

The idea of an international scientific cooperation in the Arctic has been discussed over the last 3-4 years, and has now gained support from all Arctic countries. The International Arctic Science Committee (IASC) will be founded in Canada in August this year. It remains to be seen whether IASC will meet the needs for an improved international scientific cooperation in the Arctic to serve scientists from both the Arctic countries and other regions.

Notes

1   These categories were first presented by the author in a talk in 1987 at a meeting in Sweden, "Hvorfor polarforskning--Hvilke motiver ligger bak?", published in: Lunder, Herberth (ed.): *Polarområdene. Hvite felter i politikk oq vitenskap.* Sth. 1988, pp. 73-79. A PhD student, Imgemar Bohlin, has later used and developed these concepts, see: Elzinga, Ant and Ingemar Bohlin: *The Politics of Science in Polar Regions.* AMBIO 1989, no.1, pp. 71-77.

2   See also Roots, E. Fred and Odd Rogne: *The Need for Feasibility and Possible Role of an International Arctic Sience Committee.* Ottawa/Oslo 1987.

The Creation of A Canadian Polar Commission and Its Domestic and International Role

Jack Stagg

A little less than a year ago (November 24, 1989) the Prime Minister of Canada announced that a Canadian Polar Commission would be created. This announcement was made in recognition of the need in Canada for a more focused and integrated approach in order to maintain and improve polar knowledge.

A few months after this announcement, on May 25 of this year, legislation was tabled in our Parliament, which will create the Canadian Polar Commission. (I was hoping to tell you today that the Canadian Polar Commisson was officially established, but in Canada--as in the Nordic countries--many things come to a standstill during the summer and the Bill still has to go through one or two more steps.) When the Act establishing the Commission comes into force it will give the Canadian Polar Commission legislative authority to promote and disseminate knowledge of the polar regions in Canada and elsewhere and to foster cooperation in polar science both nationally and internationally.

The initiative to create a Canadian Polar Commission stemmed from repeated and varied concerns regarding the state of polar research in Canada--concerns expressed both within the scientific community and government. In response to these concerns a study group was commissioned in 1985 by the Minister of the Department of Indian Affairs and Northern Development to investigate the state of Canadian polar science. The study group produced the report *Canada and Polar Science* which was released by the Minister of Department of Indian Affairs and Northern Development in 1987. It strongly recommended the creation of a Canadian Polar Commission.

Taking into consideration the complexity of northern science and the varied interests it served, the group reviewed and assessed existing institutions and organizations responsible for northern or polar research activities in Canada. These included twenty one federal government departments or agencies having nation-wide mandates to carry out technical, scientific, and/or knowledge-gathering activities in northern, Arctic and polar regions. In addition, over thirty universities, numerous industrial organizations, several provincial and territorial governments, as well as northern native development corporations and private organizations in both northern and southern Canada engaged in northern research, training, education, development or application of polar knowledge were also consulted.

Despite the number and diversty of the institutions and individuals involved in polar research, the findings of the Working Group revealed a widespread feeling of dissatisfaction within the polar research community and came to the following general conclusions:

-- because of a history of imposed constraints (financial and organizational), Canadian science in the North in some cases, was of less than highest quality;
-- most centres of northern study are too small to be fully effective or sustain world-class research;
-- due to demands placed on researchers, science in northern Canada is becoming schizophrenic in nature in that northern science is expected to both advance knowledge and understanding as well as be responsive to the needs and interests of northern and industrial demands;
-- development of northern technology is spasmodic and is usually directed toward short time use; and
-- there exist serious gaps in the scope and range of Canadian northern science.

After careful review, the Working Group conluded that a new major research organization with its own facilities, research staff and field programme was not what was needed and would not be practical because:

-- there already exists a number of public and private bodies undertaking polar research and a new research institute, by itself, would not be able to address and resolve most of the problems with Canadian polar research mentioned above;
-- it would be difficult to obtain the substantial funds needed to build new facilities and sustain operations considering the fiscal difficulties encountered at present by the federal government;
-- the establishment of a new research oriented institute would be opposed by much of the polar research community and by many northerners, who would see a new institute as threatening to their independence and

authority;

-- it would be difficult to achieve a consensus in Canada on the physical location of a new *national* but *northern* institute;

-- serious policy-related problems in the North, scientific independence and credibility for a new institution created by government to study northern problems may be difficult to achieve; and

-- Canada already has the legislative basis for a Canadian polar institute in the Arctic Institute of North America, which was created by an Act of Parliament in 1945 to serve as a national arctic institute, but it has not operated as such for several years. The establishment of another national body with similar mandate could raise questions as to why the first one was not used, what new mandate should be given.

The Working Group suggested that the most practical and effective course to improve polar research in Canada and to maintain Canada's position as a world leader in polar research and technology would be to undertake a number of modest, economical steps designed to build on present scientific strengths, develop a long-term Canadian commitment to polar knowledge and expertise, provide the existing polar research community with the information support it must have and increase the involvement of northerners in Canadian polar science and research.

The Working Groups recommendations formed the basis for the Canadian Polar Commission's mandate which will be to:

-- enhance Canada's international polar profile by fostering and facilitating international and domestic liaison and cooperation in circumpolar research;

-- promote and encourage national institutions and organizations to support the development and dissemination of such northern knowledge; and

-- increase international focus on circumpolar concerns such as Arctic haze, greenhouse effect, and air and water-borne toxins in the food chain.

In order to carry out its mandate the Commission will:

-- initiate, sponsor and support conferences, seminars and meetings;

-- undertake, support, publish and disseminate studies, reports and other documents relating to the polar region; and

-- recognize achievements and contributions in areas related to its mandate and encourage and support the polar research programs and activities of organizations, associations and individuals.

The activities of the Commission shall be managed by a Board of Directors consisting of a Chairperson, two Vice Chairpersons and nine other members, to be appointed by the Governor in Council, on the recommendation of the Minister for a term of three years. Persons appointed to the Board must have knowledge that will assist the Commission in the furtherance of its purpose, having regard to the ethnic, linguistic and regional diversities of Canada's polar regions.

The head office of the Commission will be in the National Capital Region; regional offices may also be established in Canada, with at least one regional office established at a place north of sixty degrees north latitude.

In keeping with the theme of the round table discussion here today, I would like to stress that the *international role* of the Canadian Polar Commission will be a prominent one as Canadians have a growing interest in international Arctic affairs. The importance of national and international polar issues in the minds of Canadians demands that the Canadian Polar Commission act as the focal point to collect knowledge about polar research in other countries and become the point of contact between Canadian and international polar research communities.

In effect the Canadian Polar Commission will take its place in international fora with equivalent foreign organizations such as the Swedish Polar Research Secretariat and the Danish Polar Center which were also established to address the growing need to coordinate cooperation in international arctic research and exchange of information.

Exercising its mandate regarding its international role, the Canadian Polar Commission would also work closely with Norwegian officials of the National Research Council, the Interdepartmental Council on Polar Matters and the Norsk Polarinstitutt, and other equivalent Nordic organizations such as the Finnish Polar Committee, the Polar Research Committee of the Royal Swedish Academy of Sciences and the National Research Council of Iceland.

Furthermore, the Commission will be expected to focus international attention on national concerns, whether they be driven by resource development, legal or jurisdictional questions, or matters related to global environmental issues.

For example, the proposal to create an International Arctic Science Committee (IASC) responsible for coordinating international scientific activity in the Arctic would see the Canadian Polar Commission as the body responsible for the coordination of Canadian participation. Although the Commission is not yet in place, I understand that the founding meeting for IASC will take place in a few weeks time in Resolute in the Canadian Arctic.

The Commission can also be expected to participate in future international deliberations regarding the Protection of the Arctic Environment also known as the Finnish Initiative. Through such a mechanism the Canadian Polar Commission will advance national objectives and ensure that Canada's viewpoint regarding such issues as sustainable and equitable development and an Arctic Environmental Strategy is adequately represented in international discussions.

An additional but primary responsibility of the Canadian Polar Commission would also be the development of a Canadian Polar Information System which would link existing data bases and create a northern information network. International access to such an information system will greatly facilitate and genuinely foster international cooperation in polar research.

To conclude, the creation of the Commission is very timely in view of recently expanded, international activities which involve the Arctic and is in keeping with stated Canadian government policy which announces our desire to develop a new cooperative ethic with our northern neighbours.

To date, the initiative to create the proposed Commission has won widespread support from the territorial governments, aboriginal people, private enterprise, research institutes and universities in Canada and has also evoked considerable international good wishes and good will.

As a major Arctic stakeholder, Canada must fulfil its responsibility as a leading nation among circumpolar countries. The need to enhance circumpolar cooperation is a practical concern and what has been addressed through initiatives such as the Canada/USSR Agreement on Cooperation in the Arctic and the North, the Northern and Cold Region Research Science and Technology Cooperation Arrangement between Canada and Norway and the Canada/Denmark Marine Environment Cooperation Agreement will be expanded upon through the auspices of the Canadian Polar Commission.

Cooperation, Conflict or Compromise? Superpower Responses to Canadian of and Nordic Policies in the Arctic

Diddy R.M. Hitchins and Bertil Liander

Introduction

Since WWII the growth in formal international relations has been enormous. This is not just a reflection of the fact that there are now more than 160 primary actors (nation-states) in the international arena, of whom all but a handful wish to be fully engaged, compared with 50 or so when the United Nations was founded. The increased activity also results from improvements in transport and communications, the creation of a global economy, and the development of a high degree of interdependence between the nation-states of the contemporary world. The rise in the number of international organizations, within the framework of which much of the increased international activity is conducted, is another indicator of the explosion. It is clear that the increment in international relations has not just occurred at the global level but also at the regional level: Europe appears to represent the area of most heightened interaction but other regions--Africa, Latin America, the South Pacific--all seem to demonstrate the same phenomenon.

It comes, therefore, as quite a shock to the student of international relations to discover that there is one region of the world which seems to have been virtually untouched by this trend: the Arctic. Unlike the Antarctic, no international regime has been created for the Arctic, and if one took as a measure of international relations activities a compilation of relevant treaties and agreements one could conclude that there is an abnormal vacuum. As recently as 1981, Lincoln P. Bloomfield in an important article ("The Arctic: Last Unmanaged Frontier," *Foreign Affairs,* 60:1, Fall 1981, 88-105) referred to the Arctic as "the last unmanaged frontier" and suggested that due to its remoteness and lack of significance, it might serve as a laboratory for U.S.-Soviet cooperation at a time of heightened superpower tension. While international relations may have had little impact on the Arctic, technological developments--both in the military/defense and security realm and in economic

297

development/resource exploitation, have relentlessly encroached upon the Arctic to the point where the increased strategic significance of the Arctic, combined with energy and resource extraction potential, environmental concerns and the organization of indigenous peoples in pursuit of their interests, has prompted attentive and well informed observers to prophesy the imminent arrival of the "Age of the Arctic" (Gail Osherenko and Oran R. Young, *The Age of the Arctic: Hot Conflicts and Cold Realities,* Cambridge University Press 1989, and Oran R. Young, "The Age of the Arctic," *Foreign Policy,* No. 61, Winter 1985-86, 160-179). Other respected authorities on the Arctic have argued that global human survival and security, in the light of newly identified ecological threats, make it imperative for there to be enhanced international cooperation in the circumpolar north (Franklyn Griffiths, as yet unpublished, presentation to Canada-USSR Conference on Canadian-Soviet Arctic Cooperation, Ottawa, October 1989). These latter observations come at a time when the tensions between the superpowers have eased considerably as a result of the new leadership (since 1985) in the USSR and against a backdrop of greatly increased transnational interaction in the Arctic arena which may precede the creation of an Arctic regime for international relations. As we stand on the threshold of such development it is worthwhile reviewing the period from 1945 until 1990 to try to understand what factors inhibited the growth of international relations in this region.

Eight nation-states are generally regarded as being 'Arctic states': USSR, Canada, USA (Alaska), Norway, Finland, Sweden, Denmark (Greenland), and Iceland. Two of these are superpowers which have been locked in tense competiton virtually throughout the whole period under consideration. Relations between the superpowers have been constrained by their competition and mutual hostility: except in a few limited and functional areas, the superpowers relations with one another in the Arctic have been in terms of their offensive and defensive military capabilities to harm one another. Such relations do not translate into instruments of international relations--regimes, treaties, agreements. Rather such relations are guarded secrets about which as little is conveyed as possible. But the other Arctic states have to exist in this environment and their governments have to make both domestic and foreign policy decisions that conform to their national interests.

We thought it would be most interesting to consider the international relations of the Arctic for the post war period specifically trying to observe and identify the dynamics between the less powerful states and the superpowers to see if we could identify why the Arctic had, until very recently, witnessed so little of the growth trend in international relations.

Setting the Scene for Arctic International Relations--
Prehistory to 1945

A major reason for the relative obscurity of the Arctic in international relations has been the difficulty experienced in trying to come to grips with the region as an entity. As eminent Arctic experts have noted, there has been inadequate conceptualization of the Arctic as a region and certain key factors have prevented the Arctic from being assigned a special status in international relations such as that held by the Antarctic. In the era of modern international relations (since the end of the Thirty Years War in 1648), the Arctic was initially conceived of as an area for exploration and territorial claims and for economic exploitation. Despite the harshness of the conditions which militated against occupation, the evidence of rich resources rendered the lands coveted prizes, thus territorial claims were asserted and economic exploitation started often virtually ignoring the existence, let alone the interests of the indigenous peoples who were sparsely scattered through the enormous region. Nineteenth century governments apparently had no inhibitions when it came to imposing their arbitrary territorial boundaries and authority on the indigenous people. Explorers and traders, however, were impressed by the ability of the natives to survive in this harsh environment which evinced an admiration in the colonizers that led to creation of the myth of the "Arctic sublime."

The Arctic was not omitted from nineteenth century international relations: the main focus of such relations were issues of jurisdiction, navigation, and commerce. Concern over exploitation of natural resources (both fish and fur seals) led to international management agreements. In the early part of the twentieth century, fisheries dominated the Arctic international relations agenda, but mammals and migratory birds were also touched upon, and in 1920 a major multilateral treaty relating to jurisdiction was entered into for the archipelago of Spitzbergen (Svalbard). This treaty between France, Denmark, Italy, Japan, Netherlands, Norway, Sweden, the USA, and the UK, created a regime that gave sovereignty over Svalbard to Norway while citizens of the parties to the treaty had the right to participate in commercial and industrial activity there.

During the Second World War, the strategic importance of the north relative to both aerial and naval warfare was amply demonstrated. Both the USA and the USSR recognized the critical significance of northern territories for access and communication. For the USA the vital importance of northern Canada, Greenland, and Iceland was amply brought home, and for the USSR the vital significance of naval access to Murmansk, which involved not only waters off Norway and Svalbard, but also access to the Atlantic through maritime passages between Norway, Iceland, and Greenland. During World War II the US entered into defence agreements with Canada, Iceland, Denmark (for Greenland) and had installations in all three locations. The wartime lessons learned made the USA unwilling to leave these locations when hostilities ceased, and made the USSR anxious to change the Svalbard regime to let the Soviet Union share in sovereignty over the island. Norway, with the support of other interested parties resisted this proposal. The US in response to a proposal from Denmark that US military installations on Greenland be dismantled, argued for perpetuation of the bases in the light of their strategic significance.

The Post War Period: 1945 to the Present--The Security Framework

With the breakdown of the wartime alliance between the USA and USSR and their entry into the Cold War in 1947, the strategic significance of the Arctic entered a new era. Whereas previously the Arctic had been only a flank, important for communications and supply, it now lay directly between two hostile emerging superpowers and on the shortest route between them. With the development first of long range bombers and subsequently of intercontinental ballistic missiles, the Arctic became a direct route between the superpowers for hostile exchanges, and for the USSR, the north became the location for its major military buildup. While both the USA and the USSR conceived of themselves as global powers, the Soviet Union is more obviously an Arctic power by geographic necessity. Since World War II the USSR has become not only one of two global superpowers with immense nuclear capacity but also a major maritime power. The major naval buildup in the USSR occurred in the Murmansk-Kola Peninsular area using northern waters both for training and for access to the oceans of the world.

From the beginning of the Cold War until the assumption of political leadership by Mikhail Gorbachev in 1985, the USSR kept its security policies shrouded in secrecy. Any geographic area which had strategic significance for the USSR was governed in the light of that criterion. The whole Soviet North was exploited and developed to serve national security objectives in absolute secrecy in a closed authoritarian system. Reasons of state security were sufficient to ensure that no constraints were put upon military activities or economic development to support military objectives. Since the USSR has no warm water ports with direct access to the world's oceans, it has had to concentrate its naval buildup in the north.

The initial Cold War threat to the domestic territory of the USA was posed by Soviet long-range bombers approaching from the north over the Arctic. In response to this threat, the USA entered into defence arrangements with Canada and Denmark to create the DEWline. Distant Early Warning stations were constructed in an arc across the north from Alaska to Greenland. Although these arrangements were under the umbrella of NATO, the US concluded bilateral agreements with both Canada and Denmark, thus essentially removing the defence of North America from the NATO agenda. Likewise, the US concluded a defence treaty with Iceland which, though technically within the framework of NATO, operated more as a bilateral arrangement until the 1980s when Iceland decided to participate in NATO meetings.

The experience of defeat by Germany in World War II made Norway anxious to secure its defence by alliance after the war was over. A founder member of NATO, Norway was only too aware of the strategic significance of its territory and its coastal waters for the USSR. In joining NATO Norway wished to ensure its own defence but did not wish to exacerbate tension with the USSR, thus Norway has striven to make it clear that it recognizes that Soviet military might is not directed at immediate neighbors but is part of a global situation. By prohibiting the stationing of NATO troops or nuclear weapons in peacetime and not allowing any manoeuvers close to the Soviet border, Norway tries to demonstrate responsible restraint.

Amongst the Arctic nation-states, all of the Arctic Ocean littorals are organized into the East-West confrontation framework, but the two non-littoral states, Sweden and Finland, are not. Finland had to make territorial concessions to the USSR after World War II, but in pursuit of its continued existence entered into a Treaty of Friendship and Mutual Assistance with the USSR which recognized its neutrality on condition that Finland would prevent violation of its airspace. Sweden had been the protagonist of a Scandinavian Defence Alliance prior to the proposal for NATO, but rather than join NATO pronounced adherence to its traditional neutrality and non-alignment. The Swedish view at the time was that an overwhelming NATO presence on the USSR's northwest border might aggravate the USSR to respond in a way that would endanger Finland, thus Swedish neutrality supported Finnish neutrality.

Despite the fact that the Nordic nation-states have differing relations to the superpowers--Norway, Denmark, and Iceland being NATO members, Sweden and Finland being neutrals, and Finland and Norway being neighbors to the USSR close to its major military installations, there is a shared concern amongst them for their region to be a region of stability peripheral to the tension between the superpowers. Each Nordic nation-state has made efforts to try to lessen tension through reassurance, deterrence, and screening.

Through the phases of the Cold War superpower relationship the threat has evolved from long range manned bombers, to intercontinental ballistic missiles and more recently to air and sea launched cruise missiles. As the technologies and strategies have evolved so has the strategic significance of the Arctic waxed and waned. Initially, with the long range bomber threat there was considerable military activity in the Arctic to construct early warning installations (DEWline in the west). As the bomber threat declined and the nuclear threat developed in the 1960s ballistic missile warning radar stations were constructed (BMEWs in the west). In the 1980s the developing threat is from cruise missiles both air and see launched, including the submarine launched cruise missiles that have under-ice capability. The response has been to further upgrade the detection facilities (NWS in the west) but also to research alternative defence systems (SDI and the Air Defence Initiative in the West). Despite the continuing secrecy regarding defence developments in the USSR we can assume that they have passed through similar stages and upgrades. Throughout the period, the North has been an area of strategic stand-off between the superpowers with mirrored developments on both sides. Since the Arctic has been in the strategic forefront for the superpowers, it is an area of extreme sensitivity for both of them, an area where they prefer to keep developments quiet and undetected under the cloak of national security.

That has been easier for the USSR than for the USA. The USSR occupies over half of the Arctic littoral--and it is the Russian Republic that occupies the north--least subject of all Soviet republics to ethnic problems. The population of the Russian Republic had been inured to secret government (up until Gorbachev's reforms).

Not being an Arctic littoral state (except via Alaska which is a non contiguous state) the US has had to rely on allies for the implementation of its Arctic defence policies. Such reliance creates a less than perfect situation for a global superpower and opens up the potential for lesser power initiatives in pursuit of their own interests.

With the East-West conflict as the framework for international relations in the second half of the twentieth century, what role have the lesser powers played in Arctic international relations? What initiatives have they taken in pursuit of their own interests?

Lesser-Power Initiatives in Arctic International Relations

As the introduction indicated, there is a surprising dearth of Arctic international relations in the post World War II period. Research indicates that the tense security relationship between the superpowers in the region apparently inhibited the growth of normal relations. While sentiments amongst the populations of the lesser Arctic powers indicate a great yearning not to be caught up in the dangers of the global superpower stand-off, geography is unyielding and the governments of the lesser Arctic powers had to accept the constraints of the security relationship upon their actions. Nevertheless, the Nordic states participated in an initiative to demilitarize and to recognize their nuclear-free status from the early 1960s onwards. The initial proposal for a Nordic Nuclear Weapons Free Zone was made in 1958 by Soviet Premier, Marshal Bulganin, in letters sent to the prime ministers of Norway and Denmark as part of a Soviet plan to forestall American intermediate range missiles in Europe. Although both Norway and Denmark had already refused the American missiles, their response to the USSR was to ask whether the Kola Peninsula would fall within the NNWFZ. Premier Khrushchev repeated the proposal in 1959, extending it to the Baltic; this time Sweden, along with Norway and Denmark, responded by asking whether Soviet territory was to be included. The Soviet reply was that to include Soviet territory made no practical sense. In 1961, having decided not to become a nuclear power, Sweden took the initiative and put forward a proposal for a Nordic "non-nuclear club," and in 1963 President Kekkonen of Finland formally proposed the creation of a Nordic Nuclear Weapons Free Zone, arguing that creation of such a zone would only render de jure what was already de facto since "the Scandinavian states already form a nuclear free zone." Such an act would, however, have been a significant change since the Scandinavian NATO members' pledge not to have nuclear weapons on their soil was conditional, applying only to peacetime. The response of the Scandinavian states to Kekkonen's proposal was to insist that the proposal must be considered within the framework of a broader European arms control agreement, following upon the achievement of a compehensive test ban.

Although this initiative met with little enthusiasm in the 1960s, when it was renewed and reproposed in the 1970s it received more Swedish support and was further resuscitated in the early 1980s by Norway. As a result, interest in the zone has been rekindled throughout Scandinavia. The issue was put on the official agenda for the Nordic Council foreign ministers in 1981 and gained sufficient support to become an ongoing process. In response the USSR announced in 1981 its willingness to unilaterally guarantee such a zone and even to consider the application of ancillary measures to apply to adjoining Soviet territory. Subsequently, in 1983 Yuri Andropov repeated this offer and Soviet General Chervov elaborated when he explained on Swedish television that the USSR was prepared to withdraw six Golf class ballistic submarines from the Baltic. Since these submarines were very old, their withdrawal was regarded more as a gambit than a real concession.

By December 1984 the parliaments of all five Nordic states supported the Nordic Nuclear Weapons Free Zone proposal. Since 1986 a Nordic inter-parliamentary working group has been working on the proposal, while since 1987 a joint working group of Nordic governmental experts has been studying the proposal. Meanwhile, a Soviet response to this initiative was to announce in 1986 some "thinning down" of intermediate range nuclear missiles on the Kola Peninsula and other adjacent areas as demanded by Sweden, achieved by the dismantling of launchers and the redeployment of several operational-tactical missiles battalions. While Nordic governments generally found these Soviet gestures encouraging, military critics were skeptical, arguing that the offers only represented post facto announcements of changes that had already been carried out in pursuit of modernization of Soviet forces and weaponry. At the same time the USA, throughout the discussion of a Nordic Nuclear Weapons Free Zone, has remained strongly opposed. In relative terms, even though all that has been achieved in pursuit of a Nordic Nuclear Weapons Free Zone is a process and an intergovernmental working group, this can be regarded as a successful lesser-power initiative in Arctic international relations. Proposals made by individuals and organizations to make the whole Arctic region nuclear-weapons free have met with less success since they have not been taken up by Arctic state governments to pursue as international agenda items. Of course the Arctic states are parties to a number of global and regional multilateral arms control regimes that apply inter alia to the Arctic region, such as the Partial Test Ban Treaty (1963), the Seabed Treaty (1971), and the Final Act of the Conference on Security and Cooperation in Europe (CSCE). These proposals essentially reflect an Arctic-wide expressed desire on the part of lesser powers to see the Arctic region demilitarized, however, the desire has run counter to reality which has actually witnessed the increased militarization of the north.

The proposal for a Nordic Nuclear Weapons Free Zone and its acceptance throughout the area can be seen as one more gesture in a pattern of behavior that tries to demonstrate that the Nordic region, while determined to maintain its sovereignty and independence from the USSR, nevertheless, seeks at every opportunity to reassure the USSR that it poses no threat. Each of the Nordic states has undertaken unilateral actions to demonstrate this situation: Finland through its attempts to disengage itself from superpower confrontation via neutrality but reassuring the USSR with frequent gestures: the Treaty of Friendship and Mutual Assistance; Finland's undertakings to ensure that Finnish

Lapland would not be used as an attack route to the USSR; Kekkonen's NNWFZ initiatives and assurances that Finnish airspace would not be used for cruise missile attacks on the USSR; and the 1965 proposal for pacification of the Finnish-Norwegian border--an early confidence building measure (CBM).

Sweden, in its original decision not to join NATO and throughout its subsequent period of armed neutrality, has sought to demonstrate that it poses no threat to the USSR. As an early proponent (1961) of a Nordic nuclear free club and a strong supporter of the Finnish NNWFZ and in its expressed view that the Baltic should be included in that NNWFZ, Sweden has played its part in trying to lessen the strategic significance of the area. Sweden's low key response to repeated and continuing Soviet submarine activity in its waters has likewise contributed to this goal, although Sweden is also determined not to be manipulated by the USSR against the USA and in this light has been a proponent within the UN for naval arms control.

Norway has perhaps been the most demonstrative of the Nordic states as it occupies the most central strategic position. Norway takes every opportunity to draw attention to its policies of restraint vis-a-vis the USSR and to demonstrate that despite its NATO membership it is not a channel for superpower destabilization of the local region. This is accomplished by prohibition on NATO troop or nuclear weapons deployment; use of Norwegian rather than NATO patrols in the Barents Sea and restrictions on NATO manoeuvers in sensitive regions; and recent proposals for preventing incidents at sea by having CBMs on naval exercises, and an international convention to ensure that offshore petroleum installations should not be used for military purposes, all of which measures are designed to reassure the USSR. At the same time on practical nonmilitary and resource development issues, Norway does have ongoing disputes and negotiations with the USSR.

The aggregation of these various measures designed to reassure the USSR that the Nordic area poses no threat to Soviet security, can be regarded as a combined Nordic initiative involving all three nation-states. The initiative emanates from a shared fear arising from their own vulnerability in the face of the military might of their close superpower neighbor.

Both Greenland and Iceland are, by virtue of geography, caught up in the Arctic strategic stand-off between the superpowers. Where Greenland is concerned there has been a consensus in Denmark: Denmark cannot defend Greenland and does not want the Soviet Union to gain a foothold there. The Danes do not want tension with the USA over Greenland. It therefore is the best policy to have an agreement with the USA for the US to defend Greenland and for Greenland to serve as Denmark's contribution to NATO. Thus

Greenland has been a host to US bases, a DEWline and BMEWs site and the location for development of surveillance activities. NATO membership, defence, and Arctic policy were very low key issues in Denmark so long as Greenland was ruled as a colony but with the emergence of the Home Rule government in the 1970s, which is opposed to the militarization of the Arctic, debate over these issues has surfaced. During the 1980s there has been concern in Greenland about any link between the installations at Thule and the USA's Strategic Defense Initiative (SDI) and whether modernization at Thule runs counter to the ABM treaty. It is however the case that, when the new North Warning System (OTH-backscatter locations from Alaska to Labrador) becomes operational in 1992, Greenland's role in the defence of North America will be largely ended.

The population of Iceland has, like the population of Greenland, been essentially anti-military. Iceland is an unarmed nation that entered NATO in 1949 to deter aggression and entered into a defence agreement with the USA in 1951 that allowed the USA to maintain an air base at Keflavik for air defence and anti-submarine warfare.

Since 1964 Iceland has had a policy not to allow nuclear weapons on its soil, which the US has respected. Proposals for a north Atlantic zone of peace have come from the Icelandic parliament and political parties. During the 1950s and again in the 1970s, Icelanders declared that they would terminate the agreement with the US because of the cultural impact of the US base personnel on an island with a population of only 250,000. In response to these concerns the US has limited base personnel to 3,000 and has restricted their movement to the base area. As the strategic technology has developed, the US has constantly upgraded Iceland's surveillance and defence capabilities, particularly since the Home Rule government in Greenland has opposed upgrading of the facilities there. During the 1980s, Iceland has moved from its minimalist involvement in NATO to becoming an active participant. In 1986 the government of Iceland announced a policy not to allow chemical weapons on its soil.

For Canada, being the ham in the superpower sandwich, has been equally as problematic as being the mouse "in bed with an elephant." Ever since the immediate post-war period, when Canada realized that "its Arctic" was full of Americans and US military installations, Canada has been faced with a dilemma: with a population of only 25 million in a northern territory second only in size to the USSR, Canada has been virtually at a loss as to how to both defend the Arctic and exercise its sovereignty. In the face of the Soviet threat at the beginning of the Cold War, as soon as the US realized that the USSR had developed a bomber with intercontinental range, Canadian territory was vital to

American defence: the obvious and necessary location for early warning stations. Canada was a founder member of NATO and soon thereafter entered into NORAD which separated North American from European defence thus making it bilateral not multilateral. Despite statements about mutual decisions it is clearly the US that is in the driver's seat in NORAD. During the 1960s, particularly during the period of the Vietnam War, there was much discussion in Canada regarding their ally's global policies: widespread criticism refocussed on the US/Canadian relationship, but the constraints of the security relationship prevented Canada from embarking upon any independent initiative until other non-defence related issues became intertwined in the situation.

There were major connected developments in two specific practical areas in the 1960s that triggered Canadian action. The first was the discovery of huge oil fields in the North American Arctic in the late 1960s. Exploration for oil had been continuous since the Second World War but only with the strikes was the question of transportation of the oil studied. Pipelines and tankers were both options to be considered. Humble Oil, a subsidiary of Exxon, decided to test the feasibility of tanker delivery of Prudhoe Bay oil to the US East coast, by sending the *Manhattan,* a refitted tanker, through the Northwest Passage in August/September 1969 and for a second try in April/May 1970.

Meanwhile, Canada had been engaged since 1958 in multilateral negotiations organized as a series of conferences to codify international law into a new Law of the Sea Treaty. Major issues being dealt with in the Law of the Sea negotiations were the extent of territorial waters and of exclusive economic zones and the rights of coastal states in regulating shipping within these zones. Within Canada, an ongoing debate continued about the legitimacy of a sovereignty that could not be defended. Canada relied upon the United States for the defence of the North. The North played a very significant part in Canadian identity. The sending of the *Manhattan* through the Northwest Passage constituted no special challenge to Canadian sovereignty but the accompanying US Coast Guard icebreaker was considered by Canada a military vessel which needed Canadian permission to pass through internal Canadian waters. The US rejected Canada's claim that the Northwest Passage constituted internal waters insisting rather that it is an international strait. Canada's behavior in the ensuing years has focussed on the importance of sovereignty for reasons of environmental protection: in 1970 Canada enacted the Canadian Arctic Waters Pollution Prevention Act thereby attempting through unilateral action to protect both the sovereignty and the marine environment of Arctic Canada. Subsequently, Canada successfully negotiated for the inclusion in the Law of the Sea Convention (1982) of an article (234) which made special provisions for

Arctic shipping that essentially supported Canada's Arctic Waters Pollution Prevention Legislation. Then, in response to the intrusive voyage of the US icebreaker, *Polar Sea,* through its Arctic waters in 1985, Canada announced the enclosure of its Arctic waters and its willingness to have the International Court of Justice adjudicate this issue. The responses of the USA have been predictably the actions of a major maritime power not wishing to have its flexibility of naval operations constrained by international legal regimes. Although the USSR has publicly supported Canada's position on the Northwest Passage, it has adopted the same position as the USA relative to Norwegian attempts to increase its jurisdiction under the new LOS contintental shelf provisions as applied to the Svalbard area. That is to say, predictably, both superpowers have resisted new LOS provisions that might encroach upon the naval freedom of the seas. Despite the fact that 20 years has now elapsed since the *Manhattan* voyage, the US and Canada are no closer to resolution of their differences over the issue having formally agreed to disagree in January 1988. The sour Arctic international relations between the two friends and allies on this issue is significant. For this issue to serve as the basis for an independent initiative for one of the lesser Arctic powers within the Arctic security context, it had to touch upon a matter even more criticial then defence, namely, the very existence and integrity of the state. Canada would not have risked friction with its superpower ally in the Arctic unless the issue was vital, which it was, pertaining to sovereignty over an area of Canada that is a critical element in Canadian identity and which Canadians feared was compromised by their dependence on the USA for its protection.

The initiatives that we have considered so far are of the most vital significance for all nation-states, namely, defence and sovereignty. There have been other Arctic initiatives which have been far more prosaic related to rather obvious and practical matters, generally connected to economic development and its impact on the environment. Though practical in nature, one initiative actually has resulted in the only specifically Arctic instrument of international law to which all five Arctic Basin states are signatories: the Agreement on the Conservation of Polar Bears ("The Polar Bear Treaty"). The initiative came from Soviet scientists and was taken up by the USA then by the International Union for the Conservation of Nature and Resources (IUCN) and then by Norway. The initial alarm that polar bears might become extinct came from Soviet scientists in the early 1960s. The Soviet Union had been conserving its polar bears since 1956 and their studies estimated a world wide population of only about 10,000 bears while annually 1,000 were being killed by hunters. In the spirit of the UN Year of Cooperation (to celebrate the 20th Anniversary of the UN), Senator Bob Bartlett of Alaska convened a First International Scientific Meeting on the Polar Bear at the University of Alaska Fairbanks in 1965. Delegates from five nation-states with polar bears--Canada, Denmark (Greenland), Norway (Svalbard), the Soviet Union, United States (Alaska)--exchanged information on existing knowledge of polar bears, research and management activities. They agreed to coordinate polar bear information through the International Union for the Conservation of Nature and Natural Resources (IUCN), an international organization. A meeting of scientists engaged in polar bear research was held in Switzerland in 1968 funded by the Conservation Foundation, a US organization. Delegates to this meeting organized themselves into the IUCN Polar Bear Specialist Group and planned to convene to exchange information every two to three years. The IUCN took the lead in preparing drafts for an international polar bear agreement, which members of the Polar Bear Specialist Group took to their governments for review. In November 1973 the Norwegian government convened a conference to prepare the final text of an agreement, which was signed and ratified by all parties and came into force in 1975. In 1981 the parties met to review the Agreement and decided to keep it in force indefinitely. The Management regime is carried out by the contracting parties. The Agreement represents an example of international Arctic cooperation that has surmounted political differences--a kind of "scientific detente."

Perhaps the greatest volume of Arctic international relations relates to economic activities: fisheries and resources. While security concerns may dampen international relations the prospect of economic activity has generally activated such relations, particularly where development of a resource is being constrained by questions of international jurisdiction. Even nation-states engaged in generally hostile relations may find it to their advantage to deal with each other for practical purposes. Some of the earliest nineteenth century international instruments dealing with the Arctic related to fisheries (US/UK 1885, 1888, 1908, 1923; Finland/USSR 1922: US/Canada 1930; Denmark/Norway 1924; Denmark/ Sweden/Germany/Poland 1929; etc.), and to fur seals (US/UK 1891, 1892, 1894, 1911; UK/Russia 1893; US/UK/Russia 1911; etc.). The chill of the early Cold War post-war period even succeeded in putting a damper on these mundane matters of international relations but two developments led to significant activity in these fields: one was the realization in the 1950s that the plethora of different international laws and agreements relating to the oceans needed standardization. Over a period of more than 20 years, the majority of nation-states participated in a series of conferences that culminated in the Law of the Sea Treaty of 1982. On December 10, 1982, 119 nation-states signed the United Nations Convention on the Law of the Sea. This treaty represented a comprehensive legal regime for the management of the oceans, not only establishing new norms for jurisdiction but also new requirements for the development of marine resources. While the treaty was still being negotiated, new norms for territorial seas and exclusive economic zones were being adopted and applied with significant implications for naval activities, marine resource development, and responsibility for environmental integrity. During the 1970s and throughout the 1980s, the Arctic Basin nation-states have been moving to implement these new provisions bringing about significant changes in international maritime relations. Questions to do with the exact boundaries of exclusive economic zones (EEZs) are still being negotiated in the Arctic (e.g. between Norway and the USSR, and between Canada and the USA) and the implications of the new Law of the Sea Treaty for development of the continental shelf in the region of Svalbard raises the question of whether the 1920 Treaty or the new Law of the Sea provisions should apply. Arrangements for administering resource development in the new 200 mile EEZs are even now being worked out.

The importance of the implications of the new EEZs has only been heightened by the discovery of major reserves of oil and gas in the Arctic region both on and off shore. With technological developments that made these reserves economically exploitable, the 1970s became a decade of feverish oil and gas development in the Arctic caused to a large degree by the problems of Middle East supply as a result of the organization of OPEC and its attempts to use oil as a weapon by withholding supply. In the pursuit of secure energy supplies, the Arctic Basin states generated a development boom in the Arctic region. This soon resulted in environmental concerns. International relations associated with the changing Law of the Sea, the economic development of the Arctic, and the concern about environmental degradation is largely bilateral or unilateral but with an impact on other nation-states, and generally very practical fisheries agreements between the US and Canada; between Finland and the USSR; between Denmark, Sweden and West Germany; between the US and the USSR; between Denmark and Norway; between Canada and the USSR; Canada and Norway. All of the Arctic littoral states are involved in various bilateral fisheries agreements. They are also linked through agreements relating to marine mammals and environmental pollution. As previously noted, the 'Polar Bear Treaty' of 1973 is the only agreement with a specifically Arctic focus to which all affected Arctic states are signatories. This most active area of Arctic international relation involves agreements that are specific and limited in scope and are occasioned either by the new LOS regime changes or (and often in conjunction with) economic development activities resulting from technological progress or environmental concerns arising from the economic activities. The agreements arise more from changed circumstances and opportunities than from philosophical initiatives with broader goals. In other words, such international relations represent the prosaic accompaniment to economic activity that happens to occur in areas subject to international interest. Superpower military competition in the region does not prevent such relations occurring (though it may substantially decrease the volume) since economic success and development is regarded as an absolutely vital corollary of the state: without economic success there would be little or nothing worth defending. Economic development is the very life of the state, prior to its defence, therefore, despite tense Arctic relations, bilateral and multilateral agreements for the exploitation of economic resources will proceed even though the negotiations may be drawn out. The overriding value here is economic necessity, and pursuit of such development is hardly regarded as initiative but "business as usual."

There is a topic area for Arctic cooperation which embraces all of the others and that is scientific cooperation. The need for cooperation in scientific research has been articulated over a long period and frustrated scientists point to nineteenth century sharing of scientific knowledge of the Arctic and point to the universal nature of science. Despite such protestations there is still as yet no institutionalized international scientific research regime. After decades of frustration during which scientists from all Arctic nation-states had expressed their conviction of the need for cooperation and collaboration, an initiative in the mid 1980s resulted in considerable progress. A series of major planning meetings were held between 1986 and 1989. In Leningrad in 1988 a task force identified priority areas for Arctic scientific cooperation and scientists were anxious to proceed but the formal instruments to create an International Arctic Science cooperation have yet to be produced. In the eyes of the other seven participants it is the USA that is thwarting this development on the basis of residual concerns about technology transfer to the USSR and the prevailing strategic stand-off in the Arctic which might be affected by free interchange of scientific information. The USSR is, not surprisingly, anxious to see Arctic scientific cooperation proceed since they wish to benefit from western knowledge and technology in northern development with environmental safeguards. With the current strains on the Soviet economy in transition, Gorbachev seems eager for demilitarization and arms control to free up Soviet financial resources for economic development. The Soviet Arctic would be a focus for both elements of such policies.

The final initiative to be mentioned here is of very recent origin: the Finnish initiative to protect the Arctic environment was launched in February 1989. It arose from a sense of the interrelatedness of questions raised about the Arctic, namely militarization, economic development, the absence of international Law or Arctic scientific cooperation, and the emerging problems of pollution of the Arctic environment. The initiative seeks to establish comprehensive multilateral measures for the protection of the Arctic environment. The response from the USSR has been positive--the Finnish initiative is seen as a response to Gorbachev's Murmansk speech ideas. The other Nordic nation-states have expressed their positive support, as has Canada. As yet the USA has not demonstrated any more urgency to this than on other environmental concerns.

The foregoing section has included a brief survey of formal Arctic international relations in the period 1945-1990 focussing on the subject matter of those relations and their progress.

Analysis/Conclusions

What emerges from reviewing the international relations of the Arctic region for the post-war period is a fairly clear picture: the continuous tense relationship between the superpowers constrains the development of Arctic regional international relations. All other activities are subsumed beneath the hostile military/strategic competition. As Willy Ostreng has put it,

> ...the East-West conflict was of a decidedly hegemonic nature. By this I mean a conflict taking place between competing political systems that develop cumulatively, in that conflict in one issue automatically spills over into the others. Purely hegemonic conflicts do not permit issues to be kept outside the conflict realm: here military conflict spreads to embrace the entire range of interests and all points of contact between the parties...hegemonic conflicts demand unambiguous national answers....No sector or segment of society, not even research can free itself totally from conflicts of this type. Consequently the hegemonic features of the Cold War contributed at an early stage to the creation of what we could call a fully integrated, multi dimensional security concept for the Arctic. The linkage between military and scientific fields became almost absolute, with few or no distinctions made between the two areas. This situation remained more or less unchanged until the beginning of the 1980s. (Willy Ostreng, "The Militarization and Security Concept of the Arctic" in *The Arctic: Choices for Peace and Security*. Proceedings of a Public Inquiry, Thomas R.Berger et. al., Vancouver, Gordon Soules, 1989, p. 119.)

Throughout our review of the material the evidence was clear: the military/security aspect of the Arctic with its superpower stand-off provided the prism through which all other issues had to be seen. The linkages between militarization and defence, environmental questions, scientific knowledge, economic development, and sovereignty could all be subsumed under the umbrella of national security and/or national interest for the superpowers. For the superpowers, projection and defence of their power in the Arctic was its primary value. For the lesser powers, the superpowers' actions in the Arctic sometimes threatened their integrity and national interests, but only when such interests were seriously challenged would reasons of state persistence activate the lesser states to take the intiative, thereby challenging the superpowers dominance in the region and risking displeasure. The lesser states constantly pronounce their commitment to peace and stability in the region--in so doing they demonstrate their alienation from the interests of the superpowers who had jockeyed for ascendancy of power.

Although from 1948 until 1985 it was the USSR that was closed and secretive, it was no more unresponsive to lesser power initiatives than was the USA, indeed, in its positive response to the proposal for a NNWFZ, in its support of Canada's position regarding the Northwest Passage, the USSR demonstrates more positive responsiveness to lesser-power initiatives in the Arctic than does the USA. Where progress was made and agreements were entered into was in the limited, practical, focussed realm of resource developement. Here the interests of all the Arctic states coincided. Norway in particular in its foreign policy demonstrated a degree of success in dividing issues into practical measures with limited implications that could be proceeded with through painstaking negotiation, and recognizing those issues that had broader implications where effort would be unlikely to be rewarded.

It is important to note that the key factor is apparently *not* the degree of militarization of the Arctic but the level of tension between the superpowers: during several periods between 1945 and 1985 the level of militarization of the Arctic was not so high but tensions were and no cooperation was possible. Since 1985 the level of militarization of the Arctic has never been higher, but tension between the US and the USSR has significantly diminished and Arctic-wide cooperation has flourished with the decrease.

As to the question in our title, the prevailing response to initiatives in the Arctic region during the period 1948 to 1985 was conflictual: the superpowers were unwilling to cooperate or to compromise during this period and generally did not welcome lesser power initiatives in the Arctic arena which merely served as irritants only giving the other superpower the opportunity to score.

served as irritants only giving the other superpower the opportunity to score. In general the relationship between the USA and its Arctic NATO partners was one in which the dependence of the lesser powers on the US for defence ensured that they would not embark on initiatives in pursuit of their own interests without prior consent or agreement unless their very existence was threatened. Really the only identifiable lesser power initiatives do arise when their very existence is threatened--by nuclear weapons, by the environmental time-bomb, or, in the case of Canada, by loss of sovereignty over a most symbolically significant portion of their territory. More mundane and limited initiatives were undertaken in pursuit of economic development: the foundation of the state's existence.

Finally, what we may conclude from this study is that the appropriate analogy for the Arctic is the Mediterranean, not the Antarctic. The Antarctic is a unique case in international relations since its land is not the sovereign territory of any state and it has no permanent population. Not qualifying to be a state, it requires a special international regime. The Arctic, however, is an international region where states come into conflict over questions of jurisdiction, exploitation, militarization, and environmental degradation. The Arctic is a region where interaction between states occurs when superpower tension declines, and this interaction increasingly needs some comprehensive organizing framework, be it a treaty of cooperation or an ongoing, functioning institution.

References on Polar Bear Treaty

Proceedings of the First International Scientific Meeting on the Polar Bear, Fairbanks, Alaska, 6-10 September 1965, US Department of the Interior.

Conference to prepare an Agreement on the Conservation of Polar Bears, Oslo, 13-15 November 1973, Final Act and Summary Record (unpublished).

Jack Lentfer, "Agreement on Conservation of the Polar Bear," *PolarRecord* 17:108 (1974) 327-30.

Jack Lentfer, "Specialist Group with a Difference," *IUCN Species Survival Commission Newsletter,* May 1985.

Thor Larsen, "We've Saved the Ice Bear," *International Wildlife* 14 (1984) 4-11.

Consultative Meeting of the Contracting Parties to the Agreement on the Conservation of Polar Bears, Oslo, 20-22 January 1981, Report of the Meeting: Summary and Conclusions (unpublished).

Sources/References/Bibliography

Johan J. Holst, "Norway's Search for a Nordpolitik," *Foreign Affairs,* 60:1 (Fall 1981) 63-86.

Willy Ostreng, "Soviet-Norwegian Relations in the Arctic," *International Journal,* 39:4 (Autumn 1984) 866-887.

Oran R. Young, "The Age of the Arctic," *Foreign Policy,* 61 (Winter 1985-6) 160-179.

Thomas R. Berger, et. al., *The Arctic: Choices for Peace and Security,* A Public Inquiry by The True North Strong and Free Inquiry Society, Vancouver, Gordon Soules, 1989.

The True North Strong and Free?, The True North Strong and Free Inquiry Society, 1987, Edmonton.

William E. Westermeyer and Kurt M. Shusterich (eds), *United States Arctic Interests: The 1980s and 1990s,* New York, Springer Verlag, 1984.

Gail Osherenko and Oran R. Young, *The Age of the Arctic: Hot Conflicts and Cold Realities,* Cambridge University Press, 1989.

Donald McRae and Gordon Munro (eds), *Canadian Oceans Policy: National Strategies and the New Law of the Sea,* UBC Press, 1989.

Kari Mottola, *The Arctic Challenge,* Westview Press, 1989.

John Honderich, *Arctic Imperative: Is Canada Losing the North?,* University of Toronto Press, 1987.

Franklyn Griffiths (ed), *Politics of the Northwest Passage,* McGill-Queen's University Press, 1987.

R.B. Byers and Michael Slack, *Strategy and the Arctic,* Polaris Papers No. 4, Canadian Institute of Strategic Studies, 1986.

Ronald G. Purver, *Arctic Arms Control: Constraints and Opportunities,* Occasional Papers No. 3, Canadian Institute for International Peace and Security, 1988.

B. Stonehouse (ed), *Arctic Air Pollution,* Cambridge University Press, 1986.

Terence Armstrong, et. al., *The Circumpolar North,* Methuen, 1978.

"L'Arctique," Numero Special, *Etudes Internationales,* 20:1 (March 1989).

The North and Canada's International Relations, Report of a working group of the National Capital Branch of the Canadian Institute of International Affairs, Canadian Arctic Resources Committee, 1988.

Shelagh D. Grant, *Sovereignty or Security: Government Policy in the Canadian North 1936-1950,* UBC Press, 1988.

Joseph T. Jockel, "Canada-US Relations in the Bush Era," *Canadian-American Public Policy,* 1 (April 1990).

Looking North: Canada's Arctic Commitment, Department of Indian and Northern Affairs, Canada, 1989.

Security Cooperation in the Arctic: A Canadian Response to Murmansk, The Canadian Centre

Suzanne Holroyd, "Canadian and US Defense Planning Towards the Arctic," unpublished
paper, 1989.

Notes on Contributors

Peter Allen: Asisstant Deputy Minister, Department of Economic Development and Tourism, Northwest Territories.

John Andersen: Assistent Professor, Department of Political Science, University of Western Ontario.

John Bekale: Senior Negotiator for Dene/Metis Negotiation Secretariat on Land Claims; former Vice President, Dene Nation.

Gurston Dacks: Professor of Political Science, University of Alberta.

Billy Diamond: Chief of the Waskaganish Band of James Bay Crees; former Grand Chief of the First Cree Nations.

Richard J. Diubaldo: Professor of History, Concordia University, and Director of its Centre for Continued Education.

William S. Grodinsky: Partner, law firm of McMillan Bull Casgrain, Montreal; Legal Counsel for the Grand Council of the Crees of Quebec.

Roald C. Halvorsen: Managing Director, North Norwegian Institute of Trade and Industry (VINN).

Stephen Hazell: Executive Director, Canadian Arctic Resources Committee.

Diddy R. M. Hitchins: Professor of Political Science, University of Alaska.

Bertil Liander: Professor of Political Science, University of Massachusetts, Amherst.

Aqqaluk Lynge: Member of Greenland Legislature; Vice President, Inuit Circumpolar Conference.

Gregory P. Marchildon: Assistant Professor, Center of Canadian Studies, Johns Hopkins University.

Douglas C. Nord: Professor of Political Science, University of Minnesota, Duluth, and Director of its Institute for International Studies.

Sven-Roald Nystø: Deputy Director, Norwegian Sami Parliament, Karasjok.

Zella Osberg: Lawyer, Environmental Consultant, Ottawa.

Nelda Knelson Daley Pearson: Professor, Department of Sociology and Anthropology, Radford University.

Odd Rogne: Executive Secretary, International Arctic Science Committee; former Director, Norwegian Polar Research Institute.

Per Seyersted: Professor of American Literature, University of Oslo; Vice President, Nordic Association for Canadian Studies/Association Nordique d'Etudes Canadiennes.

Lennard Sillanpää: Analyst with the Circumpolar and Scientific Affairs Directorate, Indian and Northern Affairs Canada.

Carsten Smith: Chief Justice, Norwegian Supreme Court; 1980-85 Chairman, Sami Rights Commission.

Heather Spears: Canadian graphic artist and poet, living in Denmark.

Jack Stagg: Director General, Constitutional Development and Strategic Planning, Indian and Northern Affairs Canada.

Tom G. Svensson: Associate Professor of Anthropology, University of Oslo, and Curator of its Ethnopgraphic Museum.

Knut Vollebæk: State Secretary, Norwegian Ministry of Foreign Affairs.

Geoffrey R. Weller: Vice President (Academic) and Professor of Political Science, Lakehead University.